click here.

web communication design

by raymond pirouz

developed with lynda weinman

New
Riders

New Riders Publishing, Indianapolis, Indiana

Click Here.

By Raymond Pirouz
Developed with Lynda Weinman

Published by:
New Riders Publishing
201 West 103rd Street
Indianapolis, IN 46290 USA

© 1997 by New Riders Publishing

Printed in the United States of America 1 2 3 4 5 6 7 8 9 0

Library of Congress Cataloging-in-Publication Data

```
***CIP data available upon request***
```

ISBN: 1-56205-792-8

Warning and Disclaimer

Associate Publisher	*David Dwyer*
Marketing Manager	*Kourtnaye Sturgeon*
Managing Editor	*Sarah Kearns*
Director of Development	*Kezia Endsley*

Product Director
John Kane

Development Editor
Jennifer Eberhardt

Project Editor
Dayna Isley

Copy Editor
Phil Worthington

Technical Editor
David Boles

Senior Editor
Suzanne Snyder

Assistant Marketing Manager
Gretchen Schlesinger

Acquisitions Coordinator
Stacey Beheler

Editorial Assistant
Karen Opal

Manufacturing Coordinator
Brook Farling

Cover Designer
Bruce Heavin

Cover Production
Nathan Clement

Book Designer
Glenn Larsen

Director of Production
Larry Klein

Production Team Supervisors
Laurie Casey
Joe Millay

Graphics Image Specialists
Steve Adams
Sadie Crawford
Wil Cruz
Tammy Graham

Production Analysts
Dan Harris
Erich J. Richter

Production Team
Dan Caparo
Kristy Nash
Laure Robinson
Elizabeth San Miguel
Maureen West

Indexer
Kevin Fulcher

About the Author

Raymond Pirouz is Senior Partner and Creative Director of R35, a digital design studio (**http://www.r35.com**), and an expert in developing compelling visual communication.

An honors graduate of the prestigious Art Center College of Design, Mr. Pirouz was granted the World Studio Foundation award for design and advertising excellence.

With a strong foundation in the use of traditional media, Mr. Pirouz has been at the forefront of developing marketing content targeted toward the Internet audience. While Art Director at Rubin Postaer Interactive, he quickly established himself as an expert in the field of advertising on the Net, creating award-winning campaigns for major clients:

- Rubin Postaer Interactive
  Interface Concept and Design
  for Web Site
  Shockwave Game Concept
  and Design
- American Honda
  Banner Ad Campaigns
  College Microsite (Honda Campus)
  Classic Golf Tournament Web Site
  Los Angeles Marathon XII

- Fidelity Federal Bank
  Naming of Fidelity's Online
  Presence: "ibank.com"
- American Century Mutual Funds
  Banner Ad Campaign
  Interface Concept and Design for
  Web Site
- Cathay Pacific Airlines
  Banner Ad Campaign

Raymond's most recent clients have included:

- Virgin Records / Amnesty International
  Interface Design
- Caltech's Multi-Res Modeling Group
  Identity Design
  Web Design
- Observant Investigation Services
  Identity Design
  Web Design

- .comCompany
  Identity Design
  Web Design
- States of Art
  Web Design for JPL's
  Pathfinder landing on Mars
  Hosted by Digital

Raymond Pirouz currently works with a select number of clients, writes books, designs web sites, and instructs a course on Advanced Web Design for UCLA Extension.

Mr. Priouz can be reached via e-mail at **rpirouz@rpirouz.com**.
His personal web site is located at **http://www.rpirouz.com**.

Developed with Lynda Weinman

Lynda Weinman is the author of the best-selling *Designing Web Graphics.2*, *Deconstructing Web Graphics*, and *Coloring Web Graphics*, as well as the recently published *Preparing Web Graphics* (all by New Riders Publishing). She is renowned for her groundbreaking research into web design issues and ability to communicate and teach digital design techniques in an easy-going and relaxed writing style. Lynda is a featured columnist on web design, video, animation, and screen-based design for many periodicals, including *Web Techniques*, *Web Studio (Japan)*, *Step-by-Step Graphics*, and *New Media* magazines. Lynda has trained some of the best digital design talent in the industry and is a faculty member at the highly regarded Art Center College of Design in Pasadena and San Francisco State Multimedia Studies program.

Trademark Acknowledgments

All terms mentioned in this book that are known to be trademarks or service marks have been appropriately capitalized. New Riders Publishing cannot attest to the accuracy of this information. Use of a term in this book should not be regarded as affecting the validity of any trademark or service mark.

Netscape Communications Corporation has not authorized, sponsored, endorsed, or approved this publication and is not responsible for its content. Netscape and the Netscape Communications Corporate Logos are trademarks and trade names of Nescape Communications Corporation. All other product names and/or logos are trademarks of their respective owners.

New Riders Acknowledgments

New Riders publishers would like to thank all the individuals and companies who granted us permission to reprint their web sites. We admire your creativity and appreciate the opportunity to include your sites in *Click Here*.

Dedication

For my **mother**, who taught me love, compassion, humility, and forgiveness—thank God for womankind.

To my beautiful fiancé, **Dante Truitt**: Your love, support, encouragement, trust, and belief in us has made life smile.

To my **mother**, **father**, **brother**, and **sister**: May we each benefit from life's infinite abundance and maintain our inseperable bonds.

To **mom** and **dad Truitt**: It is an honor to be considered your family.

To **Universal Infinite Intelligence**: While I can't place a name, face, body, or personality upon your existence, I love the overall concept of you.

To **Lynda Weinman**: Your belief in my vision is heaven-sent. Your friendship, support, words of encouragement, and guidance are much appreciated.

To **Bruce Heavin**: Your cover art adds immeasurable value to this book—thank you.

To **Glenn Larsen**: The book is laid out and designed beautifully—thank you.

To **John Kane**, **Jennifer Eberhardt**, and **New Riders**: What can I say? The vision became a reality through your willingness to take a risk (and patiently await my chapter submissions)—thank you.

To Tom "Coach" Roberts and the rest of the gang at **Rubin Postaer Interactive** (Meridee "Media Queen" Alter, Jenni "Number 1" Beach, Tim "BenoitBalls" Benoit, Brook "WA-A-O-O" Boley, Randy "Randal" Bouverat, Gayle "Gonna-Get-Married" Brown, Avery "Cares" Carroll, Stephanie "Gonna-Get-Married 2" Charles, Stefanie "HTML Queen" Dekesel, Isabel "Iz" Faustino, Garlanda "G-LANDA" Freeze, Rona "Badona" Ho, Jennifer "Straight-Up" Holbrook, Onny "HA-HA-HA" Jap, Patty "PATTY-LATTA" Latta, Marc "Suit" Levin, Andy "Hercules" Lients, Bob "Officer" Marcoulier, Lisa "Soap Queen" McMullen, Matt "Minkidinks" Minkin, Joseph "DA KINE" Paguirigan, George "Pannini" Penner, Luis "BIG LOU" Ramirez, Heather "Hot Pants" Reid, Dan "Dan Kine" Roberts, Jack "ESQ" Rudy, Van "VANDAMMAGE" Secrist, Joseph "Khaki" Shak, Mike "Stearns" Sterner, and Edward "Black Rose" Yu): Thanks for having given me joy, tears, and your understanding of my need to "follow my heart."

Raymond Pirouz
rpirouz@rpirouz.com
http://www.rpirouz.com

Contents at a Glance

Introduces readers to the book's overall concept and covers the browser wars and cross-platform/cross-browser incompatibility problems as they relate to web design.

Discusses fundamental design principles as they relate to creating web-based graphics.

Explores issues relating to browser-safe color and file size considerations.

Introduces *concept* as a key-factor in creating successful web sites.

Discusses the key factors to successful web-based communication design, including site navigation, design, and content.

Contents

Table of Contents

Contents

Foreword

Have you ever read a great book that you wished all your friends would read so you could discuss it together? Having had hands-on involvement throughout the development of *Click Here*, my biggest frustration was how badly I wanted to discuss the ideas presented here with others, while realizing I was one of the only people on the planet who had read Raymond's words.

Now that the book is finally published, I imagine it will give many people a lot of food for thought. Raymond is not only a superb web designer and writer, but he's also a deep thinker, and the ideas in this book are provocative and challenging.

The number of books about the web is totally overwhelming, and it's hard to find one that has original content. If you are looking for a book that shares innovative ideas and teaches you how to implement them, I am certain you'll be happy with your purchase of *Click Here*.

Raymond freely shares his years of design school training and teaches design principles that will enhance your ability to communicate when applied to your web site design. His writing style is conversational and easy to read, with a nice touch of humor and sarcasm when things get too technical or nerdy.

I love this book. It represents my conviction that books need to teach, present something original to say, and fill a true need in the marketplace. There's too much copycat publishing and clone books filling the shelves. The web is a deep enough subject to warrant many books, but it's important that web books contain something fresh with true value. *Click Here* achieves and surpasses this goal.

I hope you enjoy Raymond's work as much as I do. The web is a new medium with new rules and principles. Anyone who claims to know it all is full of themselves, but there are people who clearly know a lot more than others. Raymond is one of those rare individuals who can combine design and technology, and possesses great communication skills to tell the story so others can learn too.

—Lynda Weinman

I

Introduction

Why *Click Here*?

There are two reasons to write a book titled *Click Here*:

1. No one else has done it yet.

2. *Click Here* symbolizes the core reason that mankind has created art and visual communication ever since the age of the caveman. *Click Here* is basically a cry for response. Please respond. For centuries, artists and designers have created visual communication for the sake of evoking some kind of response. Graphic design, fine art, cinema, and the like are different mediums through which artists try to communicate to their audience—but at the core of that communication is the basic desire to evoke some kind of response.

On the web, things are no different. Competition has forced web site design to elevate itself to constantly evolving levels of visual (and auditory) sophistication. As technology improves, thereby breaking down bandwidth barriers and delivery-compatibility issues, the World Wide Web will totally revolutionize the way human beings communicate and advance as a species (if it hasn't begun to do so already).

Behind the concepts, interfaces, graphics, and animations to compel user interaction will be a new breed of artists, designers, choreographers, musicians, and the like who will help sell ideas, visions, entertainment, and data to consumers of the Information Age.

The Goal of *Click Here*

The web is a relatively new communication medium. Many who call themselves "web designers" have never been "schooled" in the ways of traditional design. Although it isn't important to literally "attend" a design school to be considered a designer, design school offers fundamental design principles and exposure to many design philosophies that help to create individual designers who have unique approaches to translating communication problems into visual solutions.

Click Here introduces web designers (or those interested in designing their own web sites) to fundamental design principles that help develop a foundational design philosophy on which individual growth can occur. *Click Here* takes the fundamental design principles and actually shows how they uniquely relate to web design, introducing the reasoning behind web design. Good design is about the effective strategic visual communication of an intended message—hence, good design is about effective problem-solving.

Click Here goes beyond the "cool, hip, killer" and examines how conceptual, strategic, targeted visual communication can be utilized to create compelling web sites worth revisiting.

The web is in a constant state of metamorphoses and evolution, outdating itself monthly, weekly, and even daily. In the mass confusion and hysteria, it is easy to get lost in the struggle to be the coolest. *Click Here* introduces fundamental, timeless design principles and creative visual communication techniques that enable the reader to create compelling web sites every time, without having to rely on technology to make the site interesting.

Click Here is a philosophical approach to web design that builds on foundations and emphasizes creativity and utility. *Click Here* intends to remain a useful guide to creating compelling web design long after the technology it describes is obsolete.

What You'll Find in *Click Here*

Ideally, *Click Here* is meant to be read in sequential order, from Chapter 1 through 10. Although each chapter builds on foundations discussed in earlier chapters, it is possible to skip chapters and read ahead because major points are cross-referenced throughout the book. The following is a brief overview of what you'll find in *Click Here*:

1 **Read Me First!** Covers the browser wars and cross-platform/cross-browser incompatibility problems as they relate to web design.
2 **Before You Begin.** Discusses fundamental design principles as they relate to creating web-based graphics.
3 **Click This.** Explores issues relating to browser-safe color and file size considerations.
4 **What's the Big Idea?** Introduces *concept* as a key-factor in creating successful web sites.
5 **Click That.** Discusses the key factors to successful web-based communication design.
6 **Click Your Own.** Covers some of the leading software used to create compelling web sites.
7 **Propeller Hats On.** Uses a case-study approach to cover step-by-step techniques to create web graphics and animated GIFs and stresses creative reasoning behind every action.
8 **Engage… Full Throttle Ahead.** Covers step-by-step techniques for advanced designer HTML, JavaScript, a Java banner applet, and a Director Shockwave file.
9 **Click Here.** Discusses creativity in Internet advertising and covers step-by-step techniques to create compelling banner ads, while stressing marketing and promotion techniques, such as banner exchange, for site promotion.
10 **Conclusion.** Provides links to a multitude of online web design resources.

Contacting the Author

Click Here has a web site located at **http://www.rpirouz.com/click**.

The *Click Here* web site contains some tips beyond the scope of this book and offers updates to the text as technology shifts. Please stop by and pay it a visit.

To contact me directly, you can send e-mail to **rpirouz@rpirouz.com** or visit my web site at **http://www.rpirouz.com**.

To contact Lynda Weinman, who developed *Click Here* e-mail her at **lynda@lynda.com** or visit her web site at **http://www.lynda.com**.

We hope you enjoy the book and look forward to hearing your comments.

: -)

Raymond Pirouz

New Riders Publishing

The staff of New Riders Publishing is committed to bringing you the very best in computer reference material. Each New Riders book is the result of months of work by authors and staff who research and refine the information contained within its covers.

As part of this commitment to you, New Riders invites your input. Please let us know if you enjoy this book, if you have trouble with the information and examples presented, or if you have a suggestion for the next edition.

Please note, however: New Riders staff cannot serve as a technical resource and cannot answer questions about software- or hardware-related problems. Please refer to the documentation that accompanies your software or to the applications' Help systems.

If you have a question or comment about any New Riders book, you can contact New Riders Publishing in several ways. We will respond to as many readers as we can. Your name, address, or phone number will never become part of a mailing list or be used for any purpose other than to help us continue to bring you the best books possible.

You can write us at the following address:

> New Riders Publishing
> Attn: Publisher
> 201 W. 103rd Street
> Indianapolis, IN 46290

If you prefer, you can fax New Riders Publishing at:

> 317-817-7448

You can also send electronic mail to New Riders at the following Internet address:

> **jkane@newriders.mcp.com**

New Riders Publishing is an imprint of Macmillan Computer Publishing. To obtain a catalog or information, or to purchase any Macmillan Computer Publishing book, call 800-428-5331 or visit our web site at **http://www.mcp.com**.

Thank you for selecting *Click Here*!

1

The Arena

Communicating to the web audience at large is like trying to stand on the world stage and give a speech in one language, hoping (and praying) that the majority of people also speak your language. While limited bandwidth is the biggest dilemma constraining our abilities to effectively communicate on the Net, the second major problem facing web design and the future of web-based communication is a lack of standardization on the part of the vehicles through which we communicate with our audience. As the browser giants (Netscape and Microsoft) continue the battle for domination, they create rifts in the communication wavelength between the content provider/web designer and the audience.

1.1

Accessing Macmillan Publishing USA with Netscape Navigator.

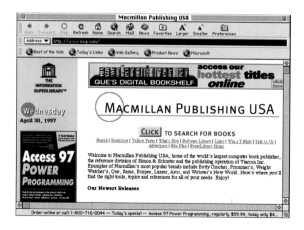

1.2

Accessing Macmillan Publishing USA with Microsoft Explorer.

Figures 1.1 and 1.2 are subtle reminders of the lack of standardization present within the web browser industry. Please take note that both browsers are Macintosh 68k versions (running on a Macintosh Quadra 840av) and have called up the same page, the Macmillan Publishing USA site (**http://www.mcp.com**). Both browsers are running on factory settings, which means that they have not been customized for the purpose of this test.

Besides the obvious interface differences between the Netscape and Microsoft Explorer browsers, notice that the Microsoft Explorer browser window defaults to a larger standard viewing area (621 pixels wide) than the Netscape browser (569 pixels wide). Notice also that the type size in figure 1.2 is smaller than that in figure 1.1. An even closer observation also reveals that there is more space in the gutter between the orange column (containing the logo and "Access 97 Power Programming" graphic) and the body copy in figure 1.2 than in figure 1.1.

So am I being picky or what? Give me a break! Browsers should be just that: BROWSERS—pieces of software that enable viewers to translate HTML code into visual web pages. There should be a standard that BOTH Microsoft and Netscape—as well as the other browsers on the market—can adhere to, so that the viewer does not have to see the same information represented differently ON THE SAME COMPUTER!

The previous example was a VERY simple study of an extremely straightforward web site. There were no plug-ins, no JavaScript or ActiveX controls, and no sound files or QuickTime movies. Because there is no set standard, both Microsoft and Netscape are doing their own thing, and forgetting, it seems, the audience who actually wants to USE these tools for what they were meant to do—help people communicate, not create dysfunctional communication.

Figure 1.3 represents one of the biggest inconsistencies existing between the two browsers. Notice that the same page has been brought up in both browsers. The page uses a background image that is composed of a white strip running through the top of a black area. The graphics that appear have been designed to appear flush with the division between the black and white background image. As you can see in figure 1.3, the background appears exactly at the same location in both browsers, but the graphics appear 4 pixels shy of their mark on the Microsoft Explorer browser. Why? Apparently, there is a 4-pixel discrepancy between the Netscape and Microsoft browsers in the way they lay out graphics. The only way to solve this problem is to create a second version of the site for Microsoft Explorer users that adds an additional 4-pixels to the invisible spacers that line the graphics up with the background image. : - (

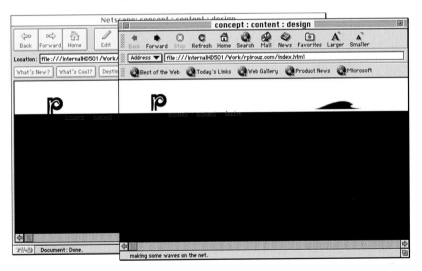

1.3

The same web site previewed on both Netscape and Microsoft Explorer.

From a designer's standpoint, if I code a piece of HTML to display a link 32 pixels in from the left margin, I want that link to appear *exactly* 32 pixels in from the left margin. Design is a very precision-oriented form of art, and it is extremely frustrating for designers to have to deal with the kind of inconsistencies brought about through a lack of standardization.

With my ranting about this issue almost complete, we arrive at a possible savior. Located at **http://www.w3.org**, the World Wide Web Consortium (W3C) is the governing body that has been trying to push for an all-out HTML standard for years.

The W3C has proposed the HTML 3.2 standard and, if both Microsoft and Netscape adopt it, will create a model by which consistent communication can take place across platforms and browsers. Sadly, it seems as though both Netscape and Microsoft have gone their separate ways with this next level of technology as well.

Dealing with Limitations

As a designer, it is important to know your limitations. If the arena in which you communicate is unstable and constantly shifting direction, you must be aware of the shifts and attempt to go with the flow until stability sets in. If Netscape and Microsoft Explorer (both running on a Macintosh) produce different web browsing results, imagine what would happen if we were to compare an image seen on Macintosh Netscape with the same image as seen on Unix Netscape or PC Microsoft Explorer. An immediate visible difference is the fact that HTML type shows up sometimes BIGGER, sometimes SMALLER (depending on many uncontrollable variables) on PCs than on Macs, among a host of other inconsistencies between the browsers. An excellent resource for identifying browser discrepancies has been created by Kevin Ready, co-author of *Hybrid HTML Design: A Multi-Browser HTML Reference* (ISBN 1-56205-617-4) and can be found at **http://www. browserbydesign.com/resources/appa/apa1.htm**.

The font issue is one of several that the browsers have not yet truly addressed. Although Adobe (**http://www.adobe.com**) and Bitstream (**http://www.bitstream.com**), among others, have proposed standardization schemes, we have yet to see a solution to the font dilemma. For now, designers are limited to either setting pixel-based typography and saving it as GIF or JPG files to be imported as images in web pages, or using the <FONT> tag to specify base fonts.

What's a designer to do? For now, I would recommend one of the following four options:

- **Design on a PC, for PCs.** The majority of users are on PCs. If the content of your site is general in nature, you are apt to attract more PC users than Mac users. Therefore, it makes sense from a statistical standpoint to design for PC users.

- **Design on a Macintosh, for Macintosh.** If your target audience uses Macintosh (artists, designers, photographers, architects, and so on), you are safe designing your site on a Macintosh. Keep in mind, however, that there are some artists and designers who are on PCs, and if they visit your site, they may not like what they see.

- **Own both Mac and PC and design for both.** Yes, the best of both worlds, and the most costly if you have to purchase two systems and two copies of Photoshop, Illustrator, Director, and so on. However, with this setup, you are sure to deliver cross-platform, consistent communication at all times.

- **Own one of the two platforms and check your design on the platform you don't own.** Of course, this requires that you have access to the other platform (the kind of access that allows you to go back to your computer, tweak a piece of code—or two—and come back quickly to check how that tweaking affects the site on the other platform). This can be a major pain if you're constantly driving back and forth to a friend's house.

The major factors that create inconsistencies between the browsers and platforms are the browsers' unique interpretation of HTML tags for creating spacers, of designating font sizes/font faces, of embedding sound files, and of gamma differences between the platforms (which I discuss in Chapter 2, "Before You Begin") to name a few. If you design a web site that treats every element as an image (GIF or JPEG), import your body copy as GIF or JPEG images, and also center everything to avoid spacing problems, you will encounter no formatting inconsistencies between the browsers. Many designers do this so they can stay sane. For the time being, this technique is the closest thing to cross-platform consistency.

Browsers for Days

Web design is still imperfect, constantly evolving and ever improving. Within a couple of years, issues of cross-platform and browser inconsistencies should no longer apply (let's keep our fingers crossed). For now, it's important to know that a major problem does exist in the flow of communication from designer to viewer as a result of the browser wars. Exactly how many different browsers are there, and who accepts what, and why is it all just one big mess? Let's take a look at figure 1.4.

Webmonkey (**http://www.webmonkey.com**) is an excellent overall web design and HTML resource on the Net. Figure 1.4 illustrates Webmonkey's Browser Kit (**http://www.webmonkey.com/browserkit/**). With this utility, you can get a listing of all the browsers available for your particular system configuration, with bullet points representing the technology each browser supports. A complete browser capabilities and comparison chart (containing all platforms, browsers, and supported technology) is also available at Webmonkey Browser Kit. Figure 1.5 presents what my request for such information served up.

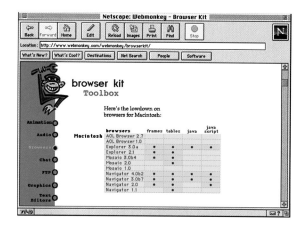

1.4

Webmonkey–Browser Kit. (Copyright©1994-97 Wired Digital, Inc. All rights reserved.)

1.5

Browser capabilities and comparison chart compiled via Webmonkey Browser Kit on April 30, 1997. (Copyright©1994-97 Wired Digital, Inc. All rights reserved.)

Imagine having to give a speech to people that come from six different continents, each speaking one of up to four different languages. Better start taking those language lessons! So what do you do? Which language should you choose to present your speech? Should you use the language that the majority of your audience has in common? Do you prepare your speech in all languages? Can you or should you provide alternatives for those who don't speak your language? The answer is not an easy one, but you will want to communicate with as many people as possible.

The same is true with browsers—different programs, different languages. Chances are, if you don't have all the time in the world on your hands, you'll probably want to narrow down your focus to communicate to the browsers whose language you speak the best. Figure 1.5 represents the arena. Study the chart and you will notice that while Netscape Navigator is available to four out of the six platforms, Microsoft Explorer is available to only two of the six platforms (a Unix version has been announced, but not yet available at the time of this writing). This may not be important, given that a large number of users are on either Macintosh or Windows platforms. Therefore, if we narrow the potential audience down to those two platforms, we will find that while both Macintosh and Windows users have plenty of choices when it comes to browsers, only Navigator and Explorer support the vast majority of available technology that makes web sites sing. If we rate on technology and availability alone, we definitely end up with Netscape and Explorer as the browsers of choice (hence the browser war giants) for PC and Mac users.

> "A good rule of thumb is to design for the environment you are comfortable in and try to learn how to design for the alternative environment in your spare time."

What does this mean? Exactly what we discussed earlier: Design only for Mac, only for PC, or for BOTH—there's no alternative for the time being. What if you don't have the resources to design for both? Let's face it: Not everyone can afford to hire a full-time webmaster and an entourage of HTML fiends. My recommendation, and a good rule of thumb, is to design for the environment you are comfortable in and try to learn how to design for the alternative environment in your spare time until you master both. It is important to maximize on the potential web audience, and as long as your audience is using different browsers to view your site, it's your responsibility to make sure that everyone gets a chance to see your work—it's good netiquette.

Warning Users and Creating Alternatives with JavaScript

Before continuing, now is a good time to introduce one of the best things that could have happened to HTML: JavaScript. You've probably heard of Java by now. Java, developed by Sun Microsystems (they almost bought Apple, remember?), is a *platform-independent* (meaning, it will work on any computer, regardless of operating system or hardware—*hallelujah!*), object-oriented programming language like C++. Java needs to be coded and compiled, which is a post-coding process that takes the raw code and creates an application out of it (and that means it's hard as hell for designers to learn).

JavaScript, on the other hand (without getting too technical) is simple code. Without any compiling, you can type JavaScript straight into your HTML and watch your web pages come alive. The only trick here is to learn JavaScript, which is not all that difficult to pick up. Although you don't have to learn how to program, *per se*, if you can handle HTML, you can pretty much handle simple JavaScript tasks. Although Chapter 8 does discuss JavaScript in greater detail, the following basic concept is appropriate to this section.

For example, assuming that you have designed your site for the Macintosh with Netscape 3.0, the JavaScript code will detect the user's browser and platform. Basically, the code says, "Hey, if you're not using Netscape, OR if you're not on a Macintosh, I'm going to give you the following alert:"

```
<SCRIPT LANGUAGE="JAVASCRIPT">

<!—//

IF (NAVIGATOR.APPNAME !="NETSCAPE" ||
NAVIGATOR.APPVERSION.CHARAT(NAVIGATOR.APPVERSION.INDEXOF("(")+1)!="M")

{

ALERT ("This site has been designed on a Macintosh and is optimized for Netscape 3.0. If you are
using another platform with a browser other than Netscape, you may notice some irregularities in
the site's layout and design.")

}

//—>

</SCRIPT>
```

R35, a digital design studio (**http://www.r35.com**) is a Macintosh-based web design shop that doesn't
have access to PCs, Unix machines, or WebTV. Figure 1.7 illustrates the R35 contact page.

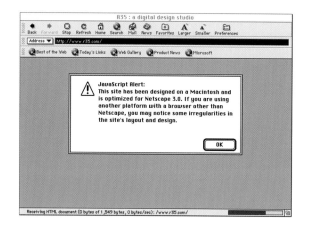

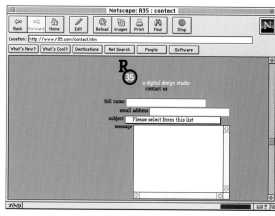

1.6

R35 accessed through Internet Explorer 3.0.1β on a Macintosh.

1.7

R35 contact page accessed through Netscape Navigator on a
Macintosh.

Viewed through Netscape on a Macintosh, this page shows up quite nicely. Notice the attention to detail
with regards to the unique typographic layout. Every detail has been designed and crafted to a point
of precision in terms of placement. Now, witness the same page as viewed through Microsoft's Internet
Explorer 3.0.1β (their most recent version at the time of this writing), in figure 1.8.

Notice that the two are nearly identical, except for one HUGE eyesore: the text entry field that shows up
unexpectedly large and out of place on the Explorer version. The HTML code is the same—it has not been
altered. Internet Explorer's translation of R35's HTML, however, has created this dismal sight. What's a web
designer to do? This is the VERY reason that the disclaimer appears for non-Netscape or non-Macintosh
viewers on R35's home page.

1.8

R35 contact page accessed through Internet Explorer 3.0.1β
on a Macintosh.

The alternative to including this kind of warning is to create a separate
web site for each possible browser combination, and in all honesty, it's
really not worth the trouble.

Seeing how the code to create the warning disclaimer uses JavaScript
to detect the browser and platform, what if visitors have browsers that
do not support JavaScript? Will they still be able to see the warning?
The answer is NO, because if their browsers do not support JavaScript,
they will not be able to process the code that creates the warning.

Do you begin to see the kind of nightmare this cross-platform/cross-
browser stuff is? Just when you thought it was all over, however, a solution: The following code of HTML, if you place it in your home page
after your JavaScript code, will "sniff" out those users incapable of supporting JavaScript and send them to a new page, where you can either
supply them with a stripped-down version of your web site or tell them
to download the newest version of Netscape and try again:

```
<NOSCRIPT>
<META HTTP-EQUIV=REFRESH CONTENT="0; URL=NEWPAGE.HTM">
</NOSCRIPT>
```

That's all there is to it. Simply replace "NEWPAGE.HTM" with the name
of the page you want to direct them to, and off they go if their browser
doesn't support JavaScript!

Now that you have a better understanding of the playing field, let's take
a look at your goals in creating successful web sites.

The Challenge

> "It's much more important to deliver compelling content to your *intended audience* than to concern yourself with pleasing everyone all of the time."

No matter what browser you're aiming for, the challenge is still the same: to create memorable, compelling web experiences worth returning to. It is important to always keep your goals in mind at every stage of the game. The problems associated with cross-platform/cross-browser issues and whiz-bang technological overdose can often cause you to stray from your goals (discussed further in Chapter 5, "Click That"):

- Identify your site's "key" purpose.
- Identify your target audience.
- Design an overall identity/brand image for your site.
- Structure an intuitive navigation.
- Create an overall "look and feel" per the site's identity.
- Plan a strategy to attract visitors into the site.
- Deliver your content in easily digestible packets of information.
- Entice your visitors to return.

These points comprise your challenge when set out to create compelling web sites. The technology is often over-emphasized and over-hyped. Technology is ever changing and evolving. For you to constantly try to keep up with every nuance of change takes away from your ability to do what you do best: design compelling web sites. The simple warning message illustrated in figure 1.6 saved R35 hours of research and programming. Although it *is* good netiquette to give all users a chance to see your work, it's much more important to deliver compelling content to your *intended audience* than to concern yourself with pleasing everyone all of the time.

That's the Ticket

I've discussed the arena, some of the major cross-platform issues you face as a web designer, and touched on the crucial points of your challenge in creating successful web sites.

Through the rest of this book, I expose you to the kind of thinking that will enable you to design well–thought-out and memorable web sites—one chapter at a time.

2

Control Freaks Beware!

The first limitation placed on you as a designer is the fact that you are communicating to an audience whose means to the Net varies (Microsoft Explorer, Netscape, AOL, WebTV, and many others). Each browser is unique in its interpretation of HTML code and its translation to visual imagery. Besides browser differences, your users may be viewing your site through Macs, PCs, Unix machines, or even the television. You have no "total" control over how the colors you select look on each platform. For a designer, this lack of "total" control over the transmission of work is a major problem. After all, one of your goals is to lay out the overall "look and feel" of a page. If you cannot be sure how your design looks to your many potential users (without having access to a Mac, PC, SGI, Sun, and WebTV), you're out of luck. Fortunately, some standards have been set, and some problems pointed out.

Among the major problems pointed out (and not yet resolved) are the issues relating to gamma differences between platforms. To put it simply, *gamma* is a measure of your computer monitor's brightness, controlled by your computer's hardware (standard on Macintosh and SGI; third-party graphics card required for Suns and PCs) and system software—this alone should hint at possible inconsistencies across platforms. Above and beyond the gamma problems, however, an even more important issue fortunately HAS been addressed: cross-platform color. Cross-platform and cross-browser color consistency is possible only through the use of *the browser-safe color palette*, which I discuss shortly.

I begin this chapter with an overview of the gamma issues as they relate to inconsistent image displays between the platforms. I then continue with cross-platform color on the Net and provide solutions for "safe" color usage, offering the designer a good degree of control (we don't have "total" control … yet). I conclude the chapter with issues that concern keeping your users waiting. Nobody likes to wait. In this Information Age married to the "now" generation, most web junkies (hi) are willing to wait only for entertainment. Unless you provide the greatest game since *Space Invaders*, chances are your visitors will hit the "stop" button followed by the "get me out" button on their browsers if your graphics take too long to load. We've got plenty to cover (and it's only Chapter 2), so let's get to it.

GammaRamma

To truly understand the meaning of gamma and its ramifications for computer monitors, you would need a degree in electrical engineering (or check out a detailed explanation at **http://www.cgsd.com/papers/ gamma.html**). Therefore, to simplify our lives, let's just say that your computer's gamma setting is a measure of how bright your images will appear on your monitor. Lower gamma ratings translate to brighter images. For the purposes of this book, and your future as a web designer, you should know that inconsistencies abound when it comes to this subject. The table on the next page demonstrates the average factory system gamma settings (based on platform).

Platform	Factory Setting
Macintosh	1.8 gamma
SGI	1.7 gamma
PC and SUN	2.5 gamma

As you can see in the preceding table, the gamma setting for PC and Sun computers is set to 2.5. This means that the same image will appear darker on the PC and Sun than on the Macintosh or SGI.

Notice that figure 2.1 was designed on the Macintosh and looked fine at its standard gamma setting. When viewed on a PC, however, the same image is much darker (fig. 2.2) because of the PC's higher gamma rating. Even if you were to purchase a third-party graphics card for the PC and Sun (the only way to change their gamma settings) you would not be able to match cross-platform gamma. Sound frustrating? Well, it is. Besides the different gamma settings, each computer treats gamma correction in its own distinct way. In actuality, the gamma problem is more of an issue to Macintosh and SGI users than to PC and Sun users. That's because the Macintosh and SGI have a lower gamma setting and must compensate UP to the 2.5 gamma setting (standard on PCs and Suns, and THE STANDARD setting that ALL monitors share).

2.1

An image designed and viewed on a Macintosh monitor.

2.2

The same image as in figure 2.1, viewed on a PC monitor.

The Solution

The only immediate solution to the "Gamma Dilemma" is *contrast*:

- If you have a Macintosh or SGI, know that your images will appear a tad darker on PCs and Suns and, therefore, create high-contrast images and graphics (white on black, for example), rather than low-contrast images (gray on black, for example).

- If you have a PC or Sun, know that your graphics will look lighter on Macintosh and SGI machines. You need not do anything else, as you are setting the standard to which Macintosh and SGI users must adhere.

You can always wait for the new graphics format, PNG (Portable Network Graphics), to be accepted and adopted by the industry. The PNG format will determine the platform that is viewing the image and gamma-correct for it accordingly. You can also wait for cross-platform gamma standardization (good luck). For now, there is still no way to "truly" please all of the viewers, all of the time.

Color Me Safe

Cross-platform and cross-browser color consistency is possible only through the use of the browser-safe color palette. Netscape Navigator, Microsoft Explorer, and the rest of the browsers share the same color palette management scheme. This is to say that they translate colors in the same manner, with a specific *color lookup table* (CLUT). This CLUT is derived from the 256 (or 8-bit) color system palette that the browser is operating on. Before we continue with the CLUT, it is important to have a good understanding of *bit depth*, which is a measure of the number of colors your system is capable of displaying. Each bit can display two colors. For the purposes of this book, know that the higher the bit depth, the more colors you can display:

1 bit	2 colors
2 bit	4 colors
4 bit	16 colors
8 bit	256 colors
16 bit	thousands of colors
24 bit	millions of colors
32 bit	millions plus 8-bit grayscale mask

Each of the different operating systems (Macintosh, Windows, Windows 95, and the rest) comes with an 8-bit standard system palette that the browser uses to display color images. Each system, while containing the 8-bit (256 color) palette, reserves 40 colors for its own use. Therefore, 216 common colors exist between the platforms. These 216 colors make up what is known as the *browser-safe palette*. The palette, therefore, is both cross-platform safe as well as browser-safe.

What can happen if you don't use the browser-safe palette, and design your image in millions of colors (fig. 2.3)?

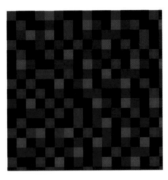 

2.3

Dithering in a non–browser-safe image versus smooth color in a browser-safe image, both images magnified 300%.

The left image in figure 2.3 started out as a solid patch of color, similar to what we see on the right side of the figure. Unfortunately, because the left side was created with a non–browser-safe palette, dithering has occurred. *Dithering* is a result of having reduced an image down to a limited palette, containing colors unavailable to the limited palette. The result is often a placement of multicolored pixels close together to echo the original color (similar to what happened in figure 2.3). If you do not use the browser-safe palette to create your artwork, you will encounter dithering in all of your limited-palette, Internet-ready images.

The Browser-Safe Palette

In the age of "safe" things, isn't it wonderful that we have access to a means of safety in cross-platform color? Lynda Weinman's "browser-safe palette" is the first such wonder.

Lynda's color lookup table (fig. 2.4)—available for download through her site at **http://www.lynda.com** (fig. 2.5)—is your color safety net. And best of all, it's free.

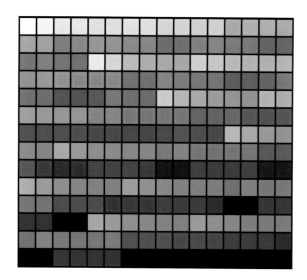

2.4

Lynda Weinman's browser-safe color lookup table (CLUT) or browser-safe palette, containing the 216 colors shared between the multiple-platform web browsers. Using colors from this palette will ensure safe, undistorted cross-platform color delivery.

2.5

Lynda's Homegurrrl Page, a web designer's virtual resource.

Without getting too technical on you, this is how it works: When a browser is launched on a computer that is limited to 256 colors (8-bit—most computers are limited to this display), the browser automatically converts all transmitted artwork to 256 colors. Therefore, if you create a beautiful image in millions of colors and your viewer can see it only in 256 colors … guess what? : - (Better a safe than a sorry designer is all I have to say.

If you've actually taken the time to count the color cubes in figure 2.4, you have already noticed that there are actually 216 color chips in the palette. It gets a little tricky here, so crank out your pocket calculator: Each platform (Macintosh, Windows, Windows 95, et. al.) reserves 40 of its own custom colors that may or may not appear on other platforms. By pointing out and eliminating the 40 naughty colors, the browser-safe palette makes available 216 nice cross-platform colors for your safe usage. The 216-color palette is sometimes referred to as the 6×6×6 palette because it breaks down to 6 red values, 6 green values, and 6 blue values (good old RGB), ranging in contrast. Lynda Weinman's browser-safe palette is an interpretation of the 6×6×6 mathematical palette organized by color (hue) and value (lights to medium tones to darks—makes more sense to a designer). You can get rid of that pocket calculator now.

Obtaining the Browser-Safe Palette

So you're convinced of the need to play it safe and want to implement the browser-safe palette into your tool chest, eh? Hop on over to **http://www.lynda.com/hex.html**, where you can get a brief description of the browser-safe palette.

From here you can link to Lynda's CLUT ftp at **ftp://luna.bearnet.com/pub/lynda/CLUTS/** where you can download color lookup tables (CLUTs) specific to the program(s) with which you work.

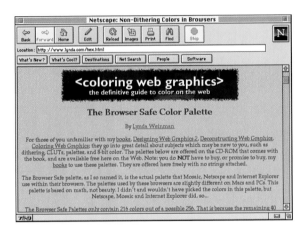

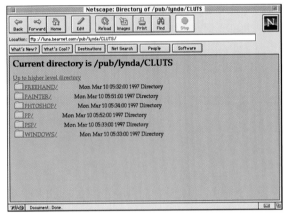

2.6

Lynda Weinman's *<coloring web graphics>* page, containing browser-safe palette information and links to other resources.

2.7

By clicking on the program for which you would like a CLUT, you will be presented with the files necessary to download for that application.

To give you an example of how an installation takes place, let's assume you would like to have access to the browser-safe CLUT in Adobe Photoshop.

1. From Lynda's ftp, select PHOTOSHOP/ and download the CLUT (by simply clicking on the file). Your browser will handle the file transfer and within minutes (or seconds, depending on how fast your connection is) you will have access to two files (the CLUT, of course, and a text file to be read for proper installation).

2. You should place the CLUT file somewhere safe; I suggest in the Adobe Photoshop folder because you will be using it with this program—but it really doesn't matter where you put this file. It just makes life easier so that you don't erase it by mistake.

3. In Adobe Photoshop, locate the floating palette that contains the Color, Swatches, and Brushes tabs. Click on the Swatches tab to bring it forward.

4. Next, move your mouse over the right triangle button (fig. 2.8).

5. Now click and hold down on the right triangle button to bring up the menu shown in figure 2.9.

6. Upon selecting Replace Swatches from the pop-up menu, you are presented with a window asking you to locate the file.

7. Select the Photoshop CLUT, in this case bclut2.aco (fig. 2.10).

Figure 2.11 shows the newly installed browser-safe colors in the Swatches palette.

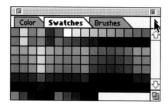

2.8

Locate the right triangle button with Swatches selected in one of Adobe Photoshop's floating palettes.

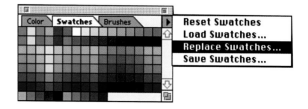

2.9

Click and hold down on the mouse to bring up the Swatch options. Select Replace Swatches to import the browser-safe CLUT.

2.10

Select the appropriate CLUT and click on Open to load the CLUT into the Swatches palette.

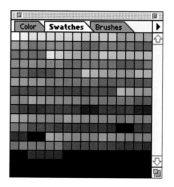

2.11

Now you can play it safe.

PANTONE's ColorWeb

Another addition to your browser-safe color toolchest is PANTONE's ColorWeb. Unlike Lynda's system (which is free), this puppy costs around $20. It can be had overnight through various mail-order vendors, such as MacWarehouse, MacZone, and MacConnection. The drawback is its exclusive Macintosh availability—sorry PC, Sun, and SGI users. PANTONE's ColorWeb is delivered in a thin box housing a floppy disk and is the most useful *tangible* web doo-dad I've ever seen. The PANTONE Internet Color System Guide is a chromatically arranged fan guide (much like PANTONE's traditional printed ink guides) that provides two useful items: color swatches of the 216 "Internet-safe" colors and the hexadecimal notation of each color. This way, when you need to HTML the color using code, it is printed right in the guide for immediate access.

Installing PANTONE's ColorWeb

Installation of the software is easy. Figure 2.12 shows the files included on the version 1 disk.

Select the Color Picker and PANTONE Internet Picker files and move them over to your System folder (Macintosh System 7.0 users and up). You will be asked if you want the system to automatically place the files where they belong—just say "yes." You may, however, get a warning message telling you that you already have a newer version of the Color Picker installed. If this happens, simply say that you do not want the file replaced and only the PANTONE Internet Picker will be installed. In any case, restart your computer and run Adobe Photoshop to start using the system. When you have Photoshop running, choose File, Preferences. In the Preferences dialog box, choose General and make sure Apple is selected under Color Picker (fig. 2.13).

After you have chosen Apple, click on OK and you will have access to the PANTONE Internet Picker upon clicking the foreground or background chips in Photoshop's toolbar. Figure 2.14 shows the PANTONE Color Picker in action.

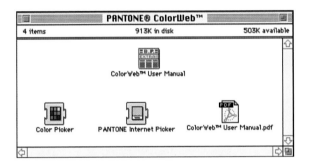

2.12

Contents of the PANTONE ColorWeb floppy disk for the Macintosh.

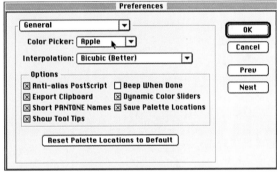

2.13

Make sure Apple is selected as Photoshop's Color Picker for the PANTONE Internet Picker to work properly.

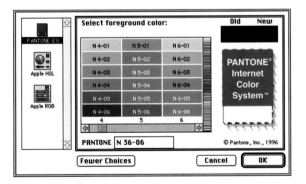

2.14

Although the PANTONE numbers assigned to each chip are irrelevant to HTML coding, they help to associate the color choices on-screen to those available in the fan guide.

By selecting from the 216 safe colors presented and clicking on OK, you ensure safe color communication across multiple platforms.

No matter which system you use or are most comfortable with (I personally use both systems and carry my fan guide everywhere), safe color communication is NOT the only reason to use the limited palette. Here are the top reasons to use the limited palette:

- They limit your file sizes, helping to speed downloads.
- They work across platforms, maximizing consistency.
- They work across bit-depths, minimizing dithering.
- They limit your color-choice availability, forcing you to be more creative in your color usage.

Hey, Let's Try to Keep That Down

Now that you have your 216 web-safe colors down, we need to cover another limitation placed on you as a designer: the need to keep graphic file sizes to a minimum.

Who Needs to Keep It Down?

Anyone designing sites for the Internet audience at large (those limited to 14.4 and 28.8 modems) needs to be concerned with the creation of minimal file-sized graphics. Three of the most widely used minimal-sized graphic files are

- **GIF** (**G**raphics **I**nterchange **F**ormat)
- **Animated GIF** (GIF87 or GIF89)
- **JPEG** (**J**oint **P**hotographic **E**xperts **G**roup)

Later in this chapter, I overview some file size optimization techniques. In Chapters 7 and 8, I tell you how to create graphics that quickly communicate your message. For now, let's take a look at a couple of sites that minimize graphic usage without losing sight of aesthetics, and all the while compel users to click.

Wired News

Wired magazine's news service hosts the coolest "haps" on the Net, while maintaining a pretty robust search engine, "HOTBOT."

Figure 2.15 demonstrates the Wired News page within a matter of seconds after you arrive at the page. As you can see, the use of graphics is sparse, yet there still exists a communication hierarchy, a nice use of contrast that makes the word "news" on top the first read, with the headlines and the HOTBOT entry field a tie for the second read. At the sidebar, notice the small graphic navigation tool indicating user location.

A couple of seconds after the initial page loads, an ad begins to flash. What is important to note in figure 2.16 is the fact that even with the ad loaded and displayed, the information is still beautifully balanced and nothing is lost to the banner ad, although user attention does shift to the banner every time it animates (as it should... after all, animation is an attraction, is it not?). The entire page layout has been conceived and carefully designed to effectively attract and communicate a message, compelling user interaction with either the HOTBOT search engine or the navigation element. Please note that nothing (except the ad) animates on this page, but that it compels interaction nonetheless.

2.15

Wired News. (Copyright©1994-97 Wired Digital, Inc. All Rights Reserved.)

2.16

Wired News with ad banner loaded. (Copyright©1994-97 Wired Digital, Inc. All Rights Reserved.)

Webmonkey

An excellent web design resource on the Net, **http://www.webmonkey.com**, is home to tips, tricks, articles, and commentary by San Francisco's elite websmiths.

Figure 2.17 demonstrates a user's initial exposure to the Webmonkey site. Not just one, but two banner ads occupy this home page to wired techno-fiends. There is no question as to what the first read is here. Advertising revenue definitely fuels this service station. Fortunately, the dismal advertising message is quickly dimmed by the friendly Webmonkey brand image implemented in a photo-journalistic style. Strong emphasis is given to HTML text, making the banner ads and the Webmonkey brand image the only graphics that need loading. This site loads quite fast and is extremely easy to navigate, as the choices are VERY minimal and clear.

One of Webmonkey's six main attractions, Geek Talk (fig. 2.18), is a classic example of good design utilizing minimal graphics, white space, a clear communication hierarchy, and link points to other sections.

Designed in a Q/A or editorial context, each of Webmonkey's sections sports the navigational tool in figure 2.18, which consists of six small graphics that not only highlight the user's location within the site, but also offer links to the other five sections.

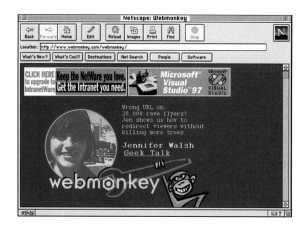

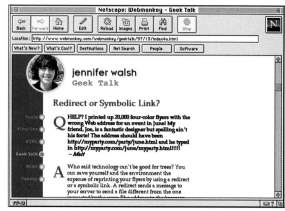

2.17

Webmonkey. (Copyright©1994-97 Wired Digital, Inc. All Rights Reserved.)

2.18

Webmonkey–Geek Talk. (Copyright©1994-97 Wired Digital, Inc. All Rights Reserved.)

R35

A digital design studio, R35 (**http://www.r35.com**) draws a blank upon initial impact. In fact, the only visible item on the page is a simple animation that begins with a "P" and animates into the R35 logo.

Figure 2.19 represents a conceptual approach at providing a compelling brand message to a targeted audience (often overwhelmed with information overload) on the Net. The animation is approximately 3k, meaning it will load and run immediately, even on the slowest connection speeds. The subtle logo animation communicates a sense of quality, substance, and confidence. Literally, the animation is meant to draw the user to the logo and compel him to click. A creatively executed brand image, such as the R35 logo animation, visually communicates more about a company and its philosophy, creative approach, and attention to detail (timing plays a key role in this) than does a press kit, company bio, or favorite links page. R35 is taking a risk by limiting the first page of its web site to a simple animating graphic—then again, those who do not understand the company's message or appreciate its design execution would probably not want to work with R35. Honesty is the best policy—even in design and marketing.

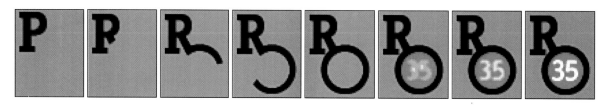

2.19

The animating R35 logo.

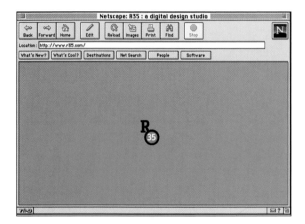

2.20

R35: a digital design studio. Upon arrival, the user is presented with a blank screen, onto which the logo animation depicted in figures 2.19 appears and compels the user to click.

File Size Optimization

The only way to keep file size down—at least until bandwidth bottlenecks are improved (we're looking at an estimated 5 to 8 years from the publication of this book)—is to create graphics that take up very little filespace. An average 1" × 1" Photoshop 32-bit PICT file (at 72 dpi) takes up approximately 15k. The same file saved as a GIF with the browser-safe palette is 2k! That's almost 13% of the original file-size, or an 87% file-size savings, translating to an 87% faster load-time for the Internet audience. It behooves you to optimize files for web usage simply on this point alone. The following are some of your developmental options for creating filesize-optimized graphics and animations:

Development Tool	Platform	File Spec	Plug in Req'd?
Adobe Photoshop 4.0	Mac/PC	GIF, GIF89a, JPEG	No*
Gif Animator 1.2	PC	GIF89a	No
GifMation 2.0a1	Mac	GIF89a	No
GifWizard	Internet	GIF89a	No
GifBuilder 0.5	Mac	GIF89a	No*
Freehand 7.0	Mac/PC	FHC	Yes*
Flash 2.0	Mac/PC	SWF	Yes*
Director 6.0	Mac/PC	DCR	Yes*

* In Chapter 6, "Click Your Own," I showcase my favorite tools in greater detail.

The above table represents the most commonly used tools to help create still images and animated graphics with quick load times. In Chapter 6, I show you how to create GIF files, and in Chapters 7 and 8, I present step-by-step lessons to teach you how to create minimal file-sized still images and animated GIFs.

That's the Ticket

By understanding the cross-platform gamma issues, as well as the browser-safe palette and how to install it, you arm yourself with a foolproof means of communication on the Net. By becoming familiar with the need to optimize file sizes for quick download times, you become more sensitive to the limitations and expectations of your viewers.

3

The More Things Change...

The evolution of human communication has been revolutionized by the World Wide Web. Our ability to quickly translate ideas and concepts into visual and auditory communication broadcast on a global scale is unprecedented. New web sites are appearing at a staggering rate, well beyond industry expectations, and the Net's limited bandwidth cannot keep up with users' demands. Sometimes the many skills needed to conceive a web site, plan its structure, conceptualize its "look and feel," and program it into existence are handled by one individual. Oftentimes, however, somewhere between the content provider, information technologist, HTML programmer, and webmaster is the web designer. The web designer does not operate on pure whim or technical savvy alone. Governing the design decisions of every astute web designer are fundamental design principles, some shaping the earliest forms of human communication. Thus, "...the more they stay the same."

> ## "The evolution of human communication has been revolutionized by the World Wide Web."

This chapter begins with an overview of fundamental design principles as they relate to the Net. When you have a comfortable understanding of the design principles, we will study the sites that play "home" to many first-time visitors on the Net. Observing how these sites lay out their graphics and information gives you a more critical design sense, which helps when it comes time to design a site for yourself.

I conclude the chapter by looking at the most popular places to hang while racking up the phone bill—search engines. These sites provide the first interactive web experience for most users. I examine them to show you how they use some of the design principles to compel visitors to interact with their sites.

Applying Design Principles to the Web

The web is still a new and ever evolving medium. However, a set of fundamental design principles exists that when carried over to the Net, helps create compelling sites. The following sections are basic overviews of each fundamental design principle: color, white space, contrast, scale, communication hierarchy, visual language, branding message, typography, and animation.

Design Principle: Color

A fundamental principle associated with drawing attention and compelling users to click is the use of color. Color is a key design element that adds vibrance to design and immediately catches the viewer's eye. With one of your goals being that of attention getting, color is a powerful tool in your electronic toolbox.

In figure 3.1, notice how your eye is immediately drawn to the red circle in the yellow box. Even though the yellow box is bright because of the nature of the color yellow, the red circle is more vivid, stronger, and demands your attention to the bottom-left of the box. Now imagine the power of color applied to web-page design. Without going too deep into color theory, it is important to study the color wheel and familiarize yourself with some new terminology before you continue.

3.1

A demonstration to show the attention-getting quality of color.

Notice the color wheel, shown in figure 3.2. It consists of the twelve basic colors and is the root through which other colors emerge. The color wheel is comprised of primary, secondary, and tertiary hues. Hue is another word for color. The primary hues (red, yellow, and blue) cannot be created by mixing other colors to achieve them; therefore, they can be referred to as absolute primaries (fig. 3.3). The secondary hues consist of orange, green, and violet (fig. 3.4). These colors can be created by mixing the primary colors in correct proportions (remember, "yellow and blue makes green"?). The tertiary hues consist of red-orange, yellow-orange, yellow-green, blue-green, blue-violet, and red-violet (fig. 3.5).

We can continue to break the hues down as we mix them. However, if continually mixed over time, colors become muddy, thus the theory of color and its complexities (which I don't go into in this book). For the purposes of this book, know this: Color, when used sparingly and strategically, can be your best ally in web design. In creating color for the web, please remember that the computer screen operates on a slightly different set of primary colors than that shown in figure 3.3.

Figure 3.6 refers to the scientific hues, or the additive primaries (Red, Green, and Blue) that, when mixed together in equal amounts, create white light (don't try that at home)—hence the term additive. Unlike the color wheel and hue breakdowns described earlier, the computer relies on science (rather than nature) to display visual information. While RGB (additive) does not literally conform to the color wheel (reflective), know that it is a subset of the color wheel, which can be an effective ally in creating compelling graphics if used harmoniously and with strategic intent.

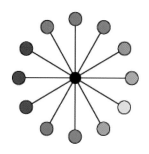

3.2

The color wheel.

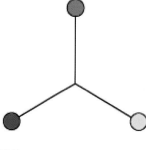

3.3

The absolute primary colors.

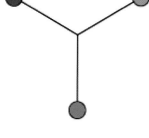

3.4

The secondary hues.

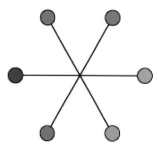

3.5

The tertiary hues.

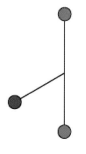

3.6

The scientific hues.

Design Principle: White Space

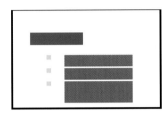

3.7

Good use of white space.

Corporate executives usually cringe at the mention of the word "white space" because it signifies a portion of communication real-estate left blank. To a designer, however, white space is a tool that helps to create a communication hierarchy (see figures on the left). A designer's use of white space tends to increase in proportion to his or her ability to use the visual language. White space can be described metaphorically as a river, leading the user through fields of information. If the river is wide, the user's travel is smooth and on course. However, if the river is narrow, with many tributaries traveling their own routes, the user can become confused and even get lost in the fields.

So how does this corny analogy relate to web design? One of the biggest design flaws you see in most sites is a failure to strategically use white space (that is, users often end up getting lost in the fields). Sites that suffer from "information overload" tend to place every link in the book on their home page. A good rule of thumb to use when dealing with white space is this: Use white space to categorize, organize, and simplify. We review many sites' uses of white space shortly.

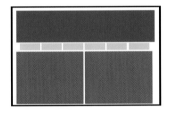

3.8

Bad use of white space.

In the meantime, take a look at figures 3.7 and 3.8. These illustrations are designed to give you a better idea of the above "river" analogy. Note that both examples use color to their advantage in creating a communication hierarchy, but do you see how it is much easier to immediately digest the information as presented in figure 3.7 than as in figure 3.8? You may remark, "Why, that's because figure 3.8 has a lot more information to deliver." Part of your job as an information provider on the web is to decide exactly how much information you want to provide in the first place. Also, part of your job is to decide how best to deliver that information. White space is a visual designer's best friend when it comes to enabling designers to create invisible signals that lead the viewer's eye through a design. The information in figure 3.8, if delivered through the utilization of white space, would result in a more pleasing and digestible page (fig. 3.9).

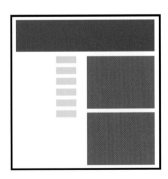

3.9

White space incorporated into figure 3.8.

As you can see, figure 3.9 presents the exact same information as was crammed into figure 3.8, but does so in a much more visually pleasing way through the use of white space.

Design Principle: Contrast

Do you stand out? This is a good definition of *contrast* without getting too "color theory" on you. What is it about the use of color that creates contrast? Remember those book reports they made you do in junior-high school, "Compare and contrast the life of Abraham Lincoln to…" You know the ones. Anyway, if comparisons are similarities, then contrasts are differences. Therefore, contrast is a measure of the noticeable difference between two or more objects … See? I told you I wouldn't get too theoretical on you. In web design, high-contrast objects stand out. I go over many effective high-contrast graphics in this chapter. For now, however, take a look at figure 3.10.

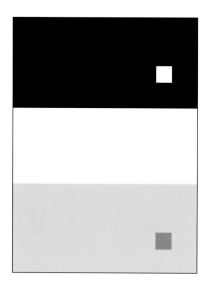

As you can see in figure 3.10, it is possible to attain contrast in color, as well as in black and white. Notice how crisply the white stands out in the black background, begging your eye for attention. In the color example, notice how the light green stands out against the yellow background. Both examples are highly effective uses of contrast. Implemented in your design, contrast can mean the difference between links that get noticed and links that go unseen.

3.10

Contrast in black/white and color.

Design Principle: Scale

Scale is a measure of the difference in size between two or more objects. When used effectively, scale can quickly draw the user's attention to a specific item over others. Most sites use scale, yet not all sites use it well. Scale is one of the tools by which effective communication hierarchy is attained (fig. 3.11).

Figure 3.11 demonstrates a good use of scale. Notice that the red "c," while bright and on top of the green "A," is much smaller in terms of scale, to the extent that the letter "A" becomes the first read. There is a danger in using color and scale together. If the red "c" were slightly larger, it might distract the viewer's eye away from the "A" as a first read. Figure 3.12 tells a different story.

Notice that although the letter "R" in figure 3.12 is smaller than the letter "Q," it is orange, and a demanding orange at that. Even though the letter "Q" has been placed first in the diagram (knowing that viewers generally start at the top left of a piece and move their eye down as if reading a book), the viewer's eye doesn't know whether to go to the "Q" or the "R" because of the color usage. This is a case of scale being misused through color to actually create confusion for the viewer. Be careful not to do this in your work.

3.11

Good use of scale.

3.12

Ineffective use of scale.

Design Principle: Communication Hierarchy

President, Vice President, General Manager. Without giving it a second thought, you just placed those titles in order from top to bottom, right? (Come on, play along.) This is an example of verbal hierarchy. A communication hierarchy places visuals or typography (fig. 3.13) in the order of prominence to supply a first read, second read, and so on. The first read is generally regarded as the most important element on the page (because it demands immediate attention). Most often, the first read is the branding message (discussed shortly), followed by a site's main features and navigation tools.

Please note: The proper use of color, white space, scale, and contrast can quickly convey the communication hierarchy.

Notice that in figure 3.13, contrast, scale, color, and white space are used to move the viewer's eye through the piece. It begins with the "R," moves to the "V," provides the hint of the "S," and ends at the "Q." Even though the letter "V" is what we see from top-down, the letter "R" is the first read based on contrast. Notice that while colors are used, value adjustments have been made to desaturate their strength so that they do not compete with the letter "R."

3.13

Communication hierarchy with type.

Design Principle: Visual Language

Don't worry, it's nothing like French. The visual language is an unspoken form of communication that transcends speech. Your mind processes information into packets and categorizes them into groups. Now, think of the words "spotted cow." Your subconscious mind is processing that information and automatically bringing up everything it associates with spotted cow: milk, cheese, bells, udders, and anything else your personal experience has placed in this category. Mind you, the visual language works only with universal symbols or visuals. A cow is more universal than, say, a RAM chip.

3.14

What does your brain associate with this image?

If your target audience is the Internet audience, you can use a more technologically rich visual language than, say, if your target audience resides in a newly discovered village. Therefore, based on the nature of your target audience, you can use the visual language to simplify the communication process. The mastery of the visual language takes years of practice and constant trial-and-error. However, after you master the visual language, you have mastered one of the keys to effective visual communication. Chapter 5, "Click That," contains more information about this subject.

Design Principle: Branding Message

Starbucks. The Gap. Microsoft. Get the message? Each of the aforementioned has a very strong brand image. We associate many feelings with the brand names (some good, others not so good). Good feelings are communicated to us by the designers who translate corporate strategy into creative verbal and visual logos, symbols, slogans, color combinations, characters, and so on. On the web, branding occurs at two levels. First, it occurs at the site level, where the host of the site promotes itself through a logo, slogan, or other memorable means. Second, branding occurs at the advertising level, where advertisers on web sites try to promote a brand message usually unrelated to the user's immediate needs. Strong branding can create positive feelings and memorable impressions—crucial if you want repeat visits to your site.

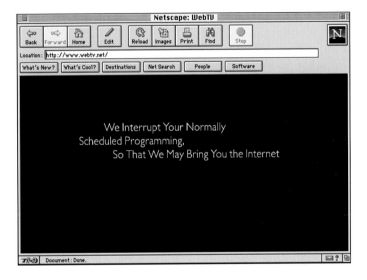

3.15

WebTV Home Page. Notice the immediate brand message.

> "The visual language is an unspoken form of communication that transcends speech."

The WebTV site (**http://www.webtv.net**) is an excellent example of a strong branding message and brand image strategy. Figure 3.15 shows what a user sees upon entering the WebTV site. Notice the immediate message, "We Interrupt Your Normally Scheduled Programming, So That We May Bring You the Internet." This is strategic thinking translated into a message through creative copywriting that throws the pitch at unsuspecting first-time visitors. This is an extremely unusual first page for a web site. Usually visitors are inundated with spinning logos and the like, and this opening actually takes hold of the user with a line of copy that demands to be read and tempts the user to find out what the meaning of the line is (it sets up the user for the brand message delivery). This can be compared to a TV commercial, wherein the first-half of the commercial grabs the attention of the audience without giving away the punch-line.

Upon going one level deeper, viewers see figure 3.16. Notice the WebTV logo and their slogan, "Tune Into What You're Into" stamped onto the page as the only graphics. No buttons, HTML text, or flying Java coffee mugs—nothing but pure strategic brand positioning and the sale of a brand message. WebTV has decided to go this route to make sure that their audience understands its mission and remembers their brand message in the future. The meat of the site is located one level deeper, past that shown in figure 3.16.

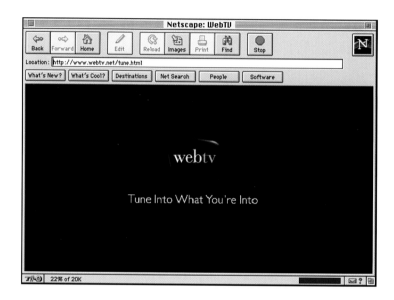

3.16

WebTV—One level deep into the site.

Design Principle: Typography

Typography is the strategic use of type to create texture, hierarchy, organization, and clear communication. Typography can be constrained and rigid or wild and boundless (to the point where type is no longer legible). There is no right or wrong when it comes to treatment of type. However, designers should create typographic layouts that are appropriately targeted to the specific audience in mind. Type can be used as navigation (through links) or simply as body copy to house the site's content. I showcase good use of typography later in this chapter.

For now, the following are good web-based typographic resources that are excellent first steps in the study of typography as it relates to the Net:

- Microsoft Typography (**http://www.microsoft.com/truetype/content.htm**)
- Typographic (**http://www.subnetwork.com/typo**)
- Yale Style Manual-Typography (**http://info.med.yale.edu/caim/manual/pages/typography.html**)

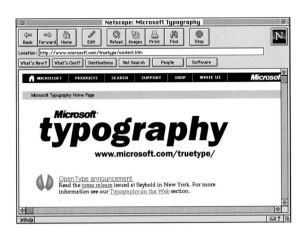

3.17

Microsoft Typography. (Screen shot reprinted by permission from Microsoft Corporation.)

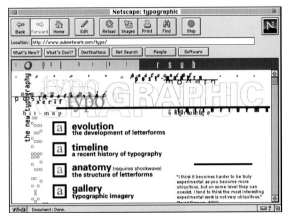

3.18

Typographic.

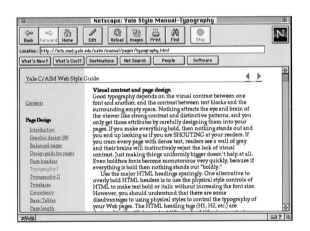

3.19

Yale Style Manual-Typography.

The best advice I can provide for typographic use is to make sure that you design for your intended audience—and the rest is really up to you. There are rules for days when it comes to creating typography, and this book is not large enough for me to even begin to list them. Your best source for typographic inspiration are the many sites that litter the web. You will undoubtedly run into a site or two that uses typography in a way that you instantly feel compelled to emulate and apply to your own design philosophy, until (over time) your will begin to form your own typographic aesthetic.

Web Design Principle: Animation

Animation is a new design principle, unique to multimedia and the Internet. Animation has helped transform the web from a quiet village to a booming metropolis. Applying simple, subtle, well thought-out and designed animation adds immeasurable value to any site. This chapter and the next showcase several compelling animation examples. In Chapter 7, "Propeller Hats On," I show you step by step how to create compelling animations that invite interaction.

Your understanding and application of these basic design principles will vastly improve the look, feel, interactivity, and excitement of your site. Now that you know the basic principles, we will use them to analyze web sites later in this chapter.

It's Not the Size That Matters

> "An accomplished designer will effectively use scale relationships to lead the viewer's eye throughout a piece of work."

Let's face it: The number one problem with the web is NOT the lack of content—it's the lack of bandwidth. With a 28.8 modem, the average web site takes approximately 20 to 30 seconds to download (assuming a 1k/second transfer rate and a 20–30k home page). Given this sad situation, it behooves a web designer to consider the size of graphic files. I cover some creative ways that sites minimize file sizes and page-load times in Chapter 2, "Before You Begin." For now, let's focus on actual graphic sizes in relation to other elements on the page: a matter of scale.

Scale Relationships

Carried forward from traditional design principles, *scale* is the relative size difference between two or more objects. You cannot judge a scale relationship if you have only one object. An accomplished designer uses scale relationships effectively to lead the viewer's eye throughout a piece of work. In web design, scale is important because it determines the order in which your audience digests the information. Of course, there are also ways to play off and balance out scale relationships through the use of color, contrast, and animation, which we covered earlier in this chapter.

The Netscape Site

A great example of scale relationships can be seen upon examination of **http://www.netscape.com**, one of the "homes" to many first-timers on the Net. Because browsers can be set to automatically load a page upon launching, they are naturally "factory preset" to take users to the browser's parent company home page. In figure 3.20, the entire Netscape home page is presented in a hyperextended browser window for the purposes of this study.

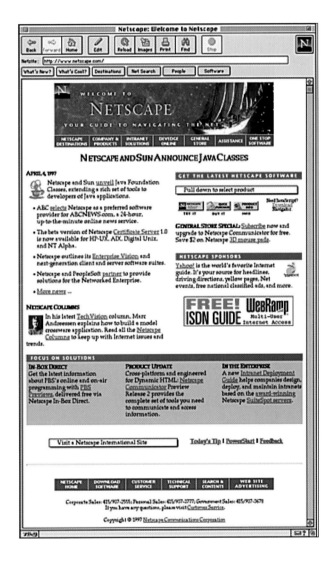

3.20

http://www.netscape.com is home to many first-timers on the Net. (Copyright 1996 Netscape Communications Corp. Used with permission. All Rights Reserved. This electronic file or page may not be reprinted or copied without the express written permission of Netscape.)

The Branding Message

Notice that in figure 3.20 the first visual read is the Netscape masthead (the top-most image on the page, welcoming users to the site). Notice the branding message communicated here. A *branding message* is a piece of communication whose aim is to reinforce a feeling (most often positive) about a product or service. Branding messages are usually conceived and designed to heighten awareness about a product or service so that if the viewer sees the image elsewhere, it subconsciously reminds the user of the positive feelings associated with the product or service. This may sound like a lot of marketing babble, but as a designer, your job is to visually convey marketing messages. Whether you are conscious of it or not, every color you use, every type style you select, everything you place on a page means something. We all—to a certain extent—speak a visual language that transcends the spoken word. Becoming intimate with this visual language (by paying attention to visual details) enables us to utilize the power of visual communication.

In the Netscape site, their masthead features an image of a sailboat on a body of water, with a superimposed semi-transparent layer containing a map of some sort—possibly an old-style celestial map. These visuals communicate a feeling of independence, adventure, the exploration of uncharted territory, and a sense of freedom and uncertainty. All the aforementioned feelings relate to the web experience Netscape hopes to facilitate and communicate quickly. There are many ways to communicate a branding message, however, and Netscape has chosen to literally communicate with a photograph.

Sometimes this kind of communication stands the risk of being taken too literally. For instance, a first-timer on the Net may think Netscape sponsors the "America's Cup Sailing Tournament." Again, this is a subjective interpretation, but think about how visuals may help or confuse your audience, especially if they are very large in scale (thereby demanding primary attention as the first visual read).

"The aim of a branding message is to reinforce a feeling (most often positive) about a product or service."

The Communication Hierarchy

Let us now examine figure 3.21, which shows the Netscape home page as an average user with a 13" to 14" monitor (640×480 display) would see it. Please note that it's a good idea to design with these viewers in mind, especially because the first graphics to appear on a page often determine whether users stay at your page. To design your best graphics and place them somewhere on the bottom of a page, hoping that users will scroll down to find them, may prove detrimental to the success of your site.

Before we continue, it is a good idea to understand the "key" purpose of the Netscape site. Although I had no part in the creation of this site, my guess is that Netscape's key purpose (as a web site) is to communicate its leadership position as a browser company and set itself apart from its competition (which we visit shortly). Notice that in figure 3.21 the communication hierarchy goes something like this:

- Netscape masthead
- Headline copy
- Date
- Java logo
- Try It / Buy It / Info buttons

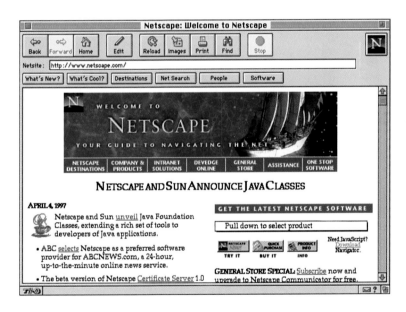

3.21

Netscape as it appears on a standard 640×480 display. (Copyright 1996 Netscape Communications Corp. Used with permission. All Rights Reserved. This electronic file or page may not be reprinted or copied without the express written permission of Netscape.)

"Once your page is loaded, you have approximately 10 seconds to compel your users to click."

In going through the communication hierarchy, my initial impression of the site's key purpose (remembering that with any communication, you have but a few seconds to attract your viewer's attention) is:

- **Positive branding message:**
  Netscape masthead
- **Technological advancement:**
  Headline copy
- **Sense of immediacy:**
  Date
- **Technological advancement:**
  Java logo
- **Marketing push to sell products:**
  Try It / Buy It / Info buttons

Through a study of the placement of Netscape's visuals, it is fair to conclude that the Netscape site has accomplished its key purpose. Unfortunately, I am not compelled to click on any of the links, due to the fact that there is a certain lack of excitement in the site.

A good rule of thumb to remember when trying to design compelling web sites: Once your page loads, you have approximately 10 seconds to compel your users to click. If you cannot compel your users to click on a link and take them deep within your site, chances are they will leave to another site—unless they came to your site SPECIFICALLY looking for a piece of information without which they will not leave. As for the Netscape site, users may come to the site looking to download the newest version of the software, in which case they will click on the Try It or Buy It links, after which they will go away, not to return until the next version of Netscape is released.

Information Overload

The Netscape site suffers from visual as well as textual information overload. What about users who are exposed to the Netscape site as their first on the Net? First-time users to the Net will be confused in navigating through the site because no particular link or set of links directly invites the user to click. Most users simply will click the Net Search button (or another similar escape vehicle) and leave the Netscape site. In general, minimizing information overload would make the Netscape site that much more successful.

How can you minimize visual or textual overload? First of all, there is no need to list the entire contents of a site on the home page. Listing all the site's contents creates a visual maze through which one must navigate (especially if the links are text-based). It is much better to create an information hierarchy. Dividing the site's contents (no matter how complex) into three to five different categories minimizes the amount of initial choices a user has to deal with. It is much easier to pick from a list of five choices than to deal with several lists (each having several choices) all over different areas of the screen, each offering a different message. As an analogy to choosing from smaller choices, consider this example: If you were to create a travel site, rather than have your users choose from a list of every country in the world, first let them choose by continent. Your list goes from hundreds down to a mere seven. Complexity and confusion in the visual design of a web site only confuses and irritates users. And worst of all, it doesn't make them click.

The Microsoft Site

Another "home" on the Net, **http://www.microsoft.com**, welcomes a host of PC and Mac users. Upon initial examination, the overall scale relationship between the visuals seems to work well. Although the word, "go" is the largest graphic on the page, it is balanced by the dark "Microsoft" logotype across the screen.

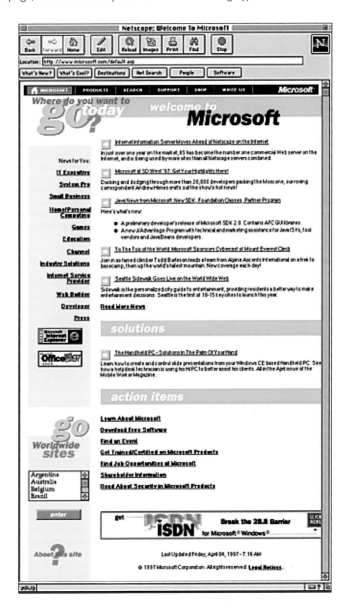

3.22

http://www.microsoft.com is home to many first-timers on the Net.
(Screen shot reprinted by permission from Microsoft Corporation.)

The Branding Message

Like the Netscape site, Microsoft's home offers an immediate branding message upon first read. The "Where do you want to go today?" tagline serves to position the company and its products as the means to some great end that's purely up to you, the user. This works very well because it brings the user into the scenario and doesn't simply talk *at* him, but rather, speaks *to* him. Unlike the Netscape site, no photographic images are used in this site, yet the brand message is just as strong, if not stronger. The simple hint of color and strong typography communicates confidence, and the strategic use of white space helps to highlight areas of importance. Although conservative clients cringe at the term "white space," it *is* a powerful design tool. "When in doubt, leave it out" sounds corny, but works well when applied to web design. The skilled designer can utilize white space to draw attention to specific information.

The Communication Hierarchy

Notice how white space is used in figure 3.23. By minimizing the amount of space the masthead takes up in a limited display size, Microsoft designers have decided NOT to cram more information into the space, but to use it to break up the information. White space does not necessarily mean space that is the "color" white, but rather, refers to any significant amount of space (can even be black) strategically utilized to divide information to make it easily digestible.

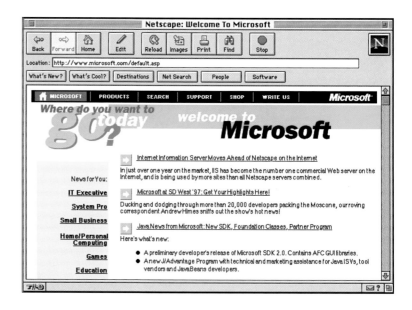

3.23

Microsoft as it appears on a standard 640×480 display. (Screen shot reprinted by permission from Microsoft Corporation.)

Notice also the use of contrast on this page. The blue on black in the top button bar and the blue on yellow in the "Where do you want to" tagline immediately draw attention to the top-left corner of the page. This is where Microsoft wants the user's eye to begin scanning the page, and a simple contrast trick is used to achieve that goal. As in the case of the Netscape site, Microsoft also suffers from information overload. However, the smart use of white space to organize the information into simple hierarchical visuals creates order out of what could possibly have been chaotic.

In analyzing the communication hierarchy shown in figure 3.23, the following are the four key points of interest:

- Navigational button bar atop the page
- "Where do you want to go today?" quickly balanced out by the Microsoft logo
- The three right-pointing arrow buttons
- "News for you:" links

Let us assume for the sake of discussion that Microsoft's key purpose for **http://www.microsoft.com** is to communicate its leadership position and set itself apart from its competition. In having analyzed Microsoft's communication hierarchy, my initial impression of the site's key purpose is:

- **Strong branding message:**
  "Where do you want to go today?"
- **Industry connections:**
  The three right-pointing arrow buttons
- **Software leader:**
  "News for you:" links
- **Sense of comfort:**
  Navigational button bar atop the page
  (with current location highlighted)

Microsoft has successfully accomplished its key purpose. Unfortunately, like the Netscape site, there is no "immediate" excitement generated as a first impression on the site. Unlike Netscape, however, the Microsoft site has two key compelling elements that are worth clicking—except they are way below the immediate field of vision (on a 640×480 screen).

Compelling Animation

Based on figure 3.22, the Microsoft site is designed so that if users scroll down halfway through the contents of the home page, they see some cool graphics that really beg to be clicked. Figures 3.24 through 3.31 demonstrate two well-designed animated links that add a sense of excitement to the page.

Microsoft Internet Explorer Button

If you've been around the web, you've seen figure 3.24 all over the place. What I love about it is the fact that someone actually went to the trouble of animating such a small, seemingly insignificant button graphic and turned it into a work of art. It is simple, subtle, yet fun to watch—it's entertaining and warrants clicking.

Microsoft Office 97 Button

This animated button is new to me. I am not a big fan of button graphics, but the dynamic way in which the information is presented in this very limited space yelps for attention. This is the kind of work that DEMANDS being clicked. Do not take the button analogy to heart, though. You do not have to create a "button" animation *per se* to get clicks in your site. What's important here is that Microsoft could have put a regular boring static graphic (nicely designed, mind you, but boring nonetheless) in the place of figure 3.28, yet they chose to create a cool little mini-ad for their product.

In my opinion, the placement of these links works well from a sense of scale and layout. However, these two buttons represent a small fraction of what could be done to make the Microsoft home page much more compelling and exciting. If you apply simple, subtle animation to your home page, you are sure to attract users' attention and get them to click. I present examples of simple animation to grab attention later in this chapter.

3.24 – 3.27

Microsoft Internet Explorer button.

3.28 – 3.31

Microsoft Office 97 button.

Animate Everything?

> "Animation is one of the most effective means to attract attention."

Does everything have to animate to be compelling? Of course not, but animation is one of the most effective means to attract attention. Like any other trick up the communicator's sleeve, animation must be well thought-out and used sparingly for maximum impact. Animation is a major key to creating compelling web sites, and I demonstrate step-by-step how to create attention-grabbing animations that demand clicks in Chapter 7. For now, it is critical to continue with our analysis to better understand how basic design principles can be applied to web design.

The Graphics We Click

So far, I have covered color, size, and scale relationships, touched on some information design tips, and hinted at the use of contrast. Now let's take a look at some of the most popular locations on the web—search engines. Many users are exposed to the search engine early in their web experience. For those new to the web, search engines act as a primary encounter with a highly interactive site. (For more information about search engines, see Chapter 9, "Click Here.")

Let me hit on one more point before we go on. Any kind of art, design, personal expression, or visual communication is judged on an individual basis, meaning, any judgment passed on visual communication is purely subjective. There is no objective means of judging design. It is purely a matter of personal taste—no more. Anyone who says otherwise is simply being subjective and assuming the world should be seen through their eyes only. Therefore, if a major portion of the population believes the color red is the best color, it doesn't necessarily make it so. Newspapers, TV, cinema, and yes, the web, may use red more than other colors, but it does not make the color yellow ugly. I make and stress this point only because I feel that everyone has the right to express themselves visually and that there is no right or wrong—just opinions. Those opinions are sometimes based on a certain level of education (taught by subjective teachers) or on personal experience (again, subjectively based). At any rate, analyze my opinions, apply them to your design philosophy if they make sense to you, and always listen to your heart.

Fueled by Advertising

All search engines (as well as the most popular sites on the Net) oper-ate based on ad revenue, meaning, they stay in business by charging advertisers space on their home page. This rented space has come to be known as the *banner* (short for *banner ad*, which is short for *ban-ner advertising*). I cover banner ad creation in Chapter 9. For now, let's just say that the function of the banner ad is to compete for the users' attention and to take them to the advertiser if they click on it. Unlike television or radio advertising, banner ads on the Net are a constant. While they interrupt the regular flow of the web (a scary thing) they are confined—for the most part—to an average 468 pixels wide by 60 pixels high (no standard size limitations have yet been set). There are no reg-ulatory agencies that decide the size of banner ads. Size limitations are usually set by the web sites that host the banners. For instance, one site may have lots of space for advertising and may choose to allot a 600 pixel wide by 400 pixel high ad space, while another site might be short of space and require advertisers to design 50 pixel wide by 50 pixel high ads. If you want to design banners, get ready to churn-out those odd sizes.

Banners usually appear near the top of a host page or along the left side margin of the page, varying in size. For example, previously refer-enced figures 3.24 and 3.28 can be considered *button ads*, because they advertise a product or service and entice the user to click on them and be swept away to another place on the web (usually to learn more about the product or service being advertised). What is different about the Microsoft button ads, however, is the fact that the sponsor is Microsoft, the site's host. In this case, you may call figures 3.24 and 3.28 *internal button ads* because they lead the user "internally" within the site.

Learn from Advertising

By paying attention to how advertisers tempt users to click, you can gain a tremendous amount of knowledge with regard to creating com-pelling sites. You don't have to use the advertising model; that is, the "banner ad." You can simply examine what exactly about banners makes them so compelling and then apply those techniques to your own site.

Netscape's Net Search

For the purposes of this study, I show you a button built into the Netscape browser called "Net Search." Upon being clicked, it takes the user to an interface linked up to the most popular search tools on the Net: Lycos, WebCrawler, Excite, Yahoo, and Infoseek.

The Net Search Template

As an overall design standard, the Net Search template works very well. Notice the banner ad near the bottom of figure 3.20. On a 640×480 pixel screen, all the pertinent information related to searching appears pretty quickly near the top due to small graphic files with limited color palettes. Netscape has done a good job of offering a modular space within which each search engine has the opportunity to show off its stuff.

Net Search: Lycos

The Lycos Net Search page is the most graphic intensive of the five—and, in my opinion, the most balanced. In terms of information hierarchy and layout, there is a branding message (are you beginning to see a trend?) as well as the tagline, "Four different ways for you to search." Don't I wish that were true? I know the copy is referring to the four "radio" buttons under the text entry field, but it looks to me as if there are 28 possible selections a user can make (because of the many mini-buttons all over the place). This is a case of information overload, without the use of white space for breathing room. However, the blue/white division creates a tolerable balance—although I would rather see all the extraneous link buttons gone. Lycos gets high praises for having a clever and bold Go Get It button instead of the standard HTML Search form button. It's a nice touch and invites interaction. I also praise the Lycos interface for good use of contrast to make the text entry field (a white rectangle atop a blue background—hard to miss) a primary read.

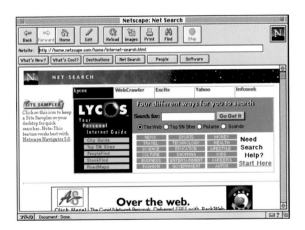

3.32

The Netscape Net Search interface with Lycos selected. (Copyright 1996 Netscape Communications Corp. Used with permission. All Rights Reserved. This electronic file or page may not be reprinted or copied without the express written permission of Netscape.)

Net Search: WebCrawler

Now we're talking white space! Figure 3.33 is a welcome relief with a serious branding message (everyone has got one). A design flaw of this page is the lack of importance given to the text entry field, where most users are looking to interact with this page. If my first read as a user is the logo, then the NEW SITES link (which is almost useless since there is a What's New? button on my browser), followed by the 18 links on the bottom and, finally, the text area and standard HTML Search form button, I would conclude that I've been taken on a wild goose chase. To fix the flaw, I'd begin by adding a solid color behind the entire interface to make the text entry field stand out (contrast) and design my graphics and links to work within the context of the background color. Let's see if Excite is a bit more … exciting.

Net Search: Excite

I like the red, black, and yellow color combination. This search environment is proof that you don't need a photograph to create excitement and warmth if you understand the use of simple, solid color combinations that work well together. My first read is definitely what I like to see, the text entry field, where I'll be keying in my search requirement. The nicely branded (here's that word again) search button in red stands out atop the yellow background, and I really want to click it because it has dimension and almost feels like the only "living" thing on the page (even though it's not animating—imagine that). Dimension is a great way to easily add an extra level of presence to your graphics. Be careful, however, of making your graphics look cheesy. Creating all kinds of 3D buttons everywhere, spinning and weaving around for the sake of looking "cool," is *not* the answer. Look at how subtle, yet beautiful, the "search" button is … I sound like I'm making a big deal about a 1k graphic … and I am! Imagine, a 1k graphic, so little in scale compared to the rest of the page, yet demanding my (and hopefully your) attention.

3.33

The Netscape Net Search interface with WebCrawler selected. (Copyright 1996 Netscape Communications Corp. Used with permission. All Rights Reserved.)

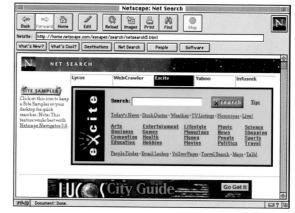

3.34

The Netscape Net Search interface with Excite selected. (Copyright 1996 Netscape Communications Corp. Used with permission. All Rights Reserved.)

I hope you are beginning to see that there is no set formula for compelling users, no special tip or trick. It is a combination of color, scale, placement in the communication hierarchy, motion, dimension, creativity, and maybe a cup or two of coffee. A compelling piece of art need not have all the above mentioned ingredients to successfully entice its visitors. However, you do need to consider all the aforementioned when creating compelling graphics for the Net. In fact, the Excite layout is so compelling that I don't even worry about the extraneous links at the bottom (even though I feel they add confusion, slow down the user, and should be eliminated).

Net Search: Yahoo!

Here is an example of *too much* white (not white space, mind you). Upon initial exposure to this interface, the branding graphic ("all right already," you say) immediately draws attention, not because it's the best-looking or most compelling graphic on the Net, but because it is the *only* graphic on the interface. Simplicity is excellent and much needed on the web. However, figure 3.35 is an example of "no design," and that's not a great thing. In fact, the Yahoo! Net Search page offers me TOO MUCH information at once, creating "information overload."

All I want is the text entry field, which is hidden in the upper-right corner of the interface, as if to say it is unimportant, a mere afterthought. The visual hierarchy of this interface leads my eye from the Yahoo! logo to the 24 links, and keeps my eye there because of its density, actually forcing me to search for the text entry field to escape the "category trap." When it comes to search engines, it is so much faster to type in a request and wait for the first 10–20 responses (that usually contain the requested material) than to wade through link upon link of categorical data, only to find out the item you needed is in an entirely different root category. For this reason, it is important that the text entry field be the first or second read in such an interface. The Yahoo! interface is very text driven, and as you find later in this chapter, so is the Yahoo! site. This is fine for those who want information—and fast—yet not so good when the mountain of text creates a mountain of information to navigate through. There needs to be a balance. Let's see if Infoseek does a better job.

3.35

The Netscape Net Search interface with Yahoo! selected. (Copyright 1996 Netscape Communications Corp. Used with permission. All Rights Reserved.)

Net Search: Infoseek

Infoseek's Net Search interface is extremely close to the Yahoo! interface, except for a few minor differences. The visual information hierarchy initially draws the user to the brand (I'll say no more). The one uncomfortable aspect of the logo is the fact that it literally touches the left and top border of the table in which it exists. I would personally advise against such brand placement. Positive branding must be comfortably situated with a fair amount of "cushion." Squishing the logo in the upper-left of the table makes it a "less important" item. Branding must be given priority and breathing room to communicate a strong presence.

The only positive aspects of this interface in comparison to Yahoo!'s version are that the text entry field is closer to the middle of the interface in figure 3.36, and instead of the word "Search" for the HTML submit button, Infoseek has decided to go with a more clever "seek," in all lowercase to reflect a brand message. Infoseek is an excellent search engine, yet could use a little color in their interface to spice things up (minimizing the links at the bottom wouldn't hurt either).

3.36

The Netscape Net Search interface with Infoseek selected. (Copyright 1996 Netscape Communications Corp. Used with permission. All Rights Reserved.)

The Search Goes On

We analyzed Netscape's Net Search page and hopefully came away with a better understanding of how the most visited pages on the Net try to service their audience's needs. Let us now evaluate a couple search engines, going beyond Netscape's "quickie search" solution.

The Yahoo! Web Site

Yahoo! is one of the first and most popular search engines (certainly the first to go public) on the Net. It loads immediately on any browser, due to limited graphic files, and sports the famous Yahoo! brand as a first read. The second read on this page, and a plus in my book, is the text entry field. Although Yahoo! does not use flashy color in its site, it delivers the option to key in an entry much faster and better than its Netscape Net Search counterpart (fig. 3.35). Isn't it incredible how much more compelling the Yahoo! site is than figure 3.35, even though no color or animation is utilized in the Yahoo! site. This goes back to what I mentioned earlier about not needing to have all the bells and whistles—just clear communication and the attempt to satisfy a user's needs. The Yahoo! site is a fantastic search tool to quickly and effortlessly retrieve information.

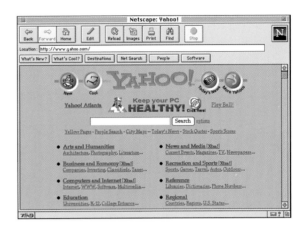

3.37

The Yahoo! web site. (Text and artwork copyright© 1996 by YAHOO! INC. All rights reserved. YAHOO! and the YAHOO! logo are tradmarks of YAHOO! INC.)

I would, however, recommend a slight animation or motion in the mast-head region—something subtle and elegant to convey Yahoo!'s coolness. For example, if the "!" in Yahoo! animated (flipping over every once in a while) the page would gain a level of character beyond what the brand currently communicates, without adding significantly to the file size of the graphic. Such a treatment wouldn't necessarily be designed to be clicked upon, but rather to enhance the brand message.

The Excite Home

The most compelling Net Search interface has a home on the web. Unfortunately, the Excite Home is not as compelling as its Net Search counterpart (fig. 3.34). The colors are muted and played down, compared to the high contrast, vibrant treatment in the Net Search version. One can argue that the colors here are muted to help focus the user on the Excite graphic in the upper-left corner of the screen, as well as the dimensional "search" button (drop shadow included). One can also argue, on the flip side, that the Excite graphic in the upper-left corner of the screen serves no functional purpose and, therefore, does not deserve such submission from the other elements and background colors.

In terms of scale, nothing immediately pops out as a first read, which is a problem. Maybe the background was left white and the strip to the left muted back to give the red logo and button more presence. Such solutions are temporary at best—as the Excite Home suffers from information overload and an incoherent communication hierarchy. A solution to this dilemma could be the reorganization of information in a clear hierarchy using scale, color, white space, contrast, and even animation. As it stands, every element in the Excite home page demands an equal amount of attention. This confuses visitors who would rather deal with a more simple, direct interface that compels full utilization.

disinformation

Now *here* is a search engine! That's what I'm talking about: Contrast baby … CONTRAST! disinformation, the subculture search engine (a project of razorfish, **http://www.razorfish.com**), hits it right on the nose when it comes to creating a compelling site—and it's a search engine at that. Figure 3.38 is an example of great contrast produced by applying white, gray, and red design elements to a black background and making it sing. The communication hierarchy of this site begins with the animated masthead, right below the cool gray barcode-like flashy-flash bar. And as a nice subtle touch, the pyramid to the left of the masthead animates, opening its eye and illuminating (figures 3.39 and 3.40).

The search engine immediately demands input through the very hard-to-miss white text entry field. In fact, even though the field is below the middle of the 640x480 page, it commands quite a respectable level of attention for a white rectangle. The only improvement this site deserves is the replacement of the HTML Search submit button with a more attractive graphic that fits into the overall look and feel of the page. I tell you exactly how to do this in Chapter 8, "Engage… Full Throttle Ahead."

3.38

disinformation

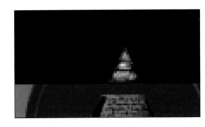

3.39 – 3.40

Animating eye atop the pyramid.

Your Search Is Over

Congratulations! You have successfully completed the analysis of several widely frequented spots and sites on the Net. You have learned to effectively equip your electronic toolbox with unified color palettes, judge good use of scale, communication hierarchy, brand positioning, and many other fundamental design issues as they relate to the web. After you understand what it takes to create compelling web sites, you are that much closer to doing it for yourself.

That's the Ticket

By feeling comfortable with fundamental design principles and how they relate to the web, you have taken one step closer to understanding what it takes to create compelling graphics that make users click. By having analyzed some of the most popular places people visit on the web, you have exposed yourself to the visual language of the Internet—a language based on the real world, but with a twist.

4

Web Design Demystified

You've equipped yourself with the right palette and understand how basic design principles relate to the Net. All you need now is the right set of techy-tools and you're ready to create some killer web sites … well, maybe not just yet. Let's talk a little about this "killer" stuff. Remember, you don't want to harm your audience. If anything, you'd like them to keep coming back for more, so let's deal with creating strategic, beautiful, compelling web sites that communicate your message and keep them coming back for more. Now that's more like it.

This chapter discusses ways to simplify site design to quickly target your audience and communicate your message in an entertaining and conceptually stimulating way.

Before we begin, let's quickly dispel a couple of myths about site design.

The Killer Website (Is Dead)

"A strong concept helps organize content into easily digestible packets of entertaining information that can quickly be retrieved by the user in search of that particular information."

A web site is usually a source of information, store of knowledge, merchant of goods, entertainer, or taxi-cab to the rest of the Net. Web sites have a key purpose—the one message they try to communicate, or the one feeling they try to have the visitor leave with in hopes of their return. When a web site designer's key purpose is to create the next "killer" web site, when he's constantly trying to out-do other competitors for the "technologically advanced, coolest features" award, he compromises the integrity of the site and risks losing touch with his target audience. Remember that the web is a communication medium, not a wrestling match. If your concept is compelling and the use of your graphics ingenious, the simplest of sites can be cool. Don't believe the hype. Target (don't lose touch with your audience), create (compelling communication to sell your message), and update (keep the site fresh). If you do all three well, you will keep users coming back.

Content Is King (Not)

Content - Content - Content. The web site needs MORE content. Too many web sites are devoid of any CONTENT. How many times have you heard people carrying on about content? What is content anyway? Who creates content? How does content relate to the web experience? Are users interested in wading through pages and pages of content, or are they interested in obtaining quick information and going about their business?

Content is important, but not all content is good. People are assuming that if they put 25 links on their home page and include 40 pages of text in their web site, they'll attain "King of Content" status.

The web is wonderful because it allows designers to create little packets of easily digestible, unmistakably branded, and entertaining content worth returning to. In this sense, it is concept, not content that is king. A strong concept helps organize content into easily digestible packets of entertaining information that can quickly be retrieved by the user in search of that particular information. After all, no matter how much stuff you put on your website. If nobody is interested in it, they'll never look through it.

Keep It Simple

"Just the facts, Ma'am," goes the old saying, and it still holds true today. The Honda Campus site (**http://www.hondacampus.com**) is a beautiful example of a strong concept, understated simplicity, powerful branding, and targeted marketing communication worth returning to.

The Big Idea

In designing a site to promote an idea, sell a product, compel users to dig deeper, or provide entertainment, you need to have an overall concept that creatively delivers the goods. Honda's microsite, in this case **http://www.hondacampus.com**, is geared toward the college crowd and promotes two of Honda's vehicles: the Civic Sedan and the Civic Coupe.

4.1

The Honda Campus home page. Notice the communication hierarchy.

Figure 4.1 shows the Honda Campus home page. Notice the attention to detail. Every element has a purpose and compels user interaction. Notice the use of white space. There is no doubt that the viewer's eye is naturally attracted to the colorful links on top. If you actually visit this page on the Net, you see the fraternity paddle sway from left to right, back and forth, to create a sense that something is definitely happening on the page (also, the paddle is linked to the **http://www. honda.com** site).

Conceptually, every detail is fully thought-out. From the site name, "Honda Campus," (remembering the target audience) to the "Delta-Sigma-Honda" insignia burned into the swinging paddle, to the creatively written section names, "Get a Career, Take a Trip, Scope a Civic, and Spot Some Overachievers." As a matter of fact, the section links double as the site's navigation, which we look at shortly.

An Effective Branding Message

Immediately upon arriving at Honda Campus, you cannot help but feel the powerful branding message and the simplicity that is unique to Honda's brand image.

In figure 4.2, the "Take a Trip" section has been selected. Notice how the navigation works here. The "take a trip" link is now in focus, with the other links appearing to have traveled to the background, fading slightly out of focus (accomplished through Adobe Photoshop's powerful Gaussian Blur filter). Notice, however, that they are still discernible for the most part, and if the user wants to go to another section, they are still active as clickable links. What this kind of navigation does is create a constant feeling of comfort for the user, who does not have to worry about remembering their exact place in the site. It also helps to strengthen Honda's brand message, subconsciously telling visitors that Honda wants to make sure you don't get lost.

Notice again the smart copy that pays homage to the Honda Civic (staying on target with the site's key purpose) and compels the user to click to go deeper by offering a "road trip" scenario up the Pacific Coast Highway. The link to go deeper, by the way, is a flashing animated GIF begging to be clicked ("Let's go.").

4.2

Honda Campus: Take a Trip.

Focused Content

Upon clicking the "Let's go" link in figure 4.2—I couldn't resist—Honda Campus presents the road trip (fig. 4.3). Notice that the communication hierarchy begins with the navigational element on top, which highlights user location in the site. White space separates the navigation from an image of the road trip queens kissing a statue. It then follows to the location head, "Santa Monica," to the bar prompting interaction to see more images from the trip, and finally rests at a new navigational element at the bottom of the page. Within a matter of seconds, what could have taken three pages of text to describe translated itself into a smart, quickly digestible, visually entertaining piece of marketing communication. Sure, the copy is fun to read and the graphics are great, but the key purpose of the site stays in focus, and the paragraph highlighting the word "Civic" in Honda's corporate blue color also adheres to it. This is a subtle, yet smart approach to focusing on the site's key purpose while delivering creative entertainment.

4.3

Honda Campus: Take a Trip: Santa Monica.

4.4

Honda Campus: Take a Trip: Tripper Images.

When the user clicks to see more tripper images, Honda Campus offers an alternative to a banner ad—in this case a commercial (within a commercial) for Arco's AM/PM (fig. 4.4). Please note how the word "Civic" is once again highlighted in Honda's corporate blue and examine its usage in the copy, "Civic Juice," instead of "get some gas for the car." Creative copywriting helps to promote Honda's image to the reading audience as a "hip" manufacturer (remember the target audience). Once again, in figure 4.4 the user is lead down the visual hierarchy to a giant collection of road trip photographs to browse through. In this case, Honda Campus is rewarding the user with entertainment for dealing with the marketing message. It is an equal exchange of advertising for entertainment (the current model of the web).

4.5

Honda Campus: Tripper Photo.

Figure 4.5 demonstrates what happens for users of Netscape Navigator 3.0 and Microsoft Explorer 3.0 or better. Upon clicking one of the photo links, the appropriate shot pops up in a new window (a JavaScript trick covered in chapter 8). Users of Netscape and Microsoft Explorer versions below 3.0 will bring up the photo in a new web page and then will have to use the browser's back button to return to the "Tripper Images" screen (browser limitations with respect to new technology are discussed in Chapter 6).

Where's the Beef?

Definition

A *rollover* is a descriptor for the act of physically moving your mouse to position your cursor over something on the screen (the word "roll" comes from the actual rolling action of the ball inside your mouse). So, if I told you to roll over an icon, I would mean for you to position your cursor over that icon … that's all.

With the key purpose of the site in mind, Honda's "Scope a Civic" section is a sanctuary of simple branding excellence.

Figure 4.6 displays an initial welcome to the "Scope a Civic" page. Notice that the navigational graphic has been updated to bring the current section into focus, fading the others out. The "Which Civic" graphic is an animated GIF and is a simple, low-filesize graphic that loads quickly and prompts the user to select either the "Sedan" or the "Coupe."

Upon rolling the cursor over the "Sedan" graphic, an image of the vehicle appears (fig. 4.7), offering user feedback. Rollovers are created by JavaScript code. (You will learn how to step-by-step create a graphic rollover for your site in chapter 8. Please note that only users of Netscape Navigator 3.0 and Internet Explorer 3.0 can view rollovers.) Upon clicking the rollover link, Honda Campus delivers figure 4.8.

Notice that the navigation changes slightly to indicate that you are in the "Sedan" section and that at any time, you may go to any of the other sections without confusion. Conversational copy entertains the reading audience while promoting the Sedan's spaciously roomy interior, and an animated navigational element (colors change continuously, prompting interaction) at the bottom of the page invites users to find out more about the Sedan through branding messages highlighting the car's key features, "Hot Laps, More Stuff, and No Worries."

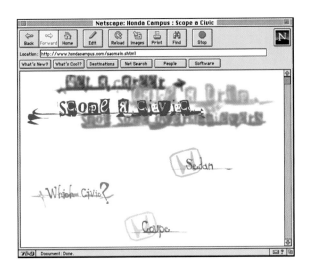

4.6

Honda Campus: Scope a Civic.

4.7

Honda Campus: Scope a Civic with rollover enabled.

4.8

Honda Campus: Scope a Civic Sedan.

Attract without Confusing

Confusing web sites are all over the place, and I hope you are starting to formulate your own design philosophy based on what we have covered so far. It is very important for you to be an individual so that your work can be as unique as your individuality. However, once you understand the fundamental issues, they will influence your design decisions. It is up to you to find a balance between instinct and rule of thumb. As long as you keep the site's target audience and key purpose in mind, you should have no problems attaining a balance in your web design and minimizing confusion. The following problems breed confusion in web site design:

> "It is very important for you to be an individual so that your work can be as unique as your individuality."

- **No Key Purpose.** Let's face it: If you don't have a goal, how can you reach it? The easiest way to obtain a key purpose for your site is to simply ask yourself, "What do I want out of this web site?"

- **Lack of Concept.** No matter how simple or complex your web site requirement, a clear concept helps to simplify the task at hand. The first step in conceptualizing a web site idea is to take your key purpose, apply it to your target audience, and ask yourself, "How can I best communicate my site's key purpose to my target audience?"

- **No Target Audience.** As you can already see, if you do not have a target audience in mind for your site, it's very difficult to creatively conceptualize a web site.

- **Information Overload.** This is the easiest way to confuse an audience. The more choices you provide, the more work your audience has to do to have fun at your site. More work does not equal more fun. A good concept helps you simplify the way you communicate your information.

- **Unintelligible Interface.** In the real world, USERS have to navigate through your site. Make things easy by simplifying your navigation and always alert the users as to where they are in your site.

concept : content : design

My personal web site on the Net (**http://www.rpirouz.com**) is a good example of a strong brand message, clear communication, simple interface, and effective animation that compels users to click and go deeper within my site.

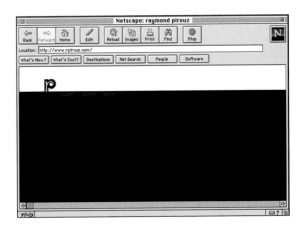

4.9

Raymond Pirouz on the web.

I have targeted my site to people who work with art directors or creatives. These can be prospective clients or creative industry people who have an appreciation for art and design. It might be argued that by targeting my site to such a limited audience (creative people or artists who love Macintosh), I am limiting the overall exposure my site can receive. It is extremely important to target, however, because it is the only way to truly and creatively express your ideas to your intended audience. If people who do not appreciate your work happen to stop by, they're free to leave; but then again, you probably do not want them to stop by in the first place if they do not appreciate your work! With that in mind, the concept of my site is to draw my target audience (those interested in working with an experienced art director to solve communication problems) to my home page, impress them with an extremely quick load-time that offers them immediate access to my site's content, offer simple graphics that are conceptual in nature, and showcase my online portfolio/design philosophy separated under the headings for which the site is titled.

Upon initially arriving at the site, the user sees only the black-and-white background (which I designed to give more visual presence to my work) and the HTML text links. Suddenly, my logo (composed of my initials) begins to sprout from the black background into the white area on top, signaling my presence on the Net (figures 4.10–4.17).

4.10 – 4.17

Raymond Pirouz animating logo.

As soon as my logo stops animating, as if to signal the second wave of graphics, a small wave begins to form across to the right of my logo, illustrated in figures 4.18 through 4.23 and visualized on-screen in figure 4.24.

Please note that the animation represented in figures 4.10 through 4.17 animates only once when the page loads and does NOT loop continuously. The animation represented in figures 4.18 through 4.23, however, loops continuously (GIF animation and looping techniques are discussed in Chapters 6 and 7). The reason behind looping your animation is this: to get attention. In the case of the wave, I felt that some users may not see it the first time since it is very subtle, so I decided to make it loop infinitely, as it adds a nice touch of motion and a sense of zen to the page. Note, however, that there is a good lag-time between loops, which balances out the repetition.

In figure 4.24, as I roll my cursor over the wave, it changes to a pointing finger (indicating that it is a link), and I receive a JavaScript feedback message in the status bar that reads, "making some waves on the Net" (I explain this feature further, step by step, in Chapter 8). My target audience, those who work with creatives and understand what to look for in creative solutions, find this a simple, elegant approach, far subtler than if I were to actually say, "Hey, look at the awards I've won…" Upon clicking the wave graphic, the awards page appears (fig. 4.25).

4.18 – 4.23

Raymond Pirouz animating wave.

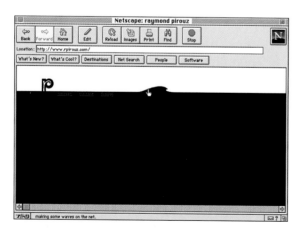

4.24

Raymond Pirouz on the web.

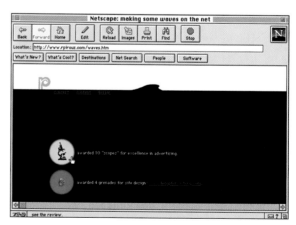

4.25

Making some waves on the Net.

Notice that my logo in this page has faded back to indicate that we are no longer on the home page. Clicking on my logo would bring back the home page. Notice the communication hierarchy in this example, along with the use of contrast to highlight the awards icons that show off some of my celebrated work. Figure 4.25 is designed to draw the user's attention straight to the awards icons. The wave graphic still operates and loops in this page, yet no link is attached to it (because we are already in the awards page). Theoretically, I could either show or not show the wave graphic in this page since it is a link on the home page and links nowhere from the awards page. I chose to show the wave as an identifier in this case, rather than use it as a piece of navigation. See how you can break the rules if breaking them makes sense?

I hope that by examining my home page on the Net, you have a better grasp for how to conceptualize, target, and design compelling web sites. Just in case you'd like to see more, however, there are two other case studies in this chapter, so let's get to them.

Going for the Dig

How do you entice viewers to go deeper within your site? Careful, here, because creative enticing techniques are not enough. You must deliver on any promise you make early on in your site—otherwise, you end up with disappointed surfers who will not return.

Before we continue with the last two web sites in this chapter, let's address one question:

What's the Ideal Site Depth?

Site depth is defined as the number of pages a user has to click through to get to the key content of the site. The answer depends on the following four factors:

- Target audience
- Site content
- Mode of transfer
- Bandwidth

A reasonable site depth can be anywhere from 1 to 5 pages. It all depends on the preceding four factors. If I created a site targeting young people and filled it with 5 pages of text, within which were hypertext links to other sections into the site, chances are my audience would not go deep within the site. Why? Younger people have a more limited attention-span and tend to be more visual than adults. While many adults (especially those in professional practice) may read copy on a page, youngsters tend to look for images that draw their attention. A five-page tease into the site's key content full of text and no imagery will NOT draw young people in.

Definition

The number of pages your user has to click through to get to the key content of your site is what determines *site depth*. The target audience, the site content, and the connection speeds of the user are all variables that will affect site depth.

The Target Audience

Generally, younger audiences are thought to be more impatient by nature. However, on the web, younger audiences spend more time on your site if you have activities to keep them occupied. If you are designing for the young at heart, knock yourself out with as many pages as it takes to strategically communicate your product or service (using entertainment).

On the other hand, the older crowd tends to want specific information and usually wants it right away. I would get to the heart of the matter within the first few pages and keep it at that. Your site should not be judged by how large it is; it should be judged by how effectively it satisfies your key purpose to the target audience.

> "Your site should not be judged by how large it is; it should be judged by how effectively it satisfies your key purpose to the target audience."

Content of the Site

As a rule of thumb, if your home page has more than 10 links on it, you might want to categorize and simplify your navigation to make information retrieval easier.

If you don't have much to say, don't cram it all on the same page, either. Use your best judgment based on the exercises we have performed so far to see if you can't create a compelling communication hierarchy.

Mode of Transfer

Will it be input or output? If the key purpose of your site is to get users to a page where you want them to input their name, address, and so on, into a form and submit it to you, you have to offer something in return (an e-mail list, guest list, newsletter, or some such) and you have to present the form early in the site. Otherwise, users get offended if you draw them many levels deep, only to give them more work to do. (For an explanation and illustration of a nicely designed form, see figure 4.30 later in this chapter.)

If, on the other hand, you are offering something the users want badly, as in the case of Apple Computer offering system software updates, you can make your users go through hell and high water—but they will get what they came for.

Bandwidth

If your target audience is on limited bandwidth (9600, 14.4, or 28.8 modem speeds) you will have to take care in limiting your site depth to anywhere from one to three pages maximum. If each page takes approximately 30 seconds for the average user to load, three pages will cause a 1.5-minute delay on your users' surf schedule. By providing the key content of your site as quickly as possible, you minimize boredom and impatience caused by slow connection speeds.

I hope these little tidbits of information help you in creating a site that best suits your needs and addresses your target audience.

Teasing Them In

Figure 4.26 shows the HotWired Network's front door (sometimes referred to as "splash screen" or "splash page").

The HotWired splash page is nicely executed in its simplicity and concept. It begins with a wired image of the planet Earth. Little does the unsuspecting visitor know that the Earth splits apart to reveal giant glowing and gyrating "Wired-like" fluorescent rings of color within the planet. The entire time this GIF animation was taking place, I as a user had the option to get rid of the introductory animation and go straight to the page via the "hotwired" link in the upper-right corner of the screen.

Figure 4.27 is the entire HotWired Network's home page at a glance.

Upon initial inspection, it seems like information overload; however, there is something about the way the information is laid out using white space to create divisions that makes the text-heavy page digestible—a section at a time. With plenty of links appearing in the left-hand column, right under the "HotWired" company logo, and links throughout the site's copy, any user can quickly become overwhelmed with all the possibilities. HotWired's use of graphics is extremely light, and minimal file-size images randomly appear in the template, making for almost immediate page-load times. The branding message is NOT as strong in this page as it could be, though.

4.26

HotWired splash. (Copyright©1994-1997 Wired Digital, Inc. All Rights Reserved.)

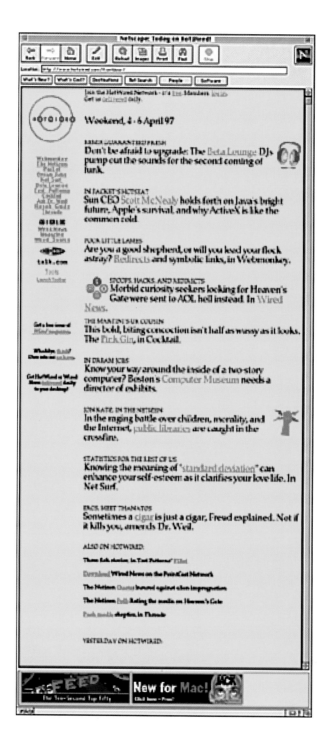

4.27

HotWired Network at a glance. (Copyright©1994-97 Wired Digital, Inc. All Rights Reserved.)

4.28

http://www.hotwired.com/frontdoor/ on a 14"
monitor. (Copyright©1994-97 Wired Digital, Inc. All rights
reserved.)

One way to make the brand stronger would be to add (drumroll, please) a subtle hint of animation. Notice that by subtle hint I refer NOT to a fully rendered, spinning 3D logo that dominates the page and takes about a minute to load. Rather, I simply refer to an interesting way to make the logo sing. By making each of the little circles that spell out HotWired flip over and spell out another word, for example, the brand could transform to something more … from a mere graphic simply placed on the page into a graphic that functions as a piece of communication. Not all graphics have to have this treatment, mind you. You don't want to see every piece of graphic doing something to get your attention—remember the communication hierarchy.

Notice that the HotWired logo takes up a great deal of space on the page, yet for a hip network of fresh industry-information, news, and up-to-the-minute happenings on the hottest trends on the Net, HotWired's identity on this page could use a little spicing up. For example, an animation to make the logo appear out of thin air would immediately attract the user's attention and strengthen the brand. Because the animation would not loop, it would create a nice introductory piece that would not continue to become an eyesore to those wanting to read the information.

Loop Factor

When considering the use of continually looping graphics, keep in mind your goal with the animation. If your goal is to attract user attention to click on an item, then loop the graphic to allow a fair amount of time to pass between loops (I show you how to do this in Chapters 6 and 7) so that it's not a continual nuisance. However, as in the case of my suggestion for the HotWired logo, do not loop graphics if they are merely an indicator or a "welcome" graphic created only for effect.

Temptation Through Typography

The HotWired network tempts users to go deeper by offering mini, stand-alone sites as links on the left-hand side of the screen (fig. 4.28). Notice the use of typography in the communication hierarchy to designate where the viewer should go first. From the brand image, the user is directed to the date, under which there is a column with industry-news highlights linked to content in the HotWired network of sites. This site is a good example of using type as visuals. If you notice the scale applied to the main body of type as opposed to the links on the left of the page, you will notice that the links to the left are an obvious third read (first, the brand; second, the date and information under it; and third, the links). In such a manner, with its use of minimal graphics (for quick downloads), along with text that demands to be read, the HotWired site tempts users to click.

Just the Facts

Observant Investigation Services (**http://www.privatedick.com**) is an international private detective agency with offices on the Net. This site is a good example of beautifully simple design, typography, and branding message targeted at viewers on the move.

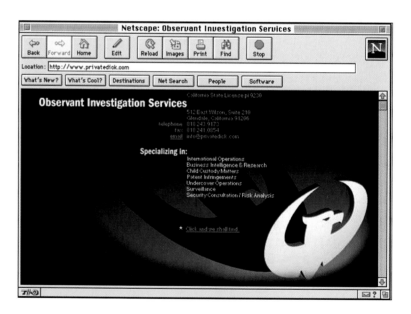

4.29

Observant Investigation Services.

The Observant Investigation Services home page quickly presents the who, what, where, when, and how. There is no overhyped marketing message because this site's key purpose is to obtain information about an individual's needs.

A simple, elegant use of the HTML <BLINK> tag is used to create a blinking "*" that immediately demands user attention but isn't a huge graphic file.

Here is the line of HTML code that created the simple attention-getting link:

```
<FONT COLOR="#ffffff" FACE=helvetica SIZE=3>

<BLINK>*</BLINK></FONT>

<FONT FACE=helvetica SIZE=1><A HREF="form.htm">Click and we shall find.</FONT>
```

Note

CGI (Common Gateway Interface) is a programming language that requires your own server to use or test, and is beyond the scope of this book. However, in Chapter 7, I tell you how to use e-mail forms with simple HTML to design your very own fully operating forms without having to know a code of CGI scripting or PERL programming.

For more information on CGI, check out Bill Weinman's *The CGI Book*, ISBN 1-56205-571-2, Shishir Gundavaram's *CGI Programming*, ISBN 1-56592-168-2, or type "CGI" in your favorite search engine, or query http://www.amazon.com for their list of books on the subject. You'll be pleasantly surprised, I'm sure.

The <BLINK> tag (a proprietary Netscape tag unsupported by Microsoft's Internet Explorer) is a great attention-getting device, if used elegantly to draw attention to a piece of information rather than all over a page (which is just annoying—unless, of course, your site is about creating annoyance).

The communication hierarchy in this site goes as follows: The oversized brand at the bottom-right of the page casts a shadow and leads the eye to the upper-left corner to the site's title. Elegant typography drops the user's focus from the title straight down the information to the blinking "*," with a link that reads, "Click and we shall find."

For the user on the move, especially for someone who does not want to spend an entire hour wading through marketing information to find out exactly who to contact and how to contact them, this site does a phenomenal job of immediately selling a service—no questions asked.

4.30

Observant's feedback form.

Upon clicking the flashing link on the Observant Investigation Services home page, you are quickly present-ed with a form to fill in with your vital information, a pull-down menu from which to select a subject, and a "Comments" box to describe your need. When you submit the form, a CGI script organizes your information and e-mails Observant Investigation Services personnel regarding your requirements, and you'll shortly be contacted with a fee schedule to service your need. Simply done and quite effective.

If your site is not a content site, but rather, is simply a marketing front-end to your business, there is no rea-son you should create confusion for yourself and your users by creating irrelevant content in the name of entertainment. If you're not in the entertainment business, do what you do best, and you will get hits.

That's the Ticket

We've covered plenty in this chapter. You are oh, so close to designing your very own site. The next step is to help you organize in your mind exactly what it is you want your web site to do. After you finalize the con-cept, content, and design issues you'll need to deal with, you're ready to get to work.

5

Communication Strategy

To get your message across clearly and quickly, you need to apply strategic thinking to your design. Before you even begin to conceptualize what you want your web page to look like, it is important to plan your mode of attack. You don't need a degree in marketing to achieve this goal. The basics of strategic planning, positioning, and marketing applied to creating compelling web communication yields the following eight-step communication strategy:

1. Develop an intimate knowledge of the site's key purpose—through research or personal involvement.
2. Not only *identify*, but also *identify with* your target audience.
3. Study the visual language that links your target audience to the site's topic (discussed later in this chapter).
4. Design an intuitive navigational system.
5. Conceptually communicate the site's key purpose to the target audience using the visual language.
6. Create a strong, memorable branding message.
7. Deliver the information in a visually interesting manner, taking advantage of current web technology to reinforce the site's topic (your message). In other words, don't use technology for technology's sake, unless your site is experimental in nature.
8. Create an environment that entices users to return.

> "Before you even begin to conceptualize what your web page will look like, it is important to plan your mode of attack."

If you follow the above guidelines for strategic communication, you're sure to successfully relay precisely the information that you want to reach your target audience. The above eight guidelines are designed to provide an overview of the basic strategic approach you should take in developing successful web sites. They represent a strong strategic foundation on which you can build successful marketing communication every time.

This chapter covers the strategic planning associated with conceptualizing and building successful web sites. I explain how to apply strategic thinking to solve communication problems, and I give you the building blocks by which to compel your Net-savvy audience, keep them interested in your site, and bring them back for more.

So You Want to Design a Web Site

There are literally hundreds of thousands of sites on the Net—from your average "Welcome to my web site, wanna see a picture of my cat?" site to the highly branded, techno-savvy, corporate-funded mega-site. There is no right answer to the question: What makes compelling web sites? Instead, you must ask

How effectively does the web site communicate its message to its intended audience?

This seemingly simple question can help give you some guidelines by which to measure effectiveness. First of all, notice that there are NO RIGHT ANSWERS. As discussed earlier in the book, all judgments are based on individual taste and are purely subjective. However, there are *degrees* of good and bad, to which the masses seem to be in agreement. If you examine the above question, you will notice that it asks, "How effectively…" This measures the *degree* of effectiveness and can be objective to a certain extent. By applying the eight guidelines for strategic communication discussed earlier, we can study a web site to determine the *degree* to which it compels its audience. The following questions help to determine to what extent a site compels (is effective):

- Is the site's content believable (honest or full of hype)?
- Does the site speak to you?
- Is the site copy-intensive, or does it use pleasing visuals?
- Is the site easily navigable, or do you get lost?
- Is the site's intent (key purpose) clear?
- Is there a strong, memorable brand message or first-read?
- Is the information delivered in a digestible manner (does it load quickly/communicate quickly), or does it use too much technology for the sake of technology (does not apply if the site is an artistic experiment)?
- Would you return to this site?

Please note that the above questions are just a general overview for measuring an immediate *degree* to which a site effectively communicates its message. You may create a site, for example, that has nothing on the page but your picture. If your intended audience is your mother, and your goal is to send her a picture of yourself, you have created a highly effective piece of communication. Things are rarely that simple, however, and you can use the above eight questions to evaluate the most intensely designed, content-rich sites. Speaking of your intended audience, the next section is designed to help you evaluate just that.

What Is the Key Purpose of the Web Site?

A *key purpose* is that which helps you achieve your site's overall goal. You can, of course, have more than one goal for your web site, but be warned: you run the risk of confusing your audience with such a scenario. Sites that have multiple key purposes (such as sales, service, product information, online gaming, chat areas, and so on) may want to consider the microsite approach (for example, Honda Campus, a microsite of the Honda site). Microsites link off the home site, yet take the user to a brand new site with its own key purpose. Thus, the home site acts as a link to several microsites, each with its own key purpose.

Amazon Books at **http://www.amazon.com** is an outstanding example of a site that has a key purpose. There is no mistaking Amazon's goal: to provide its users with access to millions of books—any and all of which are available for purchase over the Internet. Even though the site suffers from information overload and lacks an intuitive navigational structure, it is dead-on when it comes to targeting its audience (wired book-lovers) and communicating its key purpose.

You may argue that because of Amazon Books' text-heavy and navigational weaknesses, it should not be considered effective. On the contrary, if you ask any web junkie for the best bookstore on the Net, you'll undoubtedly hear the word "Amazon" as the answer. That proves that Amazon Books has associated itself with "books on the Net." Therefore, any time you think of books on the Net, you are more likely to think of "Amazon" than any other bookseller. This is, of course, due to Amazon Books' early web presence and early popularity. Regardless, Amazon Books has engraved its key purpose into the minds of web junkie book-lovers all over the world—a strategic success. The information overload and navigation issues are my personal subjective feelings and put Amazon Books in the "average" category in terms of overall site design. Nonetheless, Amazon Books successfully achieves its strategic key purpose: to sell books on the Net.

5.1

Amazon.com Books! Earth's Biggest Bookstore. (Amazon.com site as of July 1997; reprinted by permission of Amazon.com.)

Who Is the Intended Audience?

Every web site has an audience. Often, the audience has been targeted (predetermined) by the web designer who consciously sets out to communicate a certain message to them. Successful web sites target their audience based on their content. Women's Wire (**http://www.women.com**) is a good example of strategically targeted communication.

Women's Wire is designed specifically for women, to address women's issues. Therefore, it is targeted toward women in its overall site concept and design. Notice the imagery used in figure 5.2. The straw hat and glove, as used in the above context, are vocabulary words in the visual language whose target is predominately women. Therefore, in this example, art directors of the Women's Wire site have consciously chosen to use images that are more appreciated by women than by men in order to quickly communicate to their target audience. This is not to say that men would not appreciate the site's imagery. It is my opinion in this case that men are less apt to respond as quickly to the images than women are.

> "It is important for sites to not alienate the audience at large in favor of the target audience."

This brings us to the distinction between the target audience and the audience at large. The *audience at large* for Women's Wire includes men, women, boys, and girls; the entire spectrum of netizens. It is important for sites to not alienate the audience at large in favor of the target audience. For instance, figure 5.2 offers a mother's day section that can be beneficial to men and boys, as well as women and girls.

So keep in mind that, while it is important to target your audience, it is as important to keep your audience at large in mind. Chances are, if your site is strategically targeted, yet welcomes all users, you are bound to have many more return visitors.

5.2

The Women's Wire Site. (©1997 Wire Networks, Inc. All rights reserved.)

Identifying Your Target Audience

It is obvious that there will always be an audience at large. Its members may visit your site through a link or through a recommendation by a friend. Once at your site, they may or may not be interested in your content. The audience at large is usually indifferent to your site's content. However, there is always that specific target audience who is interested in (and will most likely benefit from) the content of your web site. If you decide to provide a virtual bird-watching environment, for example, with animating birds of every species, you have to think about your target audience. In this case, you would have to do some research on bird-watchers: average age, sex, geographic location, and so on. In the traditional advertising agency model, research is mainly done through the following means (in order of return based on costs involved):

- **Census data.** An official measure of population based on region—the first step to acquiring demographics information.
- **Demographics.** A collection of data used to identify consumer markets within specific regions.
- **Surveys.** Field tests, acquired either verbally or through completed forms (at supermarkets, on the Net, and so on) to determine various responses to specific inquiries by the surveyor.
- **Focus groups.** Information gathered from a select group of consumers who fit within the target market criteria of the surveyor.

Focus groups are often the most sought-after and costly means of gathering information on a specific target audience. Because of the costs involved with such statistical studies, many individuals and small businesses shy away from conducting research. The advent of the Internet, however, has allowed the average persistent "Joe" the freedom to research through the vast amount of data present in the pages of the virtual web. Unfortunately, this data can be misleading, based on the original purpose of the research and its conductor. Until more reliable sources of data appear on the Net, or companies specializing in researching specific online requirements begin to take root, online research is risky business.

Determining who your target audience is will help you communicate to them more effectively. Remember: You want to create a pleasing environment worth returning to. Knowing your audience helps you serve their specific needs and bring them back for more. In the virtual bird-watching case, for example, let's say you learn that bird-watchers live predominately in rural areas. Based on this hypothetical discovery, you may decide to create an interface that resembles deep forestry. While the interface would be pleasing to rural dwellers as well as city slickers, it would connect with rural dwellers more immediately because it would speak their visual language. It would be welcoming to city slickers who like to get away, but notice how they are not your target audience, but merely a sector of your indifferent *audience at large* in this example. You can break all the rules and offer a Martian landscape for your bird-watching site, but then again, you are bound to confuse your audience.

The key in effective targeting is to know who your audience is, identify with them, and serve them imagery that speaks their particular visual language.

Speak Visually

We've discussed the visual language and its implications in previous chapters. Here, I address the strategic benefits of applying the visual language.

Figure 5.3 displays the bookdeal.com home page (**http://www.bookdeal.com**). A virtual publishing house on the Net, bookdeal strategically integrates visual language into its interface and brand image. Notice how the top of the web page is designed to look like a typewriter rule, with the margins appearing to be set in conjunction with the HTML text on the page. It's a powerful usage of the visual language. Anyone can use the typewriter rule on their web site. It's a simple graphic to create and implement. However, the graphic would not work as well on other sites as it does in bookdeal. The visual language has been utilized here to communicate the fact that bookdeal is a "writer's" site. In this instance, the visual language is used to immediately communicate to the target audience. While the *audience at large* may or may not understand the association with the typewriter rule on top of the page, ALL writers (the target audience) will understand what the site is about immediately upon seeing the typewriter rule and the branding message.

Unmistakably raw, yet clear, the bookdeal.com branding message animates, as if being typed one key at a time, to communicate the typewriter's strikes and imprint upon the page, piquing the user's interest in a visually stimulating way. The tagline "publishing with an attitude." solidifies the brand message and leads the eye to the body copy, written in a humorous tone to describe the site's key purpose. The entire page takes fewer than five seconds to load on a 28.8 modem and communicates instantly. Notice the power of the visual language: Two minimal graphics told a story that could have taken several Shockwave files with streaming audio to describe—with much less headache and wait-time.

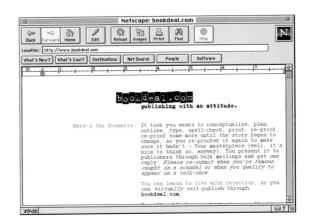

5.3

bookdeal.com: publishing with an attitude.

Click-Through Secrets

After you have your audience at your site, how do you make them go deeper? How do you entice them to click on your graphics and links to access the information you want them to see? Such answers can be had by analyzing some click-through secrets.

A *click-through* can be defined as the act of clicking on a link that takes you to another location. The word "click-through" originates from banner advertising, where click-throughs are used to record the number of times a banner has been clicked. The click-through rating measures the effectiveness of an advertising banner. For our purposes, let's say that when you create compelling graphics or links for your web site, you want people to click-through them.

In designing a web site, one of your goals is to compel users to click on HTML links or graphics that act as links. In the following sections, I examine some click-through secrets that will enable you to keep them clicking.

Never Under Construction

A well thought-out, strategic plan must account for a positive Net presence at every stage of a site's development. It's unrealistic to assume that web sites can't go live (be made ready for public access) until every page is fully designed and functional. The web is much too fluid and dynamic for such rigid thinking.

"'Under Construction' means, 'I'm not ready to have you here, so come back later.'"

Therefore, the "under construction" sign is unnecessary. The use of such imagery symbolizes DANGER—FALLING DEBRIS. It may sound funny or even outrageous, but think about it. If you see a building with a sign that says, "Under Construction," would you venture too far in its halls? This is an extreme analogy in that you can't really get hurt going through a web site, but if you believe in the visual language and what it can convey, believe this: "Under Construction" means, "I'm not ready to have you here, so come back later." I doubt you want your audience to have that kind of reaction to your site. Therefore, if your site is still under construction (100% of effective sites are always under construction) simply say nothing. Don't create links to the areas that are not yet accessible, that's all.

A beautiful example of a site still under construction, yet not coming off as such, is the Rubin Postaer Interactive web site (**http://www.rpinteractive.com**).

5.4

Rubin Postaer Interactive Front Door.

An interactive advertising agency, the rp.i site greets its visitor with three possible selections, each of which is a unique approach at delivering the same information. Basically, the rp.i site allows the user to choose between three different interfaces, as indicated by the numbers 1, 2, and 3 on the interface in figure 5.4. Now, what the user doesn't know is that there will soon be six interfaces to choose from (quite an impressive array of choices—extremely unique to the web). The art directors could have chosen to paste a big, rotating 3D "Under Construction" sign with flashing lights, announcing the site's inadequacies … but they chose instead to subtly say nothing at all and let the user be surprised on their next visit to find more numbers added to the list of possible interfaces. Remember: What you don't know can't hurt you. This applies to communicating with your audience. If the "Under Construction" sign delivers a negative visual connotation, why use it at all?

Position Your Links Within the Communication Hierarchy

Make certain that your links are visible within the communication hierarchy. I would recommend making your links the third or fourth read, at most. This assumes that your branding message is the first read, some supporting graphics or images acts as the second read, and some HTML text or copy is your third read, which leaves fourth read for your links. If at all possible, try to bump your links up to third read. Use the design principles discussed in Chapter 3—color, scale, and contrast—to structure your links within the communication hierarchy. Users like to know what their options are immediately, and often times, their options are presented through the links within a web page. By making your users' options immediately available, you add value to your page.

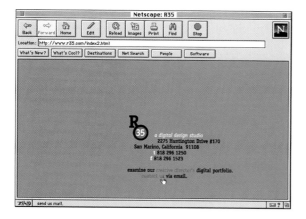

5.5

R35 content page.

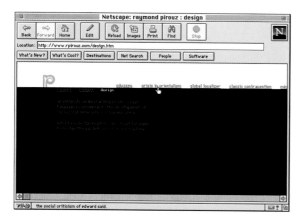

5.6

raymond pirouz: design.

In figure 5.5, notice that the two links (examine our creative director's digital portfolio and contact us via e-mail) are the third read, with the first read being the visual identity at the upper left, with the byline (*a digital design studio*) and address the second read. You can find this site at **http://www.r35.com/index2.html**.

Group Your Links

Figure 5.6 is a good example of grouped links. The only "buttons" on this page (clickable areas that actually take you somewhere else) are the underlined text links. Notice that they're grouped together not only to assist in the communication hierarchy, but also to focus the users' attention to a specific area from which they can make several choices. From a navigational point of view, it pleases users to have choices bundled together in an easy-to-comprehend manner. Staggering choices all about a web page, assuming the user will blindly click on any old link, can be detrimental to the navigational integrity of a web site—that is, don't make your navigation hard to follow.

For HTML Links, Use a Unique Typographic Layout

Figure 5.6 is also a good example of a unique typographic layout to enhance HTML link presence. The unique typography in this example draws the eye as a graphic element, while the underlined links quickly communicate their functionality and operate within the context of the page and its function (to display an artist's work).

Entice with Copy

Figure 5.7 is a good example of enticing users to click-through creative copywriting. Compelling copywriting is as effective as animated graphics in getting users to click. This figure depicts bookdeal.com's home page, where the user is tempted to click on a link to find out more. bookdeal.com could have said, "Click here" to find out more, but they chose to simply say, "Find out," and made it a link. In this example, because "Find out" is underlined, it is using the visual language of the Net to communicate that it's a link. Therefore, users automatically know that clicking on it takes them elsewhere—hence eliminating the need to say, "Click Here."

For another example of creative copywriting, you could say either, "Click to see my picture," or, "I was much more handsome at 18." The second sentence is much more compelling because it invites interaction without begging for it. The last thing you want to do as a designer is *beg* people to click. Creative copywriting is the easiest and quickest way to put HOT links on your web site without ever touching animated GIFs, Java, JavaScript, Lingo (Macromedia Director's programming language), ActiveX, or VRML.

To brush up on your copywriting skills, I would recommend that you take creative copywriting classes at your local college or university. Creative copywriting, like creative visual art, is achieved through plenty of practice and lots of research in the field. A handbook exists for the at-home do-it-yourselfer, titled *The Copywriter's Handbook,* published by Henry Holt and Company, Inc. (ISBN 0-8050-1194-3). For further study on advertising and creative copywriting, check out David Ogilvy's book, *Ogilvy on Advertising*, published by Vintage Books (ISBN 0-394-72903-X). For some online examples, you can go to my web site at **http://www.rpirouz.com** and click on "concept," whereupon you will be exposed to several examples of banner advertising using creative copywriting. You can also check out the Microscope site at **http://www.pscentral.com**, where you can take a look at award-winning banner ads, bustling with creative copywriting.

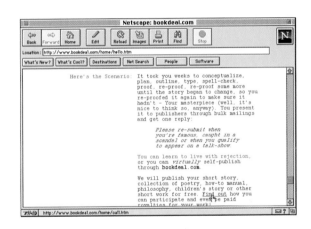

5.7

bookdeal.com.

Animate Your Graphic Links

Okay, so you weren't born a creative writer. Animated GIFs (which I cover in Chapter 6) are the easiest (and most often effective) way to create compelling communication on the web. Strategically thought-out, subtle, conceptual animations can dramatically increase click-throughs.

Reel 'Em In

After you've identified your target audience and designed a site that invites through the use of click-through techniques, it's time to reel 'em in. The following section examines how compelling animation can lead a user deep within a web site. Tools to create such animation are covered in Chapter 6, with step-by-step exercises to follow in later chapters. Using the example referred to earlier in this chapter, we will click-through one of the animated rp.i interfaces.

When we click on "2" in figure 5.8, we are presented with rp.i's interface #2 (**http://www.rpinteractive. com/pub/rpi/2/index.html**), as seen in figure 5.9. Notice the minimalist design (fig. 5.9) that draws the user to the animation that takes place. The all-too-familiar pointing finger icon moves atop the rp.i logo and clicks on it (fig. 5.10).

As the animating hand pushes in the rp.i logo, acting as a button to symbolize the "interactive" in Rubin Postaer, a new window appears as if the actual animation made it possible. Figure 5.11 illustrates the new window that opens as the hand presses the rp.i logo. This is done by using a certain JavaScript trick (which I describe in Chapter 8).

5.8

Rubin Postaer Interactive Front Door.

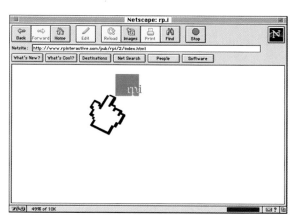

5.9

Rubin Postaer Interactive Interface #2.

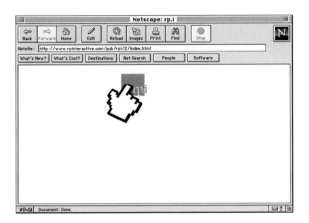

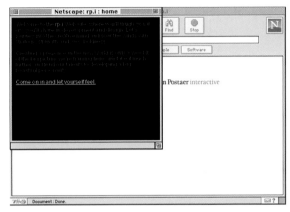

5.10

rp.i logo as a button, being depressed by the pointing finger icon to symbolize interactivity with the company.

5.11

rp.i welcome copy.

The resulting new window contains welcoming copy that compels the user to, "Come on in and let yourself feel." As an interactive advertising agency, rp.i successfully sells its services through the use of compelling visuals that entertain, while leading the user up to humorous, smart copy that compels interaction. If you have not already noticed, we have traveled into the rp.i site's content without a second thought. The site has almost taken *us* through the introduction so far, as if to lead us knowingly. This site plays itself out like a storybook, an adventure to embark on. "Come on, it's just a web site," you say! Sure, you can create "just another web site," but memorable web sites do more ... they tell a story and/or engage the user in a unique manner.

Upon clicking on the link to continue (as if we have any other choice—a strategic decision), we are presented with an rp.i disclaimer, as shown in figure 5.12.

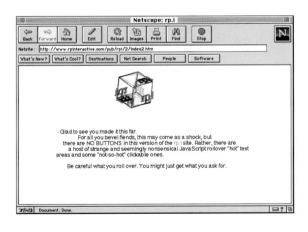

5.12

rp.i disclaimer.

The image in this figure, surprisingly enough, is a disclaimer page telling users what *not* to expect—and warning them what they should look out for. We are presented with humorous copy, "Glad to see you made it this far," quick-loading graphics (a spinning wireframe rp.i logo turned into a cube), and HTML type that quickly reinforces the message that this is an intermediary page. It is obvious by the tone of the copy on this page that #2 is somewhat of an experimental site. Therefore, it is fair to presume that it employs some technology for the sake of experimenting with user response to that technology (JavaScript, discussed in Chapter 8). Advancements in HTML and web design always take place as a result of designers who are willing to experiment.

On one hand, experimentation limits your target audience considerably (to those who have the hardware, software, and plug-ins to view your pages properly). On the other hand, without experimentation and the push to expand our limits, we would be stuck with pages full of raw HTML text and NO images whatsoever. It's a fine line, and rp.i's interface #2 tries to tip-toe through it by providing the user with some warning. You rarely see experimentation by mass-market sites (especially transactional sites), for the fear of losing business. In rp.i's case, however, because there are three possible interface selections (soon to be six), some experimentation is expected—and encouraged.

With the disclaimers out of the way, we take heed of the warning given by rp.i and roll over the animating rp.i logo, to be presented with yet another pop-up window with more text (fig. 5.13).

5.13

rp.i: here's the plan.

We are once again presented with humorous copy that introduces rp.i's team of strategists and welcomes the viewer to see how they get the job done. Notice that each time a new window opens, the original interface lays behind it, giving the user a sense of comfort concerning their location within the site. Notice also that each time a window pops open, it closes itself after the link is depressed (another JavaScript trick I tell you about in Chapter 8). This technique allows for plenty of white space to dominate the interface, beautifying the page while maximizing the communication hierarchy. As copy is needed to emphasize a point or to lead a user to the next level of a page, it can pop up in a new window, thereby keeping the overall page uncluttered with heavy text. Notice also how these intermittent pages act as teasers, enticing users to see more.

You may argue that interface #2 is too clunky, that it requires too much user interaction and awareness. And arguably, that's true. However, the rp.i site's key purpose is to communicate rp.i's unique ability to offer choices and unique solutions to communication problems. To answer this key purpose, site #2 has taken a very personal approach to web design. It's as if the web site is actually communicating to the viewer in a very personal manner and compelling interaction through the integration of technology, copywriting, and minimalist visual imagery. Interestingly enough, interface #2 does require a great deal of concentration and participation on the part of the viewer. It is not at all a passive site. You'll notice a considerable difference between each of the individual interfaces (and the strategic approach used for each) if you study the entire site on your own.

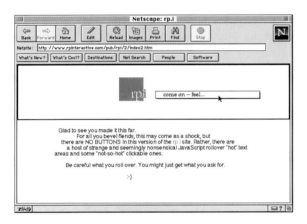

5.14

rp.i: come on – feel…

Upon clicking on the link shown in figure 5.13, the text box closes to reveal the rp.i logo, on the right of which sits a pull-down menu bar with the phrase, "come on – feel…" within it (fig. 5.14). The phrase immediately draws attention because of its simplicity and subtle command. In computer speak, for a cursor to feel, it must click. Therefore, this is another way to say, "click here," without actually saying it. Creative copywriting always adds to the compelling qualities of a web site.

At this point, we are at the heart of the rp.i web site, where we have the option of selecting from the pull-down menu (I tell you how to create your own in chapter 8). The rp.i interface #2 has successfully reeled us in using compelling animation. The following are some guidelines for creating compelling animations to reel users in:

- **Keep your animations simple.** Complex animations take long to download and distract your audience from the rest of the site's content—unless your site has no other content.
- **Use animations to draw attention or to communicate a message.** Animating your company logo, for example, can communicate a dynamic aspect of your product or service.
- **Keep your animations subtle.** 3D spinning logos for the sake of looking cool can be cool … they often succeed only to clue people that you just learned how to use your first 3D program.
- **Create utilitarian animations.** Try to implement function into your animations. If you're going to attract attention, you might as well make it count for something. If an animation is clickable and takes the user somewhere, it can be used as a successful teaser.

Notice that many of the animations in the rp.i interface "2" study fulfill these criteria. Granted, not every animation can be utilitarian and simple and communicative, but it is your responsibility as a content provider to provide compelling communication that adds value to your site, as well as to make your user's visit enjoyable and easily navigable.

Keep 'Em In

Getting users to your page is one thing. Enticing them to dig a little deeper is another, and keeping them occupied and happy in your web site determines (for the most part) whether they'll come back for more. Although the term "occupied and happy" may seem vague, it can apply to those visiting a one-page site that conveys a piece of information or a 500-page site that tries to do much more. An occupied visitor is one who is interested enough in your content to stay awhile and snoop around. A "happy" visitor is one who leaves your site with information he or she deems valuable and enjoys the experience enough to want to return.

In figure 5.15, the "Playtime" option has been selected and we are at the rp.i antics page. Notice that the cursor is positioned over the rp.i logo, which is animating. Notice also that to the left of the animating logo is a mini-image of figure 5.4, the rp.i front door. In the rp.i's interface #2, when the user rolls over the rp.i logo, it begins to animate and the mini-image is revealed (*rollover reveal* is covered in Chapter 8) to indicate that if the user clicks, he or she will be taken back to rp.i's home page, where they can select another interface. This, in effect, is the "go back home" button, but designed much more interestingly (although quite experimental in nature—I discuss JavaScript rollover techniques in Chapter 8). When the user rolls off the animating logo, the logo turns back into the solid rp.i, and the mini-image of rp.i's home page disappears.

"Inviting users to your site is almost like inviting someone over for dinner. If you don't make them feel welcome and at home, chances are they may not want to come over again."

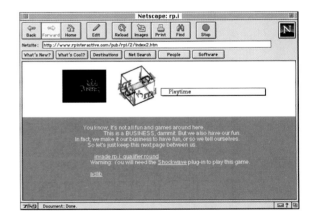

5.15

rp.i: Playtime.

The "Playtime" section offers two games, "invade rp.i: qualifier round" and "adlib." The "invade rp.i" game requires the Shockwave plug-in and "adlib" uses CGI scripts and PERL programming (more on tools in Chapter 8). Both games are attempts to create an environment in which the user will spend some time. "Why," you ask, "would I want my users to spend time on my site?" It's a good question, one worth a sound explanation. If you create an environment wherein your users are entertained and begin to associate positively with your site, you create a relationship between the user and your site. As the positive relationship is established, the user feels more comfortable exploring your site further. It's almost like inviting someone over for dinner. If you don't make them feel welcome and at home, chances are they may not want to come over again. So we crank out the party games and invite good cheer for our guests.

Speaking of good cheer, how would you like to invade rp.i? Let's get to it.

Upon rolling over the "invade rp.i" link on figure 5.10, a new window immediately opens (I cover a JavaScript rollover technique to open windows in Chapter 8) to load the Shockwave file containing the game. Shockwave is a plug-in by Macromedia, creators of Macromedia Director (covered in Chapter 6). With Director, designers can build complex interactive presentations or games containing animations, sound, and special effects. After the designer finishes putting the Director piece together, it can be saved as a compressed Shockwave file, which can be opened by any browser that supports the Shockwave plug-in. Currently, Netscape and Internet Explorer both support the Shockwave plug-in. The only major obstacle between users and Shockwave applications is the bandwidth bottleneck. On a 28.8 modem, there is an approximately 10 to 15 minute wait time to play "invade rp.i." As far as online games go, however, "invade rp.i" is well worth the wait.

In figure 5.16, the user is presented with the rules of the game, which stress that this is a "qualifier round," foreshadowing the possibility of upcoming rounds (creating the subconscious need for the user to want to return to the site). The object of "invade rp.i" is to hit 20 targets without missing more than 3. The prize, for those who succeed, is the password to invade rp.i (also foreshadowing a possible future game worth returning for).

By clicking on the screen to begin, the user is presented with a cross-hair scope with which to aim and a beam of laser light that follows the cursor as the user moves it (designed to create subconscious confusion—adding challenge to the game).

Figure 5.17 displays a target awaiting the user's bullet. The targets appear quickly and disappear even quicker, requiring a blazing hand-eye coordination. The background music adds to the overall mood of the game and creates an interesting ambiance. As targets are hit, they fall to the floor, quickly being randomly replaced by another to test the player's dexterity.

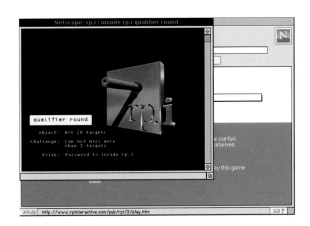

5.16

rp.i: invade rp.i qualifier round.

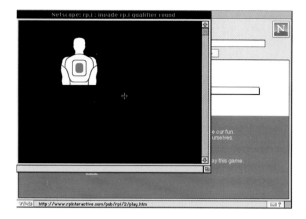

5.17

rp.i: invade rp.i qualifier round.

5.18

rp.i: Come on…

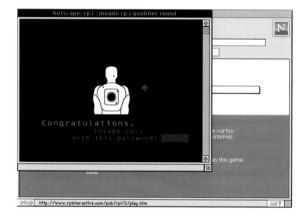

5.19

rp.i: Congratulations.

If the user misses more than three targets, the illustrious "Come on…" page appears (fig. 5.18), enticing the user to try again, adding to the challenge and urging interaction.

When the user successfully hits 20 targets without missing more than 3 (extremely hard to do … you'll see), the "Congratulations" page is displayed (fig. 5.19) along with the password to invade rp.i (grayed out this figure—sorry, you'll have to earn it).

"Invade rp.i" is the kind of entertainment that creates happy, occupied visitors. The game is simple, not overly time-intensive (unless, of course, the user is unable to win), and serves one purpose: To entertain while strengthening rp.i's image with the user.

By strengthening your image with visitors, you create what is called a "memorable" experience. Memorable experiences translate to return visitors.

> "By strengthening your image with visitors, you create what is called a 'memorable' experience. Memorable experiences translate to return visitors."

Bring 'Em Back Once They're Gone

So you've created a strategically targeted site, filled it with strong compelling content, and provided your users with memorable experiences. How do you ensure that they return once they're gone?

Offer Content Worth Returning To

Rubin Postaer Interactive's "invade rp.i" is a good example of content that makes the user want to return. Upon completing the game, a password is given with which the user can play the second game in the series. The potential for scenarios to the game is unlimited, creating an on-going dialogue between the user and rp.i. With a hooked audience, rp.i can creatively deliver agency news within the gaming interface to keep players updated with regard to rp.i's accomplishments.

> "Know your audience and deliver the kind of content they want to see."

If haven't heard of the game, "You Don't Know Jack," the beZerk site (**http://www.bezerk.com**) is definitely worth a visit. By downloading their games for your Macintosh or PC (Win95 only), you can take part in some of the most exciting online experiences available via the World Wide Web.

Gaming sites generally are bookmarked on users' browsers because of the entertaining products they offer, as well as the curiosity they instill in their audience, which is constantly on the lookout for the next step in online entertainment.

Do you necessarily have to provide entertainment to bring users back? Definitely not. Amazon Books, for example, brings users back because of their service and huge selection of books. The rule of thumb here is to know your audience and deliver the kind of content they want to see, while regularly maintaining the site, keeping it fresh.

5.20

beZerk — The Premier Online Entertainment Network.

Compile a Guest List and E-mail Updates

Using a CGI script, you can have your visitors sign a virtual guest list. In figure 5.21, Amazon Books is offering a contest and asks its users to provide their name and e-mail address to enter. The users' name and e-mail address is a very valuable piece of marketing information that can be used to send e-mail updates to prospective customers, collected through forms (see HTML in Chapter 7). Because spamming (the sending of electronic junk mail) is looked down upon by virtue of netiquette (Internet etiquette), it is wise to let users know that their information will be used to send weekly, bi-weekly, or quarterly site updates. If you decide to gather visitor information, you may want to assure your users that the information they provide will be kept confidential (if in fact you do not intend to sell or share the information). Lack of such mention may create hesitation in users who may otherwise provide personal information. This way, you don't offend anyone, and you have a sure-fire way of enticing your users to return based on new site updates.

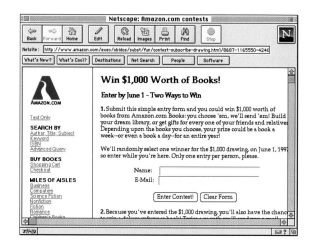

5.21

Amazon.com contests. (Amazon.com as of July 1997; reprinted by permission of Amazon.com.)

Provide Daily Updates

If you look back to figure 5.1, you will notice that in the lower right-hand corner of the screen, there exists a "Book of the Day" listing. Dedicating a certain portion of your home page to provide weekly, daily, or even hourly updates sets your site apart and makes it a much more immediate source of information. Of course, this works only if you do, in fact, continually update your site with fresh, new information. It also does you no good to go to this trouble if you have only, say, ten visitors per day. Such an undertaking requires a dedicated staff of content providers, programmers, and designers working in harmony to make your web site a dynamic entity. Figure 5.22 illustrates a highly dynamic web site worth returning to on a daily, if not hourly basis.

The CNN Interactive site (**http://www.cnn.com**) is a model example of dynamic information design on the web. The date and time updated notice near the top of figure 5.22 communicates an up-to-the-minute source of information, and the newspaper-headline style of information layout creates an unmistakable information hierarchy.

Must you invest this kind of attention to detail in order to get return visitors? Well, yes. When it comes down to the pure numbers, there's no competition between the average "Joe" and a giant like CNN. However, you can apply the same techniques that CNN and other successful sites use for getting *your* particular audience to return—and that's what it's all about. In fact, the culture of the Net is based on the "View Source-Copy-Paste" mentality. To succeed, simply look around and see what others do, examine their techniques, and apply them to your site in your particular style, and you too can be a success.

You should take a couple points into consideration when dealing with "View Source-Copy-Paste." First, you should always be sensitive to others' copyrights and should give credit where credit is due. Second, not all technologies are HTML-based. Bearing that in mind, know also that the following technologies cannot be examined using "View Source":

5.22

CNN Interactive.

- ■ **Java.** Java applets (mini-applications) are coded and complied (much like C++ programming) and reside on the web site server. They are called into action through use of the <EMBED> tag (see HTML in Chapter 7).
- ■ **Shockwave.** These programs are compressed Macromedia Director movies and are placed on the page by using the <EMBED> tag.
- ■ **Flash.** These compressed animations, created by using Macromedia Flash software, are also placed using the <EMBED> tag.
- ■ **CGI.** Designed to extend the functionality of HTML, such as with forms processing or web counters, these pieces of code reside on the website server and can not be accessed.

All of these technologies are relatively easy to learn and apply to your site if you know where to find out more. The following table contains learning as well as developmental references for each of them:

Java

Java Computing	http://www.sun.com/java
The Java Repository	http://java.wiwi.uni-frankfurt.de/
JavaWorld	http://www.javaworld.com
Symantec Corporation	http://www.symantec.com

Shockwave

Macromedia Shockwave	http://www.macromedia.com/shockwave
Macromedia Director	http://www.macromedia.com/software/director
Shockwave Support Center	http://www.macromedia.com/support/shockwave/
Shockzone	http://www.macromedia.com/shockzone

Flash

Macromedia Flash	http://www.macromedia.com/software/flash
The Leading Edge!	http://www.macromedia.com/shockzone/edge/flash/
Flash Support Center	http://www.macromedia.com/support/flash/

CGI

CGI Made Really Easy	http://www.jmarshall.com/easy/cgi/
Cabernet's CGI Cellar	http://ulc199.residence.gatech.edu/keith/cgi/
CGI Scripts	http://www.ipps.lsa.umich.edu/wn_docs/cgi.html
The Common Gateway Interface	http://hoohoo.ncsa.uiuc.edu/cgi/overview.html

The web is literally full of thousands of other resources that cover the above material. I suggest visiting your local search engine and typing in your inquiry to find out more.

That's the Ticket

Over the last five chapters, I've covered the fundamental visual, strategic marketing, and design issues that help create compelling web sites. The rest of this book focuses on informing you of how to creatively combine the skills you've learned with the technology at hand to create memorable web sites.

6

Very much like traditional designers, web designers use a variety of tools to get the job done. This chapter introduces you to the many tools available for creating compelling web design. Some of the tools are easy to learn and implement (like HTML) while others can take months—if not years—to master (like Macromedia Director).

The Tools

"Don't under-estimate the power of creative thinking: it's the tool without which all other tools are useless."

Several years ago, much of the design software was available only to Macintosh users. While technology has advanced to the point that the same software (that is, Photoshop, Illustrator, and the like) is available for both Macintosh and PC users, this chapter has a Macintosh slant, based on my own personal experience. Please note, however, that after you have a good understanding of the tools and their uses, you can achieve the same results on both Macintoshes and PCs.

Please note that this section in no way intends to replace the manuals and tutorials that ship with your software. Rather, it is meant to serve as a general overview of the tools available to you and to cover specific hints and tips associated with the tools as they relate to web design.

Your Brain—The First and Most Important Tool

Your brain is the most important tool you will ever have, both as an individual and—most important—as a designer. Don't underestimate the power of creative thinking; it's the tool without which all other tools are useless.

Adobe Illustrator 6.0 and Macromedia FreeHand 7.0 as Web Design Tools

Both Adobe Illustrator and Macromedia FreeHand are vector-based drawing tools. While GIFs and JPEGs are the most popular graphic file formats for the web, they most often start out being designed as vector images. The difference between vector-based art and GIFs/JPEGs is this:

GIFs/JPEGs are graphic files based on pixels, with 72 pixels in every inch. Vector art, on the other hand, is based on mathematical instructions between the computer and the software that produces smooth, non-pixelated lines, arcs, circles, type, gradients, and so on.

Working with vector-based drawing tools such as Illustrator or FreeHand gives the designer an unparalleled amount of control in terms of typographic layout, image creation, and initial web page skeletal design. Illustrator and FreeHand act as the buffer between the computer's mathematical capabilities and the designer's lust for perfection.

Both Illustrator and FreeHand vector images can be transferred to Adobe Photoshop either by using Copy and Paste functions or by exporting. After a vector-based image has been transferred to Adobe Photoshop, it becomes pixelated because Photoshop is a pixel-based painting and composition tool. This is our goal, however, since the majority of web communication is pixel-based.

Scaling is a major issue when it comes to pixel-based image-editing programs like Photoshop. The general rule of thumb is to never scale a pixelated image UP, as that forces your software to interpolate (or fake) a blown-up image of your original art. I have generally found it okay to scale DOWN a pixelated image in Photoshop, but I recommend that for any scaling function, you scale to the appropriate dimensions in your vector-based program and then export your artwork into Photoshop for pixelization.

Using FreeHand and Illustrator for Visualization

One of the greatest freedoms both Illustrator and FreeHand provide is the ability to lay out the foundation (or skeleton) of a web page's look and feel within the mathematical precision of a vector-based environment.

"There can never be any 'set' formulas in design. Each unique solution must address the unique communication problem at hand."

Figure 6.1 demonstrates how easy it is to set up the building blocks of a web page's layout. First, the designer needs to decide on the overall image area of the page. In the example, I have set a width of 500 pixels and a height of 350. There are no "official" size limitations or "standard" web page size guidelines. Some designers do not create scrolling pages, limiting themselves to an approximately 550×400 pixel web page, while more experimental designers force their viewers to scroll through pages of information. There is no right or wrong here. There can never be any "set" formulas in design. Each unique solution must address the unique communication problem at hand. Each page has different requirements, based on the amount of content on each page, whether the designers want their users to have to scroll down to see more information, and other factors. This kind of initial architectural thinking can help to determine many facets of a web site's look and feel.

It is important to lay out an initial skeleton of a site to get an idea of where graphics, images, or navigational elements may go on the page. After I set my boundaries, I can easily start plugging graphics in and experimenting with different looks. Figure 6.2 illustrates such experimentation for the bookdeal.com site (**http://www.bookdeal.com**). Notice that I am just playing around with placeholders for now—no need to get fancy yet. After I have the foundation I'm happy with, the details become that much easier to integrate.

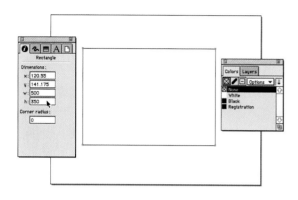

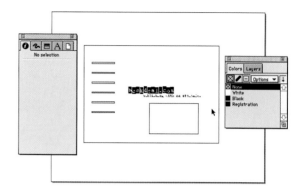

6.1

An example of laying out the foundation of a web page in FreeHand.

6.2

Laying out the initial web page skeleton using FreeHand.

Transferring from FreeHand or Illustrator to Photoshop

Once I am happy with my initial layout idea, I want to transfer what I've done into Adobe Photoshop so that I can start playing with colors and getting an idea of what things will look like pixelated instead of as the smooth lines I see in Illustrator or FreeHand.

Before taking my work into Photoshop, I want to maintain the integrity of the layout with regards to the image area dimensions I've created. Therefore, I select all the items of my layout (including the border) and choose COPY from the EDIT menu. Figure 6.3 demonstrates a tip you might like to utilize: select your screen border and turn the line white, or to no outline at all, and then choose COPY. This way, when you transfer your files into Photoshop, you don't get a box around your art. There is a way around having to create a rectangular border, and that is to create crop marks; but this trick works only in Illustrator. To create crop marks, either select your rectangular border or create a new one in Illustrator, and with it selected, go to Objects, Cropmarks, Make. This technique works only if you save your Illustrator file and import it into Photoshop. It will not work with the Copy-Paste function.

I can either save my work in Illustrator or FreeHand and then import it into Photoshop, or I can simply use Edit, Copy from my vector tool and use Edit, Paste into a new document in Photoshop. I personally prefer (and recommend) the Copy-Paste route. It can save plenty of time, and actually works quite nice. Both programs must be open at once, of course. After the work has been copied out of Illustrator or FreeHand, I switch to Photoshop and choose File, New.

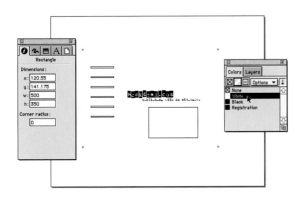

6.3

Getting ready to transfer work to Photoshop.

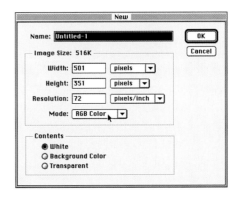

6.4

Choose File, New in Adobe Photoshop.

"The web is not a printing press."

Please note that Photoshop automatically calculates the image area (based on the perimeter screen box I created and copied along with your artwork) and presents me with the option to choose my Resolution and Mode. Notice also that the Width and Height are 1 pixel greater than that which I had originally intended—that's to compensate for the white border I am transferring along. I can easily resolve this later with the Image, Canvas Size. Resolution should remain at the default 72 pixels/inch, as all web communication transpires at 72 pixels/inch. For mode, I am presented with CMYK (Cyan, Magenta, Yellow, and Black; old-school printing terminology, probably before your time). Choose RGB, as the web is not a printing press. One word of warning: FreeHand and Illustrator are vector-based programs that operate under the CMYK palette. When I transfer my artwork from Illustrator or FreeHand to Photoshop RGB, any colors chosen in my vector-based tools will come out different through the translation between the palettes. When I click on OK, I'm presented with a blank page in Photoshop, in which I can Edit, Paste my artwork.

When you choose Edit, Paste in Photoshop to translate your vector art into pixels, you are presented with figure 6.5 and are asked whether you want to paste as pixels or paths (choose pixels). For anti-aliasing on or off, choose on. Your image then appears in Photoshop as a pixelized, anti-aliased image.

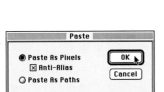

6.5

Photoshop's Edit, Paste command after coping your vector art.

Moving Type in Illustrator

Both FreeHand and Illustrator provide excellent typographic control for the traditional designer. Figure 6.6 demonstrates one of Illustrator's strengths in terms of type manipulation. In order to transfer this kind of typography into pixelated artwork for web use, you must copy and paste it into Photoshop. However, there are two ways to do this. The first, and most logical, is to simply select the object (fig. 6.6), select Edit, Copy from Illustrator, switch to Photoshop, and select File, New and Edit, Paste. Another way to do it (a much better way) is to translate the type from its original PostScript state (PostScript is a programming language through which the best typefaces are generated) into a vector-based state.

Figure 6.7's equivalent command in FreeHand is Text, Convert to Paths. Type comes out looking much richer when you translate PostScript type into vectors before you transfer the artwork into Photoshop.

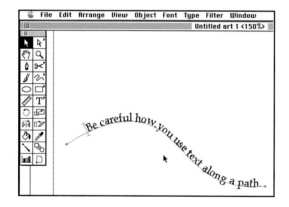

6.6

Working with type on a path in Illustrator.

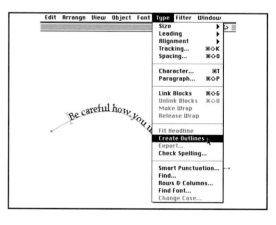

6.7

Illustrator's Type, Create Outlines command is used to transfer PostScript typefaces into vector artwork.

> "The darker the typeface, the more defined it is and the easier it is to read."

Notice that in figure 6.8, the file Untitled-1 has been created with a PostScript typeface copied in Illustrator and pasted into Photoshop. In the same figure, the file called "anti-aliased" was originally a PostScript file, later converted to paths in Illustrator, copied, and pasted into a Photoshop file. They are both enlarged 300% so that you can see the difference. Notice how the bottom example is much darker than the top example. For typography on the web, the darker the typeface, the more defined it is and, thus, the easier it is to read. Therefore, I would recommend translating your PostScript fonts into vector art before bringing them into Photoshop for web use.

Figure 6.9 illustrates the same piece of type in figure 6.16 translated into vectors, with all the points selected, ready to be copied for export. A word of advice: Always duplicate the PostScript typography you want to convert before you make vectors out of them. If you find a typo later, you have to do the whole thing over again unless you have backup copies of the work, because after you create vectors out of PostScript type, you can no longer edit it as text.

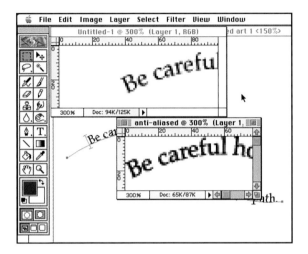

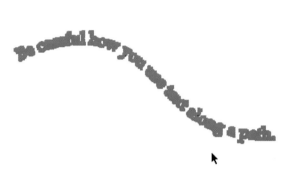

6.8

A comparison of PostScript type brought into Photoshop versus vector type brought into Photoshop.

6.9

PostScript type translated into vectors by Illustrator's Convert To Paths command.

An Overview of Adobe Photoshop 4.0

Adobe Photoshop is by far the most important electronic piece of software to hit the shelves since Aldus PageMaker revolutionized desktop publishing back in the day—remember that?

Color Planning as it Relates to the Internet...

Before the advent of desktop publishing, traditional design was done by hand and taken care of by many people. From hand-drawn calligraphy and fine lettering to pasteboards stuck with blocks of text created by typesetters, graphic art followed an archaic process from concept to print. Aldus, a software manufacturer eventually bought out by Adobe and Macromedia, produced PageMaker, which was the software that revolutionized the traditional publishing industry by creating the desktop publishing phenomenon. How does Photoshop play into all this? Well, Photoshop, created by Adobe Systems (http://www.adobe.com), was the first tool to give designers complete control over image editing. Designers deal with two things: words and pictures. Words are taken care of by the desktop publishing revolution; pictures are taken care of by the Photoshop revolution.

A highly powerful and effective photo compositing, manipulation, and effects-generation tool, Adobe has added a couple of very nice features in Photoshop 4.0 to address web design in particular. Let's get into a couple of fundamentals regarding Photoshop's web design strengths.

Configuring Photoshop for Web Design

As I discussed in Chapter 2, "Before You Begin," your most important first step is to import Lynda Weinman's browser-safe color palette (Macintosh and PC) or install your PANTONE ColorWeb software (Macintosh only).

Second, you need to set some preferences—after all, what good is a precision tool without precision settings?

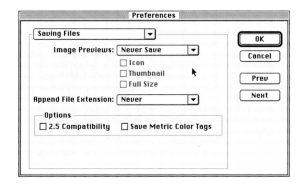

6.10

File, Preferences, Saving Files.

In figure 6.10, notice that "Never Save" has been selected for Image Previews, with none of the check boxes on the interface selected. This way, when you save a Photoshop file, it doesn't have a scaled-down preview (visible in Photoshop's Open File dialog box, and as the file's icon). Rather, it has a standard Photoshop icon. If you're searching for long-lost drawings and you have to open files one by one because they lack image previews, it can be a pain. However, image previews add a fair amount of information to your files, thereby increasing file size. When you transmit your files over to your web server, you're sending image files as raw data, which gets rid of Photoshop's icon anyhow. Basically, you don't want Photoshop to save a preview so that you can get a more accurate reading of your file's true size (discussed in the section "Judging True Filesize" later in this chapter).

In figure 6.11, notice that pixels have been selected for Units, because web pages are measured in pixels, not in inches. Also, select points rather than picas for column Width and Gutter because you work with pixels and points when you design web pages.

In figure 6.12 notice that Brush Size has been selected as your Painting Cursors and Precise has been selected for Other Cursors. When you are dealing with images that rely on pixel-accurate tools, it is best to have your settings as such so that you can take advantage of the precise control they offer.

Now that you've got your settings straight, let's create some web-safe, web-friendly images.

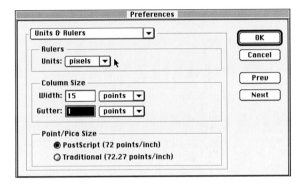

6.11

File, Preferences, Units & Rulers.

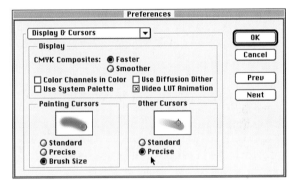

6.12

File, Preferences, Display & Cursors.

Creating Web-Safe Images

Basically, what I mean by "web-safe" are predominant file formats that all browsers understand. In this case, I cover the differences between aliased and anti-aliased graphics and how to create GIFs and GIF89s. Please note, however, that these examples represent a general overview of some of the basic principles. For a much more in-depth analysis of all your options and the many different approaches to creating graphics for the web, I strongly recommend Lynda Weinman's *Designing Web Graphics.2*, ISBN 1-56205-715-4.

Aliased and Anti-Aliased

A good rule of thumb here is this: If you're going to create GIFs with transparent backgrounds (because you use a background image on your web site and want your GIF to seamlessly integrate with it), you should create aliased graphics. I personally shy away from GIFs with transparent backgrounds because they are a pain to deal with—unless you're working on artwork that's not meant to look elegant on-screen.

The following represents scenarios where anti-aliasing is useful:

- Importing type from Illustrator or FreeHand
- Graphics without transparencies
- Creating medium- to large-sized (35×35 pixels or more) images residing on a solid background

The following represent some scenarios where aliasing is useful:

- Graphics to be placed on transparent backgrounds
- Typefaces that are "grungy" in nature, yet still readable when aliased
- Graphics with limited color palettes, containing large blocks of geometric color

Please note that the above are meant to serve as guidelines and are in NO WAY set in stone, but rather, act as a foundation upon which to experiment.

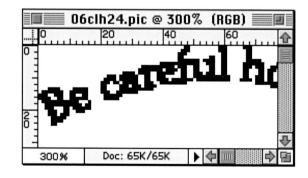

6.13

An image with aliased (bumpy-lumpy) edges.

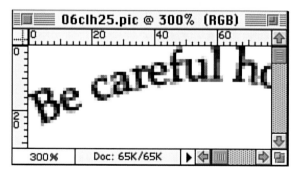

6.14

An image with anti-aliased edges (look Ma, no lumps!).

When you compare figures 6.13 and 6.14, there's no reason why anyone would want to use aliased typography. However, when it comes to solid colored shapes, you can sort of get away with it (if your shapes are very small and their lumpy edges indiscernible). Figures 6.15 and 6.16 illustrate the point further.

6.15

Closeup of aliased (bumpy-lumpy) edges.

6.16

Closeup of anti-aliased edges (look Ma, no lumps!).

6.17

Photoshop's alias-capable tools:
Lasso, Magic Wand, Paint Bucket,
and Pencil.

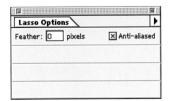

6.18

Lasso Options floating menu with
selectable Anti-aliased feature.

"Aesthetics
are extremely
important in
getting a point
across. However,
if you can save
a considerable
amount of
disk space by
creating aliased
graphics while not
degrading the
overall quality of
the image, it's
more practical to
alias the work."

In Photoshop, you can create aliased artwork through the use of the Lasso, Magic Wand, Paint Bucket, and Pencil (fig. 6.17) or you can designate an imported graphic to be aliased by unchecking the Anti-Aliased check box when you import or paste (refer back to figure 6.5).

Figure 6.18 demonstrates the Lasso Options floating menu, within which you can decide whether you want the Lasso to operate in an aliased or an anti-aliased fashion. As you select the other tools in figure 6.17, their respective Options floating menu also enables you to designate their aliased or anti-aliased nature.

When it comes to choosing between aliased and anti-aliased, consider this:

> Does anti-aliasing my artwork enable my viewer to more quickly decipher my message, or am I simply anti-aliasing for the sake of aesthetics?

This, of course, is a design decision based entirely on the designer's own point of view and personal design aesthetic. I personally never limit myself to either one or the other. My choice of whether to alias or anti-alias artwork is based on my personal design aesthetic, the importance of the artwork being communicated, and the composition itself. If the image were a fifth or sixth read, is an accent graphic, and is a small two-color image, I'd probably leave it aliased. On the other hand, for all first and second-read images, I anti-alias the artwork—unless they are one- or two-color small graphics that I want to look "rough" or pixelated.

GIF, GIF89a, and JPEG

The GIF and GIF89a formats (allowing for transparency and animations) are the most popular graphic file formats on the web, and JPEGs are a close second. The rule of thumb for choosing between GIFs and JPEGs is this: If you want to save grayscale, full-color photography or artwork that takes advantage of millions of colors or shades of gray and uses smooth gradations, save your image as a JPEG file. If, however, you want to save graphic artwork such as logos, line art, and images with less than 256 or so colors, you're better off with the GIF format. The process of saving GIFs is a lot more involved than saving JPEGs (where you simply save as JPEG), so let's take a look.

Making GIFs

When you're working in Photoshop and you're ready to export an image to GIF, please make sure that you've flattened all the layers in which you may have been working (an example follows later in this chapter).

The bookdeal.com logo in figure 6.19 is used to present the following examples. While the color scheme chosen to present the logo doesn't comprise bookdeal's official colors, they have been chosen to make the process easier to understand. To get your full-color RGB or grayscale art ready to save as a GIF, you must first reduce the number of unused colors (or shades, if in grayscale) that will be saved along with your image data. To accomplish this, choose Image, Mode, Indexed Color, as shown in figure 6.20.

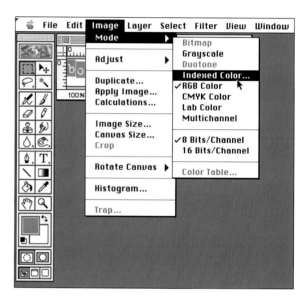

6.19

Colorized bookdeal.com logo in Adobe Photoshop 4.0.

6.20

Transforming an RGB image into indexed color, to eliminate unused colors or shades.

6.21

Selecting Palette and Color Depth options for the RGB to GIF transformation.

You will be prompted for a Palette selection, Color Depth, Colors, and the option to Dither (fig. 6.21). I usually always select an Adaptive palette (unless I have solid colors with no gradations, in which case, I choose None), with anywhere from a 3- to 6-bit color depth for GIFs. Adaptive palettes are good because they reflect the colors you are actually using in your artwork. If you select SYSTEM, for instance, you are presented with all 256 system colors—regardless of whether you are using them in your artwork. If you select Adaptive palettes, you can enter a lower number of colors within your image to save file space by decreasing the amount of information Photoshop has to embed in your file when you save it.

For the Dither option, I select Diffusion (unless I'm dealing with flat graphics, in which case I choose None). For graphics that contain blends or multicolored, anti-aliased edges, Diffusion helps to maintain the anti-aliased, smooth edges by using colors in the new color palette. There's really no set formula; you have to experiment based on the image and number of colors in the image. Just remember that your goal is to minimize file size and that the lower the bit depth and number of colors you have in your image, the smaller the file—and the faster it loads into view for your audience. In figure 6.19, it seems as though you're looking at a 2-color logo, but in reality, if you zoom up on an aliased image, you see that many shades of one color create the feathered edges that make the image look smooth, not jagged. Therefore, you must account for these shades—and this is why figure 6.21 displays a 4-bit, 16-color selection. Figure 6.22 shows the resulting indexed-color image.

But wait, that's not all. We have yet to save our creation as a GIF file. Select File, Save (or File, Save As) and Photoshop's standard "save" dialog box appears (fig. 6.23).

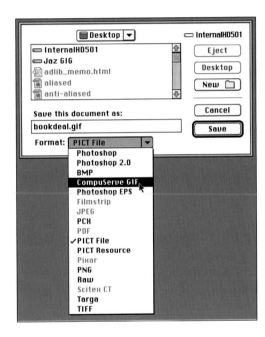

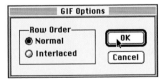

6.22

The resulting indexed-color image.

6.23

Photoshop's standard "save" dialog box, with CompuServe GIF selected for Format.

6.24

The GIF Options dialog box.

To save to the standard GIF format, you must choose CompuServe GIF from the pull-down Format menu (fig. 6.23). Upon choosing your file's destination and clicking on Save, you are prompted with yet another choice (fig. 6.24).

The GIF Options dialog box lets you select whether you would like your file to be Normal or Interlaced. I prefer everything normal myself. (Hey, it's nice to have some normalcy on the web!) If you select Interlaced, your image shows up gradually as the file loads into your viewer's browser. Some people like this; I don't.

The interlaced GIF option allows for the creation of a graphic that quickly presents itself to the viewer from a chunky image, transforming into its final state as it downloads to the user's machine. Figures 6.25 and 6.26 show the bookdeal.com logo as it appears to the viewer over time, transmitted over the Internet. Because the file is only 2k in size, it takes the logo only one "chunky" step to appear. If the image were larger, though, say 10k, it would take it approximately four chunky steps to appear. Therefore, the larger the image, the longer it takes to appear, and the more chunky steps involved. I use the word "chunky" to refer to the state of the image as downloads. Notice that in figure 6.58, it is hard to make out the actual image because of its chunky nature. The reason I don't like interlaced GIFs is that I feel that they distract the viewer and are unnecessary. It is my personal opinion, of course, but I'd rather wait to see the image in its final, intended form. If the image takes too long to load, I'm off to my next web destination.

6.25 – 6.26

An example of how an interlaced GIF appears.

Making GIF89a's

What about GIF89a? You know, the format that allows for transparent backgrounds and animation? All right, let's create a transparent version of figure 6.22 and save it as a GIF89a format. Creating transparent GIFs benefits web designers in two ways:

- Minimizes file size: The background information (if one solid color) takes up one color chip in the palette and, if removed, lowers the file size requirement of the graphic.
- Allows for placement of graphics on textured backgrounds or different colored backgrounds, without the image border (you know, that ugly square or rectanglular box called the "canvas" in Photoshop).

Let's go one step further and test it on a browser with a dark background to see how it shows up with its transparent background. Sounds good—let's get to it.

Saving to GIF89a is a different affair. I must use File, Export, GIF89a Export (fig. 6.27). A dialog box appears, similar to that shown in figure 6.28, that allows me to select an Interlace option (but I shouldn't do it) and designate the color I would like to be transparent.

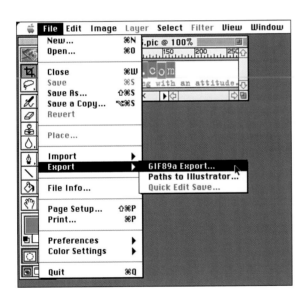

6.27

Exporting a copy of figure 6.33 into the GIF89a file format.

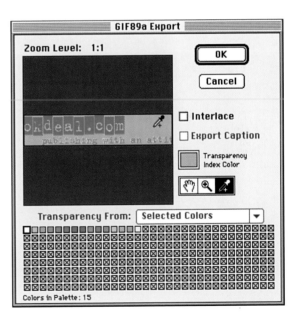

6.28

The GIF89a Export dialog box.

6.29

Both GIF and GIF89a versions of original figure 6.19 as viewed in a Netscape browser with the background set to black.

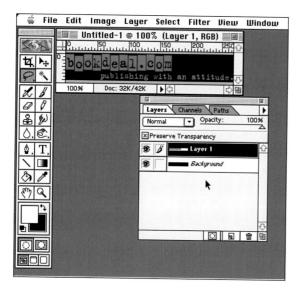

6.30

The original figure 6.19 graphic, this time with a black background.

In figure 6.28, notice that I have zoomed into my image with the Magnifying tool so I can get a better look at what's going on, and I have selected the Eyedropper tool and made the white background transparent (as depicted by the gray).

Figure 6.29 shows what happens when I display both the GIF image and the GIF89a (transparent image) in a web browser with a black background. Surprised? What happened to the GIF89a transparency? How come there's a white halo around the image, making it look cheap, cheesy, and undesignerly? Remember the section on aliased and anti-aliased images? Well, in order to avoid having a blocky, chunky graphic, the bookdeal logo was created as an anti-aliased image. Like all anti-aliased images, it consisted of many shades of the orange and red that made up the logo. Since it was composed on a white background, the anti-aliasing effect created shades of pink and light orange for the logo colors to make the edges look smooth. In the process to make the white background transparent, the light pink and light orange pixels were not made transparent because they were not white! Now I'm stuck with the kind of GIFs you sometimes see floating around on the web. Well, there's a way to fix that (well, not fix, really—more like do over).

Let's go back to the drawing board. Hopefully, I saved a copy of the original figure 6.19 Photoshop file before I flattened the image (always have backup files just in case). Sure enough, here it is (fig. 6.30), with one difference. I have now made the background color black, to match the background of the HTML page in figure 6.29.

I flatten the image (fig. 6.31) so that I can go ahead and export the GIF89a format. Once again, I select File, Export, GIF89a Export (fig. 6.32).

This time, I have zoomed in a considerable amount to witness the detail of what goes on when the background of an anti-aliased image is made transparent. Notice that in figure 6.32, the anti-aliased edges of the graphic, which are not a true black, are still left. They are made up of varying shades of black to create the relatively smooth appearance of the graphic. By saving this file and comparing all three GIFs in the browser (fig. 6.33) I am presented with the three non-animating GIF possibilities for web graphics.

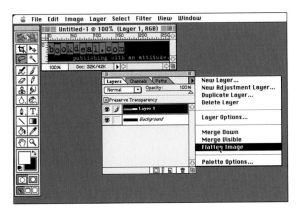

6.31

Preparing the new graphic for export to GIF89a.

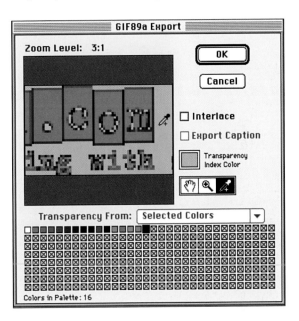

6.32

The GIF89a Export dialog box.

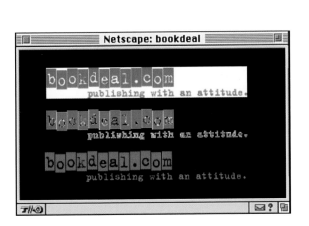

6.33

All three GIFs compared in the Netscape browser.

Why couldn't I just have saved the logo on the black background without making it a GIF89a transparent image? I could have, and it may have worked fine with black, but sometimes, during the process of converting from RGB to indexed-color, some colors tend to shift a bit. If I had a web page with a lime-green background, for example, and our bookdeal logo was also on a lime-green background, I may have run into some trouble. The lime-green may have shifted (I have noticed these shifts even on a browser safe palette) and it would have been noticeable on the web page. You may have run across many logos on web sites that appear to have a background color that's a little different from that of the overall background color of the web site. By compositing my anti-aliased image on the same color background as my web page and then converting it into a transparent GIF89a, I have no apparent shifts in color when I import my images into a browser (this, I guarantee).

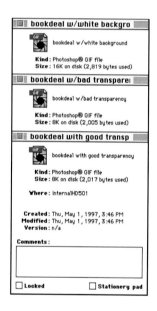

The File, Get Info command applied to the three bookdeal GIF files to measure true filesize.

Judging True Filesize

Earlier in this chapter, I skimmed over image filesize and have subtly touched on it throughout the book so far. How, then, do you measure the true filesize of your images? For people who use PCs, this is a no-brainer. The filesize you see on a PC is the file's true size, give or take a byte or two not worth fussing over. On the Macintosh, however, it's another story.

On the Macintosh, with your Finder running, select a file (not a folder) and choose File, Get Info from your system's menu bar. An info dialog box appears, containing information about the file. In the above figure, all three bookdeal GIFs' "Get Info" dialog boxes are open, revealing both image sizes on disk and total bytes used (the true filesize). As the figure to the left points out, our second bookdeal logo with the bad transparency, weighing in at a little over 2k (true filesize, 1,000 bytes = 1k) is the most compact file, with the third bookdeal logo (the one that worked best) coming in a *very* close second. 2.017k literally takes less than 2 seconds to download on a 28.8 modem. This is a *great* graphic filesize for quick, beautiful communication.

This is not to say that all your graphics should be 2k, but you should definitely aim low in terms of image size until the bandwidth problem is solved.

An Overview of Animated GIFs

Animated GIFs (a subset of the GIF89a specification) have taken the web by storm, and can be overdone at times. However, they're lots of fun and can add compelling visual appeal if properly and sparingly used.

An animated GIF can best be compared to an electronic flip-book, if you will. With a block of images, presented one on top of another, until the last is reached, animated GIFs are streaming in nature. *Streaming* refers to the process by which the first frame of the animated GIF is

"Animated GIFs are an excellent, easy-to-create, practical resource for the web designer."

presented to the audience while the second loads, and the second is presented when it has finished loading, and so on and so forth, like that, until the entire animation has presented itself. This way, your audience does not have to wait for the entire animation to download before being able to view it. Of course, during its initial stream, an animated GIF may not run at the optimal speed at which it was designed to run if your viewer is on a slow connection (because the second and following images must be transferred over the phoneline before they can be shown). Nevertheless, animated GIFs are an excellent, easy-to-create, practical resource (they don't require special plug-ins to view) for the web designer. Best of all, the software with which you can create these web wonders is free for Macintosh users at **http://iawww.epfl.ch/ Staff/Yves.Piguet/clip2gif-home/GifBuilder.html**.

If you're using the Windows/Windows 95 platform, you can obtain GIF Construction Set at **http://www.mindworkshop.com/alchemy/ alchemy.html**.

Working with GifBuilder 0.5

Although I am using GifBuilder to demonstrate a behind-the-scenes example of how animated GIFs are put together, once you understand the principles, you can use any piece of GIF animation software (or any platform, for that matter) to perform the task.

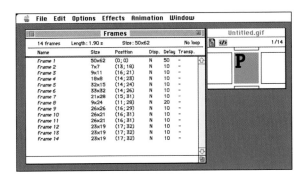

Figure 6.34 displays the R35 logo animation sequence. When I first load GifBuilder, I get the interface shown in figure 6.34, except that the Frames window and the animation preview window (to the immediate right of the Frames window) are empty. In this example, however, all 14 frames of the logo animation are visible in the Frames window, along with the first frame in the animation preview window.

6.34

GifBuilder interface displaying the R35 logo animation.

My favorite techniques for loading individual frames into GifBuilder are:

■ **Create a QuickTime Movie of my animation and import it into GifBuilder using File, Open.** Each frame of my QuickTime Movie will load into the Frames window (it might take forever if I have a long QT movie—I'd recommend making QT movies short, at 10 frames per second MAXIMUM). For optimal results, try something like 5 or 6 fps. For a 10-second movie, that's 50 to 60 frames (a whole lotta frames). Remember that animated GIFs are composed of many individual GIF files (each frame), so if each frame (or GIF file in the animated GIF) is 5k, 60 frames would net a 300k animated GIF—and that's WAY too large for the Net audience. Average animated GIF files range anywhere from 7k to 20k. If creating GIFs larger than 20k, it is best that they be the first read or the only graphic on the page because of the attention they would demand from the viewer.

■ **Create each frame of my animation by hand (the traditional way) using Photoshop and its powerful layers feature.** Then, Copy images from each layer (representing each frame in the GIF animation) and PASTE it directly into GifBuilder. I can also save my Photoshop file with all the layers ready to convert and open the file directly in GifBuilder. However, I have found that doing so produces odd color conversion results and yields larger filesizes than does manually copying and pasting each individual file … go figure.

I have found that the above two techniques work best. I especially like using the second technique. As a matter of fact, I created the example in figure 6.35 in Photoshop layers and individually copied and pasted it into GifBuilder.

Notice that in figure 6.35, GifBuilder provides me with the number of frames in the animation, the animation length in seconds (represented by the delay numbers for each frame, where 100 delay units = 1 second), and the animation size. Your favorite animation program will more than likely provide similar information, although it may place that information in different locations within the interface. Notice also that this animation does not loop (in figure 6.35, notice that it says, "NO LOOP" in the upper-right corner of the Frames window). Most of these figures can be changed simply by clicking on the individual specs, or by using the Options, Effects, and Animation pull-down menus. As with any other aspect of web design, it takes plenty of experimentation to get the most pleasing results.

In figure 6.35, Frame 5 has been selected. Notice its content in the animation preview window. The background has disappeared for the most part and its image size (32×15) is much smaller than the overall animation size of 50×62.

Figure 6.36 displays the final frame of the logo animation in the animation preview window. Basically, the logo transforms from a "P" into an "R," which forms a circle at its base as it makes itself visible, with the number "35" animating into focus upon the completion of the circle. Originally, when I individually import each frame into GifBuilder, their sizes should all be identical to the size of the first image I import in. The reason that the frames in our example are of different sizes (all except for the first frame, which is the first frame of the animation) is that they have been optimized to reduce the filesize.

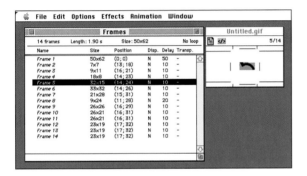

6.35

GifBuilder interface displaying Frame 5 of the R35 logo animation.

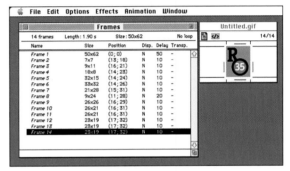

6.36

GifBuilder interface displaying Frame 14 of the R35 logo animation.

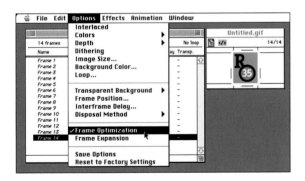

6.37

Options, Frame Optimization displayed.

Figure 6.37 illustrates the fact that Frame Optimization has been selected for this file. In fact, this is a file that has already been saved once and reopened for examination. When I am initially creating my GIF animation, I choose all of my settings, including color depth. I recommend using the 6x6x6 (216 browser safe) palette (discussed in Chapter 2) in order to ensure cross-platform color consistency. Note that I can change my settings later and resave to make them take effect. In any event, if I am sure to have Frame Optimization checked, GifBuilder will analyze each individual frame for areas that do not change over time and will delete those areas, making for smaller filesize GIF animations (a very helpful feature). Of course, this feature is mathematically generated. If I want perfect optimization, I can go into Photoshop and individually crop down the frames that I know change only in certain areas and copy and paste them into GifBuilder, positioning each graphic in my animation preview window. It's a great way to create extremely small GIF animations (yes, very time-consuming—but well worth it).

An Overview of Macromedia Director 5/6 and Shockwave

Macromedia Director has been around since the genesis of the World Wide Web and has been a leader in providing designers with the tools to create highly interactive, extremely powerful and flexible multimedia presentations, CD-ROMs, and now, web-based Shockwave files.

Unfortunately, Macromedia Director is an extremely complex program to discuss without getting into specifics, which requires an entire book in itself. However, in this overview, I cover some of Director 5.0's strengths, discuss how to create a Shockwave movie and place it within your web site, and go over some of Director 6.0's promised features.

Director's Strengths

If you want bells and whistles, music and animation, interactivity and database capabilities … if you want to create a game, design a step-by-step interactive online tutorial, create those Shockwave files everyone's talking about, and have the programming know-how, Director's your tool of choice. No piece of multimedia authoring software comes close to Director's raw power and flexibility. The only drawback to tapping its vast resources is a STEEP learning curve and the need to learn the Lingo programming language. Lingo enables you to program events and true interactivity into your presentations. It's easy to figure out how to do simple tasks with Lingo (like JavaScript). However, as you grow more knowledgeable about the language, you begin to learn that "you don't know jack," if I may so use a popular phrase. It is very difficult to integrate the TRULY amazing features Director enables programmers to accomplish if you're a one- or two-man (or woman) operation, unless you're a designer who knows OOP (object-oriented programming, like C++).

A competitor on the market, Mfactory (**http://www.mfactory.com**), has come out with Mtropolis, which is more of an icon-based, WYSIWYG approach to creating interactive titles. Available as an authoring tool for the Macintosh and Power Mac, Mtropolis has a very nice cross-platform/medium feature: it includes player files for the Macintosh, Windows 3.1, Windows 95, and Windows NT, as well as for the Internet. However, Mtropolis is not as powerful as Director in terms of its raw potential.

Creating Shockwave Content

Shockwave is Macromedia Director's product delivery vehicle for the Internet. After I've created my Director movie, the only way I can share it with my Internet visitors is to *shock* it (make a Shockwave movie out of it). The following tips are designed to help make Shockwave movies smaller in filesize (please note that the tips below are optimized for Director 5.0 and may not apply to newer versions):

- Use small stage sizes—the smaller the better. The smaller your stage, the smaller your graphics, images, and ultimately, your Shockwave file.

- Convert your RGB images to indexed-color, Web, 8-bit Diffusion in Photoshop, save them as .pict files, and import them into Director.

  Set your Director movies to play in 8 bit. I achieve this by using Lingo (Macromedia's programming language) in the MOVIE SCRIPT (COMMAND-SHIFT-U on the Macintosh). Figure 6.38 tells Lingo to set the viewer's bit depth to 8-bit (256 colors). This, along with the last tip, ensures consistent color reproduction across platforms.

- Convert your sound files to 11kHz, 8-bit mono AIFF files by using your favorite sound editing package (Macromedia's SoundEdit 16 v2 is great).

- Use only one sound channel and keep your sound files small, looping them (elegantly) when possible to create the illusion that you have a long song playing in the background.

- If using multiple movies in one page, you will get better results if they all have the same palette, and if only one plays sound.

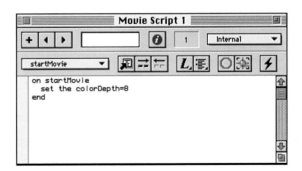

6.38

Director's Movie Script, depicting a Lingo command to set the viewer's monitor bit-depth to 8-bit (256 colors).

Shocking Your Files with Afterburner

After you've optimized your file and assembled your Director presentation, it's time to shock the sucker!

Director 5.0 requires that you use its Afterburner Xtra (available from **http://www.macromedia.com/software/director/**—select Xtras from the menu and select Macromedia's Xtras from the link that appears) to create the movie (Director 5.0 Shockwave movies end with the .dcr extension). Figure 6.39 illustrates the selection of the Afterburner utility from the Xtras pull-down menu. Users of Macromedia Director 6.0 do not need to use Afterburner. Director 6.0 creates web-ready files straight from the application.

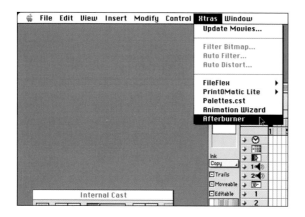

6.39

Using Xtras, Afterburner to create Shockwave content in Director 5.0.

6.40

The Afterburner dialog box.

When you select Afterburner, the dialog box shown in figure 6.40 appears, and in it you attach a filename to your presentation. Don't forget to attach the .dcr extension to the name.

In your HTML code, simply insert the following where you want your Shockwave movie to display:

```
<EMBED SRC="FILENAME.DCR" WIDTH=X HEIGHT=X PALETTE=BACKGROUND>
```

Make sure that you input the correct width and height figures based on your stage size. The PALETTE= tag, when set to BACKGROUND, loads the viewer's system palette into the movie. If you want to display the movie's own color palette, choose FOREGROUND. That's all there is to it. If your viewers have the Shockwave plug-in, they can witness your achievement.

Director 6 Aims for the Net

Director 6, Macromedia's newest and most powerful version of the popular authoring software is now available and boasts the following:

- Every movie element can be associated with a URL.
- Movies can be optimized for the Internet without having to use Afterburner.
- Movies optimized for the web can be viewed in Director.
- The new Shockwave format will stream all media types.
- JPEG images can be stored externally from the Shockwave file for efficiency.
- Shockwave movies will respond to JavaScript, ActiveX, and LiveConnect technologies.
- Java can be embedded and fully integrated into Shockwave movies.
- Shockwave movies can be embedded into Java applets.
- The Score window has been updated to allow up to 120 sprite channels.
- Director 6 will be able to read GIF and JPEG image formats.

With all of these new enhancements and many more unlisted, Director 6 promises to be an exciting and liberating product.

An Overview of Macromedia Flash

The first thing to know about Flash is the fact that it's vector-based. There are pluses and minuses associated with this fact. On the plus side, vector graphics load quite quickly and run very smoothly. On the downside, however, the quality of a vector graphics (with their computer-aided precision lines and geometric shapes) just doesn't stack up against the deep, rich color and texture available from a standard GIF, GIF89a, or JPEG. Flash 2.0 is definitely technology that can be used only for certain tasks. For instance, Flash would be a great product to use for animating cartoon-like characters or illustrations with sound and interactive roll-over effect capabilities. However, I don't quite see how it could fit into a very elegant web environment containing textured images with blends and transparent backgrounds layered with typography unless its usage is very minimal and subtle.

We're going to have to let this piece of software sift into the hands of the masses and see the kind of work that turns up. Already, many sites are taking advantage of Flash 2.0's capabilities. MSN (The Microsoft Network) is a big supporter of Flash technology. However, visit their site (**http://www.msn.com**) and judge for yourself. To me, the implementation of the technology so far has been a bit too sterile. Everyone's overusing Flash in their sites, from what I can see. It's like learning about animated GIFs and plastering your entire site with them. Sure, it's cool technology, but I like to see more of less.

An Overview of SoundEdit 16 Version 2

Give me good sound over a cheap piece of graphic any day! Sound is an oddly avoided topic when it comes to creating compelling web page design. Think about this: If you've got approximately 35k worth of information to put on your page, which would you do?

> Place your company logo, company slogan graphic, company president's welcome message, picture of company president, a couple of animated GIFs for the hell of it, and some odd links to sites you wouldn't even visit?

or

> Place your company logo and one interesting sound file? (OK, you can also put a picture of your cat up there if you like ... maybe if someone rolls over your company logo, the cat appears...)

I would personally scrap an entire list of useless items on people's home pages for some nice sound. And we're not talking MIDI either! The point is to offer your viewers something different, something interesting and engaging, as the above example reflects. If you offer them an experience, rather than a sales pitch, you can improve the quality of your web site overnight.

"Designers should definitely incorporate more sound into their pages."

SoundEdit 16 Version 2 (**http://www.macromedia.com/software/ sound/**) is a good all-around introductory sound editing program that is powerful enough to handle your average web-based sound creation and editing needs. Unfortunately, SoundEdit 16 is currently unavailable for the PC. With the purchase of sound editing cards such as SoundBlaster 16, Windows users receive sound composing software with features similar to what I describe, however. Sound editing programs allow you the opportunity to import, record, and create your own audio files and compress them to bits for use on the Internet.

Figure 6.41 is an example of SoundEdit's incredible compression power. At a sample rate of 5.564 kHz, 16-bit sound can be compressed to a ratio of 4:1. One minute of sound at this setting takes up 163k of space, so 10 seconds of sound (a VERY long time in web speak) takes 27k, and a 5-second sound file takes approximately 13.5k.

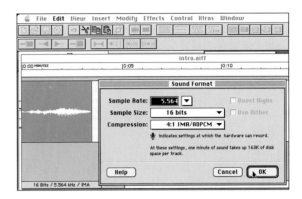

6.41

Compressing a sound file in SoundEdit 16 Version 2.

The only comment I have on the issue of sound is this: Compose, experiment, and compress. Designers should definitely incorporate more sound into their pages. The following HTML can be used to integrate AIFF or WAV files into your page:

```
<embed src="FILENAME.aiff" hidden=true autostart=true LOOP=TRUE>
```

The above HTML code embeds your sound file and makes it invisible (no controller is present; to enable the controller, type HIDDEN=FALSE). AUTOSTART=TRUE means that as soon as your page loads, the sound automatically loads and begins. If you don't want your sound to loop, remove the LOOP=TRUE tag, or simply change it to LOOP=FALSE.

An Overview of BBEdit 4.0

If you don't know how to program HTML, you should learn now. There are so many HTML resources available on the web there's no reason not to learn how to HTML if you have a web browser. Remember, when starting out with HTML programming, your best friend is the View, Document Source command from Netscape's pull-down menu (View, Source on Internet Explorer). When you're at a web site that you'd like to deconstruct (work backwards by snooping through other people's HTML to learn how they did things) you can view their document source and try to figure things out, and you'll succeed little by little. There are plenty of books out there, and probably dozens of geeky friends who could get you started.

"If you don't know how to program in HTML, you should learn NOW."

HTML has enabled designers to say, "Yeah, I can program!" It is by far the easiest programming language, despite how archaic it looks with all those funny <words between less-than and greater-than symbols>. Hey, at least someone finally found some real use for those things.

BBEdit is the ideal HTML programming tool. It color-codes my HTML as I go, making image tags and link tags different colors so that I can easily spot them (a life-saver if you're still doing your HTML in SimpleText on the Mac). The program has so many features, it takes longer to learn than HTML! The only downside to BBEdit is that it's not available for PC users … yet.

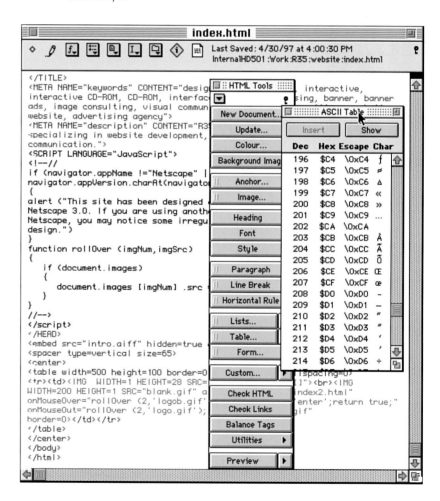

6.42

BBEdit 4.0's interface and HTML editor.

There is, however, another pretty good HTML editor called Emacs, and it's available for the Win 95 and NT crowd, as well as for Macintosh, Amiga, and Unix. It's free to those who download it via **http://www.gnu.ai.mit.edu/order/ftp.html**.

An Overview of Adobe Pagemill 2.0

If you don't know how to HTML, please learn. WYSIWYG (What You See Is What You Get) web design software such as Adobe's Pagemill is a good overall program for beginners, but I wouldn't leave myself at the mercy of a program that places design restrictions on you based on the way it's programmed to allow you to do things.

Learning HTML is a breeze. Start with the wonderful resources in Lynda Weinman's *Designing Web Graphics.2*, ISBN 1-56205-715-4. Continue your HTML tour-de-force by visiting WebMonkey's HTML Reference (**http://www.webmonkey.com/webmonkey/reference/**) and WebMonkey's Teaching Tool (**http://www.webmonkey.com/web-monkey/teachingtool/**). Once you've read Lynda's book(s), visited the multitude of links on the web, and practiced using what you learn to build your own pages, I guarantee you'll have HTML under your designer belt. Start with the basic HTML tags and work your way up to the more advanced ones. Test your work by simply opening your HTML file inside your web browser. (You can do this by using the File, Open command from your browser's menu bar and choosing your HTML file to test.)

Once you learn HTML, you will have TOTAL freedom in designing your pages. Sure, it's a little extra work, but it's well worth it, and the ability HTML gives you to fully customize your pages (an ability that WYSIWYG editors do not provide) will make your work stand out that much more. I have not yet found a WYSIWYG HTML editor that gives me full control over every aspect of a page's layout down to the pixel, additional technology (like JavaScript or ActiveX), and the integration of embedded assets requiring plug-ins.

> "Once you learn HTML, you will have TOTAL freedom in designing your pages."

I've heard of people who use Pagemill to create tables (it has a great table editor) and then save the Pagemill HTML file (which includes plenty of its own proprietary code to allow Pagemill to recognize it), copy the table information out, and paste it into their own HTML file. Pagemill's imagemap creation tools are excellent as well, so maybe you just use Pagemill for its strengths (table creation and imagemapping) and treat it as another tool in your web designer's toolbox.

That's the Ticket

In this chapter, I have covered many of the tools I personally use to create compelling graphics and web sites. While the tools presented herein are unique to my personal web design philosophy, they may not necessarily find their place in your electronic toolbox based on your personal choices and preferences. Platform differences pose a major stumbling block to clear communication of basic technological issues. However, please note that at the heart of the issues, platform differences are insignificant when compared to the bigger picture: effective visual communication of a message from designer to audience. A Unix user should be able to pick up this book, read through the chapters, and understand that although the technology discussed may not apply to him or her, the fundamental thinking behind why certain technologies are implemented over others does. Even though SoundEdit 16 v2 may not be available for PC users, I'm sure that another sound editing program is. PC users, then, should apply their ultimate cerebral design tools to create beautiful, ambient, compressed sound to their pages by using whatever technology is available to them.

The only tool you ever really need is your brain. All the software and hardware discussed in this book will be obsolete in a matter of years (if not weeks or months). In the long run, perhaps the most useful information in this book is the stable and timeless creative communication strategies interwoven within each chapter—with the technological issues acting as their current delivery vehicles doomed to extinction by their technical offspring.

The rest of this book focuses on how to apply creative visual design strategies and concentrates more on the actual process of designing specific site content.

7

Delivering Technology to Your Audience

Thus far, we've covered the communication bottlenecks and hurdles that we must overcome as a web community, the fundamental design principles as they relate to the web, and issues regarding strategic planning and creative implementation of a strong concept. We've arrived at a stage where the basic tools available to us have been overviewed. It is now time to start putting the pieces together.

One of the fundamental questions you should be asking yourself is, "How is my audience going to use the technology I deliver them?" That's really what it's all about. At the end of the day, you won't be the one sitting in front of your PC or Mac being exposed to your web site for the very first time on God knows what browser, accessing some local ISP (Internet Service Provider; for example, Earthlink, Netcom, AOL, to name a few) at bottleneck rates.

How will the technology you decide to incorporate into your web site help your ultimate viewer better understand who you are (or who your client is) and what you're trying to say?

Do you decide to go for the gusto, leaving the millions of potential AOL subscribers in the dust because their browsers won't be able to access all the whiz-bang goodies your site has to offer? There's an interesting dichotomy here between designers wanting to communicate, and at the same time, wanting to demonstrate their skills. Well, if the audience isn't ready to see what you've got to show because the technology isn't there yet, who are you designing for?

"One of the fundamental questions you should be asking yourself is, 'How is my audience going to use the technology I deliver them?'"

These are issues we should all consider as designers faced with extremely challenging, fascinating, technologically evolving, and thought-provoking times. The safest route (limiting web sites to standard technologies such as animated GIFs and tables, as opposed to Shockwave, Flash, and frames) may not always yield the most technologically advanced or "cool" site of the week. On the flip side, the safest route will yield the widest possible viewership and enable true communication (mass communication, not selective communication for the elite) to take place.

If the goal of your web site is to sell a product or advertise a service, it behooves you to design for mass audience viewership. On the other hand, if you are designing for an elite group of designers who have the fastest PCs or Macs and all the plug-ins, then more power to you. Again, there is no right or wrong here. Good design is about effective problem-solving. If you address your target audience and serve them through the appropriate visual language and technological means, you will succeed.

In this case-study chapter, I examine a web site from concept to completion, as well as provide a design analysis for the reasoning behind all graphics, animation, and typographic treatment.

Design for the Sake of Communication

While design is an extremely subjective artform, relying on each designer's (and each client's) personal philosophy, aesthetic, and problem-solving skills, you should *always* have a reason (or concept) behind each and every piece of graphic, imagery, typography, color selection, and page layout decision you make in the design process.

Gratuitous design for the sake of design can be nice to look at as art—but it doesn't always work as communication design. Successful communication design is clear, bold, aesthetically pleasing, and unmistakably memorable.

Gratuitous design is fashionable and functional as decoration, but it isn't always clear, and it isn't always well-thought-out, let alone memorable. Trends and fads in design (the overuse/misuse/abuse of "grunge typography," for example) often stem from designers who deploy a singular "HOT LOOK" to communicate their message. Although these styles are often aesthetically pleasing, they tend to wear on viewers after a brief period of time, giving rise to the next "star designer." The conceptual communication designer utilizes "grunge typography" when communicating to an audience who responds to it instead of using it as a mode of personal expression.

There is nothing wrong with gratuitous (or decorative) design, so long as you use it sparingly and with purpose. The skilled designer should incorporate both classic design thinking and decorative design elements to strategically communicate a message on any medium.

.comCompany Case Study

.comCompany(LLC) is an Internet-based information resource for corporate executives, university professors, market researchers, and anyone else interested in the acquisition of information. The company offers several services (InfoDig, QuickDig, and TrendSpot, among others) that fall under its .comResearch(SM) branch.

Figure 7.1 represents .comCompany's home page (**http://www.comcompany. com**). In this case study, I analyze the many aspects of conceptual and strategic development, design, and production of the .comCompany web site. While the final outcome of the site is unique to .comCompany's requirements and in no way reflects the "coolest" or most technologically intense web site in the universe, my intention in analyzing it here is to help you conceive of and develop more thought-out, strategically targeted, and compelling web sites.

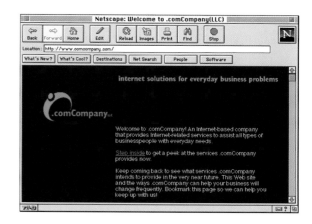

7.1

.comCompany Home Page.

Identifying .comCompany's Key Purpose and Online Strategy

You need to translate the key purpose of a web site (the site's goals, communicated through verbal language) into compelling visual imagery without losing the original intent of the key purpose. One way to judge the effectiveness of a site is to see whether you can decipher its key purpose and message. Take a look at a site you think is effective and go through it page by page. Try to arrive at the site's key purpose based on your visit. If you cannot decipher the site's purpose and message, it was not effectively communicated to you the visitor. Please point your web browser to **http://www.comcompany.com** and thoroughly analyze the site. See how closely your analysis of .comCompany's web site matches the following key purpose:

- To introduce .comCompany and its unique services to first-time visitors
- To entice prospective clients to take advantage of the company's services

The above points can be broken down and flushed out to represent .comCompany's online strategy more fully.

To introduce .comCompany and its services to first-time visitors:

- To create an attractive overall look
- To quickly present a striking branding message
- To engage the visitor with animation
- To quickly convey a descriptive tagline
- To offer an immediate link to the next layer of information

To entice prospective clients to take advantage of the company's services:

- To offer descriptive copy
- To educate visitors about .comCompany's benefits
- To entice prospective clients with animated graphics
- To provide an easy-to-use navigational interface
- To showcase each service
- To provide a contact-vehicle for feedback and interaction

To effectively translate .comCompany's written key purpose and online strategy into a compelling web experience, designers should consider the following:

- Logo design
- Logo animation considerations for the web
- Typographic treatment
- Color palette
- Visual language
- Information design
- Information hierarchy
- Page layout
- White space
- Scale relationships
- Navigational interface design
- Feedback-form layout and design

The key purpose, online strategy, and initial design considerations are preliminary thinking associated with the creation of successful web sites.

Identifying .comCompany's Target Audience

As a designer, you don't need to worry about the research that goes behind strategic audience targeting—your clients will more than likely provide you with a "creative brief." A *creative brief* is a sheet (sometimes several sheets) that breaks down a project by goals, target audience, and other information pertinent to the job at hand. It *is* a good idea to ask for a creative brief before you begin a project. The creative brief clears up the communication between you and your client by placing the client's expectations and your responsibilities on paper, and helps minimize problems down the line.

"As a designer, your job is to keep the target audience in mind when conceptualizing the site's overall look, navigation, and graphic treatment."

If you are designing your own site, brushing up (to say the least) on marketing 101 (if not 102 and 103) will enable you to better assess your target audience. If you are creating a site for other designers, you don't need to analyze your target audience; you know your peers well enough. I recommend conducting research only when you're not familiar with the audiences that you're trying to target.

.comCompany is a merchant of marketing information. As such, its target audience consists of people involved with the day-to-day consumption of highly specific data. The immediate potential users who come to mind are marketing managers, professors and research assistants, analysts, advertising account executives, and business development managers, to name a few. Generally, this target audience is highly educated and familiar with the Internet (this is the kind of information you might see on a creative brief) as a source for information.

As a designer, your job is to keep the target audience in mind as you conceptualize the site's overall look, navigation, and graphic treatment. For example, using a progressive, hard-to-read typeface to design .comCompany's navigation would not be wise. Marketing managers and professors, among other consumers of data-based information, prefer legibility and the ability to speed through easily navigable layers of information.

By keeping the site's key purpose in mind and aiming to design for the intended target audience, you equip yourself with a well–thought-out design strategy.

The .comCompany Brand

A strong brand can enhance a company's visual image, strengthen the "believability" of its presence, and portray a dynamic symbol representative of its products, services, and reputation.

On the Internet, the logo has evolved to represent one of the first visible signs of a "civilized" or "serious" presence. A home page with a beautifully crafted (and often animated) logo is much more compelling and inviting than a page that lacks any visually aesthetic symbol or identifying mark. After all, it's no wonder that corporations have paid upward of hundreds of thousands, if not millions, of dollars toward the creative conceptualization, development, and creation of compelling visual logos. There is a reason behind the vast amounts of cash layouts for those cute little circles with lines running through them: They work. A strong logo/branding message can equate to a powerful and compelling first impression, which is every bit as important as the company's product, service, and reputation. In fact, a memorable logo can encompass all three over time (and become a priceless asset, adding to a company's net worth).

7.2

The .comCompany logo.

7.3

The .comResearch logo.

"A strong logo/branding message can equate to a powerful and compelling first impression."

The .comCompany logo (fig. 7.2) is an example of an effective logo/logotype treatment that lends itself beautifully to the Internet. One of the client requirements for the logo was that it be easily adaptable to work within all of .comCompany's divisions, one of which is .comResearch. Figure 7.3 displays the .comResearch logo.

Notice that everything about the logo shown in figure 7.3 is the same as the one shown in figure 7.2, except for the word "Research(SM)" in place of "Company(LLC)." Because of the unique versatility the Internet provides content-developers, it's easy to segment services to help break up the information overload to reduce large chunks of information down to smaller groups. Traditionally, in print media, a much more elaborate printing budget is necessary to output each and every unique logo configuration, stationery, brochure, and catalogue considerations ... typically a morass of chaos, paperwork, and confusion. In designing a logo that can adapt to cost-saving electronic alterations, however, you need to take consistency into consideration. A separate graphic could have been made for the .comResearch logo, as well as all the other services that .comCompany provides. Instead, one singular look was chosen to represent the umbrella of services, with only the service name changing between each company division (as shown between figures 7.2 and 7.3). Once viewers become familiar with the .comCompany symbol, they will immediately recognize the slightly adjusted version of it when they see it atop the .comResearch logotype. This technique helps to ensure brand recognition as the company grows.

Logo Production for the Web

Creating logos for web site use is not much different than creating logos for traditional use—they both start out the same, anyway. After you spend days or weeks coming up with the graphic that most appropriately symbolizes the corporate image, you need to use a vector-based drawing tool to make the crisp-clean lines, arcs, circles, ovals, and fully editable typography. I suggest you use Adobe Illustrator or Macromedia FreeHand to do the job. My personal software of choice is FreeHand 7, and figure 7.4 illustrates the .comCompany logo in FreeHand's Preview mode.

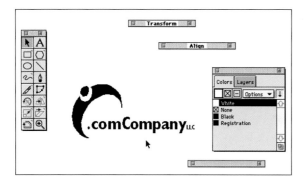

7.4

The .comCompany logo in FreeHand Preview mode.

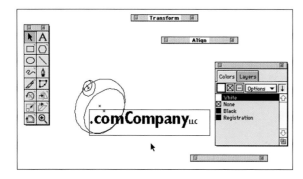

7.5

The .comCompany logo in FreeHand Keyline mode.

7.6

The non-optimized .comCompany logo transferred to Photoshop.

Notice that the logo still is black and white. I do not apply colors to logos I create in FreeHand for web use, simply because the colors tend to shift when I export them into Photoshop (and I am going from a FreeHand CMYK to a Photoshop RGB image here). I save the coloring exercises for after I port the image to Photoshop. Before exporting the graphic shown in figure 7.4 to Photoshop, however, let's take a look at the logo's keyline view (View, Preview in FreeHand; View, Artwork in Illustrator), shown in figure 7.5.

Notice that in figure 7.5 the logo is made up of several ovals and a block of type. The ovals are laid on top of one another, a black oval at the bottom, covered by a smaller white oval on top, which looks like a single arc when you view it in Preview mode. This logo has not yet been optimized for export to Photoshop. Please note that in traditional design practice, such nuances are unimportant because the PostScript processor mathematically punches out invisible areas when sending files to a printer. In the electronic world, however, the nuances are very important. Next, I take this image as-is into Photoshop and let you see what happens.

Figure 7.6 shows the .comCompany logo copied from FreeHand and pasted into a new Photoshop RGB file. Everything looks okay so far. If I hide the background layer by clicking on its Eye icon in Photoshop, however, I am presented with the problem.

Notice that in figure 7.7, two white ovals show up as opaque areas on the logo, when in fact those ovals are supposed to be transparent. What happened? Photoshop translated the PostScript code literally, which created a black oval with a white one on top of it, as designed in FreeHand. Why is this a problem? When you color items in Photoshop, you get best results by placing the areas you want to color alone on a transparent layer so that individual items can be selected easily (using the Lasso, Magic Wand, or Marquee tool) without background colors getting in the way of the process. So what's the solution? Punch out those ovals.

7.7

The non-optimized .comCompany logo viewed with its background turned off in Photoshop.

Figure 7.8 illustrates how to punch out those pesky opaque shapes from your illustrations (Modify, Combine, Punch in FreeHand; Filter, Pathfinder, Minus Front or Filter, Pathfinder, Minus Back or Object, Compound, Paths, Make in Illustrator). Simply place two graphics atop one another, select them both, and perform the punch operation.

Figure 7.9 displays the arc shape as it was originally intended. Next, the "dot" atop the arc needs to be punched out, and the typeface needs to be converted to paths (Text, Convert To Paths in FreeHand; Type, Create Outlines in Illustrator) for optimal conversion.

Figure 7.10 represents the optimized .comCompany logo (punched out and typeface converted to paths), ready for export to Photoshop. After I copy and paste the image into a new RGB Photoshop document by removing its background layer, I get what you see in figure 7.11.

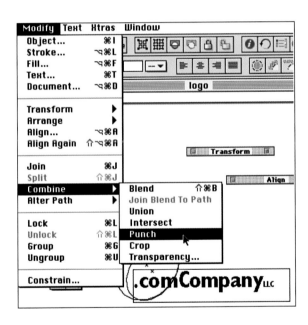

7.8

Punching out the opaque ovals in FreeHand, thereby optimizing the logo for transfer to Photoshop.

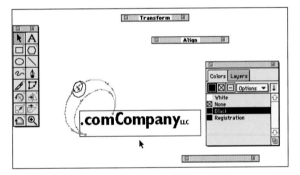

7.9

Arc shape created by punching one oval into another.

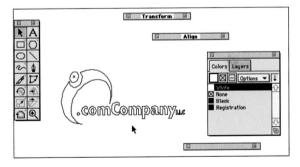

7.10

Optimized .comCompany logo, ready for export to Photoshop.

7.11

The optimized .comCompany logo viewed with its background turned off in Photoshop.

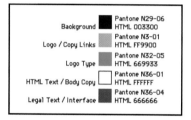

7.12

The .comCompany browser-safe web site color palette.

> "A cross-platform, cross–browser-safe color palette for consistent color application and communication throughout the site is essential to the success of any online presence."

Figure 7.11 represents the ideal black-and-white artwork (easily selectable because there is no background present) for browser-safe color (see Chapter 2) experimentation and application.

The .comCompany Browser-Safe Color Palette

A cross-platform, cross–browser-safe color palette for consistent color application and communication throughout the site is essential to the success of any online presence (I covered the browser-safe color palette in Chapter 2).

While .comCompany prints its identity across an entire line of print literature using traditional CMYK (Cyan, Magenta, Yellow, and Black [K]) and PANTONE inks, their online color palette consists of 0s and 1s. Figure 7.12 shows a breakdown of .comCompany's online color palette, starting with the background color for the web site (PANTONE N29-06 [if you have PANTONE's ColorWeb fan guide, see chapter 2] or HTML 003300). Yes, the palette in figure 7.12 is just a limited five-color solution; it is simply a guideline for the most effective combination of colors. For example, while the yellow-orange (PANTONE N3-01) designates a link when used in body copy, it also serves to create current-page markers in the user interface (which I cover later in this chapter).

Other colors can be incorporated into the web site, as long as the web site's senior designer approves them. Color palettes, if decided upon early, help to serve as a guide in structuring the web site from an aesthetic, color-coded point of view that helps to break down information and simplify color-related decision making down the line.

The colors in the palette here were chosen not only for their unique and aesthetically pleasing hues, but also to ease prolonged reading and web site browsing. The .comCompany color palette has been chosen with the notion that dark backgrounds with light foreground text make reading the text less demanding on the viewer's eyes. Generally, white backgrounds with black or blue body text are not the most suitable color combinations for on-screen reading (gray on white and gray on black, for example, are better solutions). Because the .comCompany deals with lots of textual information, it is a good idea to structure an interface using a color palette *designed* for usability beyond simple aesthetics (the .comCompany color palette achieves both).

7.13

The .comCompany color palette applied to the .comCompany logo.

Figure 7.13 reflects the .comCompany color palette as applied to the .comCompany logo. With the color palette and the logo settled to our satisfaction, it's time to create a stunningly memorable animation of the .comCompany brand image.

Animating the Brand

In designing a logo for online application, it is important to consider an animated version. Not every logo must be animated to be effective. Given the luxuries that the Internet provides, however, animations are relatively easy to create, and they can add life, vibrance, and impact to an otherwise static logo.

Like every carefully crafted piece of communication, animated logos should have a reason for existence, as well as a nicely choreographed beginning, middle, and end. There is one drawback to animating logos—they can be cheesy if not artfully crafted. Cheesy logo animations can simply be described as rendered, beveled, gray 3D nightmares (with highlights and lens flares). Anyone who has access to a 3D modeling/rendering program can quickly piece together an extrusion or lathe (3D modeling terminology) and make it spin. Crafting a unique logo and making it animate gracefully takes much less horsepower than that of a 3D modeling engine. In fact, all it takes is a bit of creative brainpower and a good understanding of traditional animation techniques.

> "Not every logo must be animated to be effective."

As a matter of fact, the only two pieces of software you need to create an animation are Photoshop and a GIF animator (I use GifBuilder 0.5 for the Macintosh). Although many designers use Adobe After Effects (an extremely powerful video and animation editing/composing tool) to create complex animations, it is not NECESSARY to use it—although it can help you create dazzling effects not available through "traditional" Photoshop methods. If you are going to use After Effects to create your animations, consider the following:

- Although After Effects imports PICT, Photoshop, and various other graphic file formats, it does NOT import GIFs.
- Create your animation in After Effects for export to a QuickTime movie or a series of PICT images that you will import into your GIF animation program.
- Export your animation to a QuickTime movie or a series of PICT images using a minimum Frames Per Second (5–8) to cut down on the frame editing you have to do later to make your GIF files smaller.
- Import the QuickTime movie or PICT images you created with After Effects into your favorite GIF animator program.

- In your GIF animation program, cut the number of frames down to an acceptable level (based on final filesize—you'll have to experiment with this based on the filesize objectives/limitations you have regarding your resulting GIF)
- Save your final GIF animation using the browser-safe palette (sometimes referred to as the 6×6×6 palette)

Before you create an animation, have a purpose for doing so. Directors spend much more time conceptualizing, planning, and setting up a shoot than they do yelling "Cut!" during taping. Designing compelling web graphics is no different; it requires talented conceptual thinking as well as beautifully executed visuals.

The Storyline

The .comCompany logo animation presents the company to the viewing audience in a unique, interesting manner, helping to:

- Give the .comCompany logo a grand entrance
- Promote positive feelings about the company based on the attractive animation

Believe it or not, the power of visual communication can most definitely create positive feelings about a product or service simply through its presentation. The choreography I'm about to show you is what enables the .comCompany animation to arrive with a "bang" and impress its audience.

7.14

Animation begins on a dark green background.

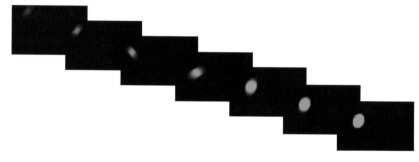

7.15 – 7.21

From deep within cyberspace, a dot circles toward the viewer, zooming in as it approaches.

7.22

The dot stops on impact with the screen to form the upper oval "dot" of the logo.

The graphics on the right visually describe a continuously looping animation. (I tell you how to create it in the next section.) The animation symbolizes .comCompany's information retrieval capabilities, and it can be summed up thusly: "From the depths of cyberspace, .comCompany will appear, disappear with it your information requirement, and return with an answer." Regardless of whether the viewer immediately gets this message upon witnessing the logo animation, you can see that there is a "real" strategy behind the logo animation. It's not just animation for the sake of animation. Designers must carefully conceptualize the purpose of each animation so that they tell a story—something you want to keep in mind as you strive to create compelling, memorable animations.

Animation Station

The following are some points to consider when creating web-based GIF animations using Photoshop:

- Use the browser-safe palette to avoid being surprised by color shifts after you do all that hard work.
- Work in layers; it's the only way to create animations and still maintain your sanity.
- Name your layers to avoid confusion.
- Always save your original Photoshop file.
- Save often—crashes suck.

The animation loops to the beginning

The "dot" zooms back out into cyberspace

The glow behind the "dot" erupts again to signal change

The arc sweeps up into the "dot"

After a brief pause, the logotype fades away

7.23 – 7.30

A glow suddenly erupts from behind the "dot" and the arc portion of the logo sweeps in (in a digging motion) to reveal the logotype, ".comCompany(LLC)."

For an online tutorial on how to effectively use layers to create imagery and set-up animations in Photoshop, visit the *Click Here* web site at **http://www.rpirouz.com/click**.

Figure 7.31 demonstrates the .comCompany animation setup file I've created in Photoshop. Notice that I am working with layers and have named each layer for my own sanity. Notice also that as your eye moves up the layers, from Photoshop's *Background* layer, on up to my Dot 1 and Dot 2 layers, and on up, you can begin to see the animation take place in a flip-book style (the way traditional animation has taken place for years, and, in fact, continues to take place today).

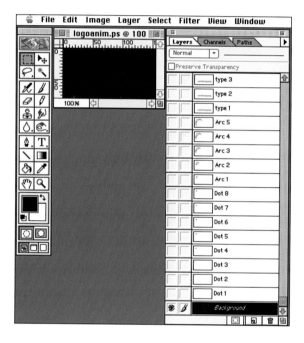

7.31

The .comCompany logo animation setup file in Photoshop.

Traditionally, animators worked with an original background image, laying transparency after transparency atop it to draw the differences in each frame of the animation. Therefore, each layer of transparency acted as each frame in the animation. What I'm demonstrating in figure 7.31 is nothing more than applying this traditional animation principle to the electronic model, as made possible by Adobe Photoshop 4.0.

Let's take a look at the layer named Dot 4. Figure 7.32 shows a layer that represents a frame in the logo animation (shown earlier in figures 7.14 through 7.30). To give the "dot" a sense of motion, to make it look as though it's zooming by, I am applying the Motion Blur filter (Filter, Blur, Motion Blur) to my image. The beauty of working with layers in Photoshop is that you can apply filters to each individual layer without disrupting the artwork on other layers. To create the motion of the "dot" traveling in a semicircle over time, I simply applied the Scale (Layer, Transform, Scale) and Rotate (Layer, Transform, Rotate) functions to copies of the original "dot" on several different layers to create the sensation of it appearing from a distance and moving toward the viewer.

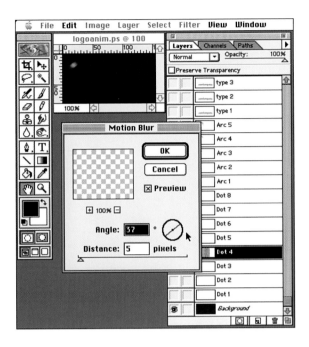

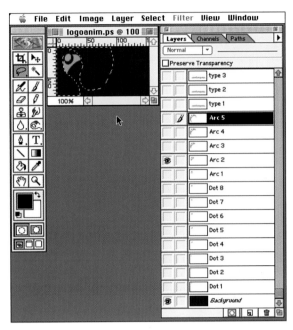

7.32

The "dot" with Photoshop's Motion Blur filter applied to it.

7.33

Using Photoshop's Lasso tool to make the "arc" appear.

"Most web-based animation is achieved through cheap tricks and visual spoofs."

Very much as with movie special effects, most web-based animation is achieved through simple tricks and visual spoofs. Figure 7.33 demonstrates how I made the "arc" of the .comCompany logo "appear" to be coming out of thin air. The original "arc" was copied several times and each successive layer was edited (removing a small piece of the "arc" in each layer until it looked as though it appeared over time) by using the Lasso tool in Photoshop (fig. 7.33).

If there's one filter web designers can't do without, it has to be the almighty Gaussian Blur filter (Filter, Blur, Gaussian Blur). Figure 7.34 demonstrates the filter's power, by showing how applying the filter to the .comCompany logotype makes it appear to "fade in" over time. Applying the Gaussian Blur filter to an image on a transparent layer enables you to blend the image with whatever you happen to have on the *Background* layer. Applied to two consecutive layers of the logotype, the first at a radius of 2.5, and the second at a radius of 1.5 (fig. 7.34), the logotype appears to get less blurry (or foggy) over time, thereby creating the illusion of fading in.

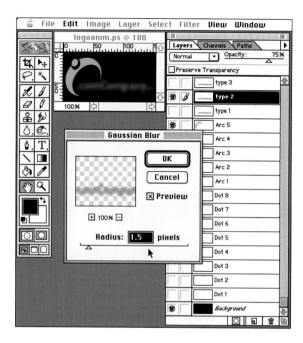

7.34

Fading the .comCompany logotype into view.

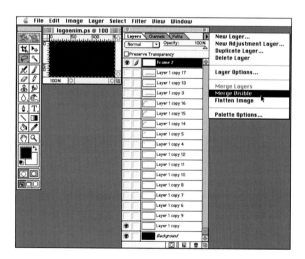

7.35

Merging layers in preparation for export to a GIF animator.

Notice that I am creating each specific frame of the animation, thereby having complete control over each and every single frame that will end up in my animated GIF file. For pure control freaks, there's nothing like being able to do as you please with each frame of a 17-frame animation.

After the animation is set up and looks great, it is time to prepare the file for export into your favorite GIF animator. I'll need to flatten each layer so that whatever has been chosen as the *Background* image replaces the transparent backgrounds in each layer. This action needs to take place because when I go to copy each of the animation frames and paste them into my GIF animator, I want Photoshop to maintain the width-height proportions of each frame with respect to the original canvas size. (With transparent layers, Photoshop will select only the image area that is opaque, creating odd-sized image files in the system clipboard.)

Here's the step-by-step breakdown:

1. Count the number of frames in your animation (the .comCompany animation yields 17).
2. Create as many new layers for your image as frames in your animation.
3. Make the *Background* image visible (click on its Eye icon).
4. Make the first transparent layer visible (click on its Eye icon).
5. Select your first new layer (by clicking once on its name).

6. Click and hold down the arrow to the right of the Layers menu (fig. 7.35) and while holding down the Option key on your Mac (PC users hold down Alt) select Merge, Visible from the pop-up Layer menu.

You should now have a combined merge of the *Background* image with the first frame of your animation in the new layer.

7. Repeat steps 3 through 6 for the remaining frames of your animation until all your new layers are filled and represent your animation over time (fig. 7.36).

8. I almost forgot … SAVE, SAVE, SAVE! And SAVE often. Be sure to always create a backup of your original unaltered file, just in case. :-)

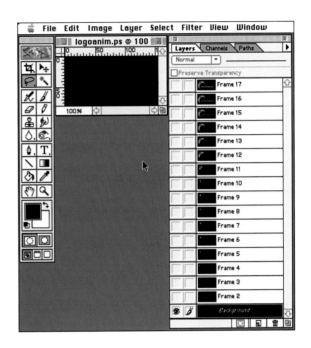

7.36

Merging layers in preparation for export to a GIF animator.

Figure 7.36 represents a completed layer merge of all transparent layers to the *Background* image. After I save this file, I have three options:

- Save the file as a Photoshop file and (if my GIF animator supports a Photoshop with layers translation) import the file into my GIF animator.
- With both Photoshop and my GIF animator open at the same time, copy and paste each individual frame from Photoshop into my animator.
- Save the individual frames of the animation as separate GIF files and import them individually into a basic GIF animator.

I personally use GifBuilder 0.5 to compose my animated GIFs (**http://iawww.epfl.ch/Staff/Yves. Piguet/clip2gif-home/GifBuilder.html**). Although it imports Photoshop files and translates the layers and places all the frames into the Frames window for me, I have found that it tends to shift my colors slightly. I personally prefer choice number two from the above three choices.

With Photoshop and GifBuilder open at the same time, I begin by selecting the first frame, which happens to be the *Background* frame (fig. 7.36), and then I Copy it, and finally, I go over to GifBuilder and paste it in. After I repeat the Copy-Paste function for all the frames in the animation, I end up with a Frames window that contains the 17 separate frames of the animation. Remember, however, that early in the conceptual phase of the animation it was decided that the logo would appear, stay still for a while, and then disappear again, looping forever. Since I have all my frames in GifBuilder, I can use its Copy-Paste function to add further frames to the animation to make it look like the logo fades back out (all I'm doing is Copying-Pasting the original frames again, only in reverse order this time), so that I eventually have a 32-frame animation (fig. 7.37).

The first frame has been selected in figure 7.37, and its corresponding visual is presented in the Untitled.gif window to its right. Notice that we are presented with some information atop the Frames window:

- The animation consists of 32 frames.
- Its length is 11.10 seconds (1 DELAY = 1/100th of a second).
- It is 155 pixels wide and 80 pixels high.
- It is set to loop forever (Options, Loop).

Even though I used browser-safe colors in preparing the artwork in Photoshop, it is a good idea to make sure that a browser-safe palette (sometimes referred to as the 6×6×6 palette) is chosen in GifBuilder (Options, Colors, 6×6×6 Palette) to ensure cross-platform compatibility when GifBuilder saves the animated GIF.

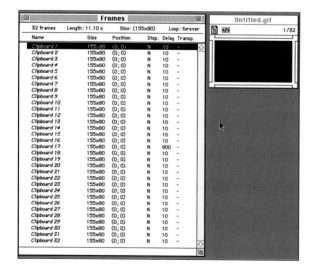

7.37

"Frames" view in GifBuilder 0.5.

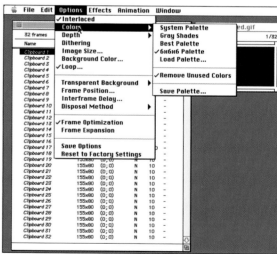

7.38

Selecting the browser-safe color palette in GifBuilder.

Frame 17 (the pause in the animation), shown in figure 7.39, is set to a Delay (Options, Interframe Delay) of 800 (equaling roughly eight seconds). All the other frames have been set to a Delay of 10, meaning they will appear as fast as the browser can handle it. You have to experiment with DELAY settings to get the best results with your particular animation.

With the animation set to my satisfaction in GifBuilder, I save it and take a look at its size (fig. 7.40).

Notice that in figure 7.40, the animation only takes up approximately 5.4k because of GifBuilder's compression scheme—not bad for a 32-frame, 155-pixel, streaming, multi-colored, animating logo. Remember the following points to achieve minimal file-sized web graphics or animated GIFs:

- **Image size.** Smaller image sizes equal smaller filesizes
- **Frame rate.** Less frames are better (if animating)
- **Frame optimization.** Deletes recurring imagery to save room
- **Color depth.** Less colors are better
- **Bit depth.** 72 dpi (monitor's default resolution)

To see why GifBuilder can save animations using such little disk-space, take a look at figure 7.41. It represents the 5.4k file reopened in GifBuilder after I saved it. Now compare figure 7.41 with figure 7.39. Notice that the numbers under the Size and Position columns have changed drastically, except for the first frame, which has remained the same (the first frame is used as the foundation for the animation and is not altered by GifBuilder).

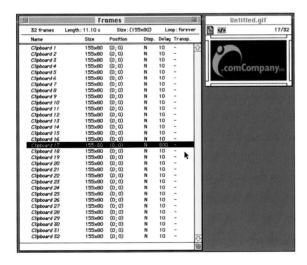

7.39

Pause frame selected in GifBuilder's Frames view.

7.40

Filesize info on the .comCompany GIF animation.

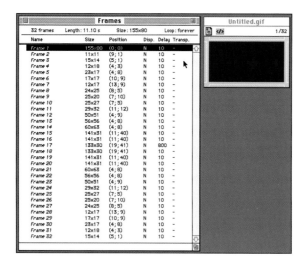

7.41

.comCompany animated GIF re-opened in GifBuilder.

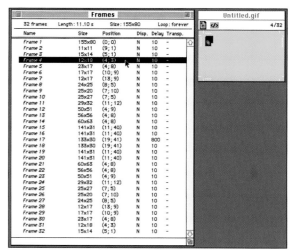

7.42

Looking at Frame 4 of the optimized .comCompany GIF animation.

Figure 7.42 demonstrates what happens when I examine Frame 4 of the animation. Notice that the background is now gone. The only image in this frame is the moving "dot." This technique is called *GIF optimization* and is a feature that GifBuilder (OPTIONS>FRAME OPTIMIZATION) and other GIF animators use to rid the animation of areas that stay constant throughout the animation. By going through each frame and mathematically determining/removing the unchanging areas that the first frame has in common with later frames in the animation, GIF animators can dramatically cut down resulting filesizes.

Every other animation in the .comCompany site was created using the guidelines and techniques mentioned earlier. With animations in the .comCompany site covered, the next consideration is an intuitive interface that enables users to find information quickly and easily keep track of where they are in the site.

The .comCompany Interface

Once users are compelled to enter a site based on its overall look and feel, they need to be able to access information quickly without getting lost in the process.

An *interface* is that which your audience interfaces (or interacts) with. Arguably, the entire web page is an interface, as are your web browser, your system software, and your computer as a whole. For this example, we are dealing with interfaces within interfaces. System software is created to ease the level of interaction between you and your computer hardware. In this sense, you create a web site interface to make your visitors' journeys through your web site more pleasant. An intuitive interface acts as a roadmap to the contents of your site. If the map is confusing, your users will get lost. If the map is easy to follow and lets users know where they are, you are bound to have many of your pages viewed.

Figure 7.43 illustrates .comCompany's second page (the "Step inside" link from the home page brings users here). While the .comCompany home page acts as the introduction to the company and its services, the "About .comResearch(SM)" page (fig. 7.43) is the main page from which users can travel throughout the site. Notice how the interface works: The yellow-orange text highlights the user's present location within the site and the gray links represent pages available to the viewer.

7.43

One level deep into the .comCompany site, with its interface present as a second read.

Designing .comCompany's Interface with the Client-Side Imagemap

Because the .comCompany interface essentially is a GIF image (the only way to represent unique and consistent fonts with non-editable sizes on the web), it has to be laid out and designed in a vector-based program, such as Illustrator or FreeHand, and imported into Photoshop for conversion to its pixel-based, browser-safe GIF format (using the same steps and techniques discussed earlier in this chapter).

Figure 7.44 shows the imported and fully colored interface in Photoshop. Notice that six possible selections can be made from the interface (Contact us, InfoDig, QuickDig, TrendSpot, .comCompany, and About .comResearch—.comCompany sends the user to the main **www.comcompany.com** home page). Therefore, six different layers have been set up to represent each of the five possible destination pages (fig. 7.45) as well as the standard interface layer used in pages that are not main destinations (there is a link off one of the pages that takes users to a "resources" page, for example).

Before the interface can be used within the .comCompany site, each layer must be saved as a GIF file and called from the HTML code. To use the interface as a clickable graphic with links to the six possible destinations, however, takes some more work.

To create a single GIF file that contains *regions*, or "hot" areas, that are clickable, you must produce an *imagemap* of the image. An imagemap is a piece of code that tells the browser that certain areas on a referenced image (selected by you) are links to URLs (defined by you).

There are two kinds of imagemaps: client-side and server-side. Server-side maps require that you create a separate map file to be placed on your *server* (the storage area that houses your HTML documents, GIFs, and other files that you want to make accessible to web users). Because of the reasons stated above, server-side maps are a pain to deal with, and I personally don't like to use them.

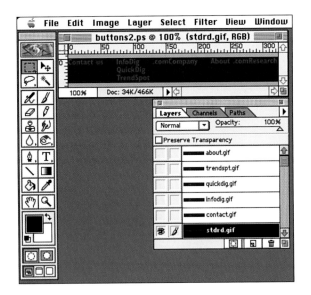

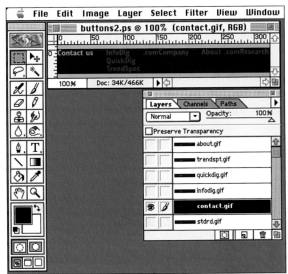

7.44

The .comCompany interface in Photoshop.

7.45

The .comCompany interface in Photoshop with the contact layer visible.

Client-side imagemaps reside within the HTML document you create and can be added and modified easily after you understand the basics:

- You need a GIF or PICT file of the image you want mapped.
- You need a program that creates imagemaps. (I recommend Adobe PageMill.)
- You need to follow the tutorial on creating imagemaps (coming up).
- You need to know how to Copy-Paste.

1. Open Adobe PageMill and import the figure you want to animate. Figure 7.46 shows Adobe PageMill open, with the standard .comCompany interface GIF imported.

2. Double-click on the image to make the imagemapping tools available (fig. 7.47).

   Notice that you can select from a box, circle, and polygon. These are the kinds of "hot" areas that you can make using Adobe PageMill's imagemapping feature.

3. Select the box and then position your cursor on the lower-right corner of the first link you want to create (fig. 7.48). Please keep in mind that you will in no way be able to edit the GIF with these actions. The imagemap is created mathematically by PageMill and made available later for HTML implementation.

7.46

Adobe PageMill, Edit mode, with the standard .comCompany interface GIF in view.

7.47

When you double-click on the .comCompany interface, the imagemapping tools become available.

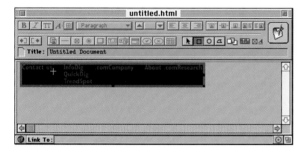

7.48

Having selected the box, I move to create my first "hot" spot.

7.49

The first link is created and the "Link To:" field filled.

4. Next, click and drag the mouse to create the hot area for the first link. The `Link To:` prompt at the bottom of figure 7.49 lights up, awaiting user input. For now, put the word **contact** there. Ideally, you would want to put the actual page to which the link will take the user if clicked.

5. Repeatedly select all the areas you would like to make "hot" and input `Link To:` locations for them. You should end up with something similar to that shown in figure 7.50.

6. To create an HTML document that contains the imagemap you just made, you can either save the file to your hard disk or simply go to Edit, HTML Source (fig. 7.51).

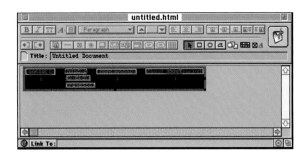

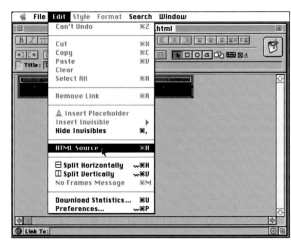

7.50

All the "hot" areas have been selected.

7.51

To view the imagemap, select Edit, HTML Source.

Now it's time to view the imagemap.

Figure 7.52 displays the HTML code for the page put together here in steps 1 to 6. The imagemap is the body of type starting with <MAP NAME="STDRD"> and ending with </MAP>. All you have to do is select the imagemap, copy it, and then paste it into the HTML document. The only other piece of code you have to worry about is adding USEMAP="#STDRD" within the <IMG> tag. The following code listing is an example of the <IMG> tag and imagemap used on .comCompany's second page:

```
<IMG SRC="about.gif" WIDTH="324"
HEIGHT="35" BORDER=0 ALT="navigation"
USEMAP="#trendspt">
```

7.52

PageMill's HTML Source mode.

```
<MAP NAME="trendspt">

    <AREA SHAPE="rect" COORDS="129,0,202,9" HREF="home.htm">

    <AREA SHAPE="rect" COORDS="73,24,128,34" HREF="trend.htm">

    <AREA SHAPE="rect" COORDS="73,12,119,21" HREF="quick.htm">

    <AREA SHAPE="rect" COORDS="73,0,111,9" HREF="infodig.htm">

    <AREA SHAPE="rect" COORDS="-1,0,54,10" HREF="contact.htm">

</MAP>
```

It is common practice to place imagemaps within the HTML document *after* the <IMG> tag and *between* the <BODY></BODY> tags. Since there are no HARD rules for this, you can follow common convention or experiment on your own. If you experiment with the HTML code placement, be aware that you *may* experience technical difficulties.

HTML: The Final Frontier

The Hypertext Markup Language (HTML) is both a blessing and a curse to web designers. It's a blessing in that it allows designers to learn its relatively simple code and put together beautifully crafted web sites. It's a curse in that not all browsers support many of its more progressive technologies as discussed in chapter 1.

This section covers some HTML issues as they relate to designers, using the .comCompany case study to exemplify the points.

I Need My Space

The <SPACER> tag is a wonderful piece of code that allows designers to create a blank area simply by typing a line of code. You can think of the <SPACER> tag as the HTML equivalent of pieces of lead in traditional typesetting. To create a spacer 50 pixels wide, for example, you would type <SPACER TYPE=HORIZONTAL SIZE=50>. Conversely, to create a spacer 50 pixels high, you would type <SPACER TYPE=VERTICAL SIZE=50>.

> "One of the fundamental issues that web site designers must deal with early in the implementation of HTML for page layout is the use of white space."

Unfortunately, although Netscape 3.0 understands the <SPACER> tag, Microsoft's Internet Explorer does not. Why am I making such a fuss about a spacer issue? One of the fundamental issues that web site designers must deal with early in the implementation of HTML for page layout is the use of white space (a fundamental design principle that I cover in Chapter 3). The only cross-browser–compliant method for creating consistent white space is what I refer to as a *fake spacer*.

A fake spacer is a transparent GIF file (GIF89a, discussed in chapter 6) that measures 1 pixel wide by 1 pixel tall, and which HTML code calls to create white space.

Figure 7.53 shows Photoshop's "New" image dialog box, wherein settings for a fake spacer have been keyed in. After you create the image and convert it to a 2-bit Indexed Color document (Image, Mode, Indexed Color), you export it as a GIF89a (File, Export, GIF89a Export).

Figure 7.54 demonstrates making the 1×1 pixel spacer transparent. You don't have to choose the Interlace option, because there will be no image to appear over time. Clicking on OK gives you a fake spacer to play with in your HTML.

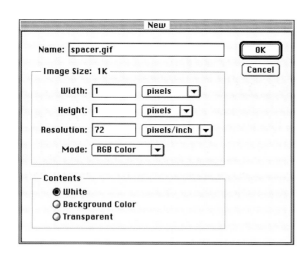

7.53

Creating a fake spacer in Photoshop.

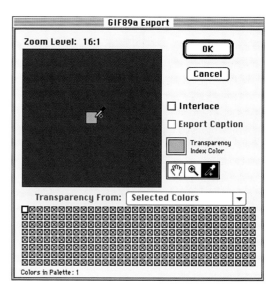

7.54

Exporting the transparent 1×1 pixel fake spacer.

The following line of code calls the fake spacer and creates a 50×50 pixel invisible box (because it's a transparent GIF) that you can use as white space:

```
<IMG WIDTH=50 HEIGHT=50 SRC="SPACER.GIF" ALT="[]">
```

Calling All Images

The <IMG> tag is used to call all images. For optimal results, there are a couple nuances that you should consider when you use the <IMG> tag. Take the following <IMG> tag, for example:

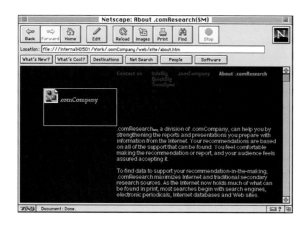

7.55

The ALT addition to the <IMG> tag in action.

```
<IMG WIDTH=155 HEIGHT=80 SRC="LOGO.GIF"
BORDER=0 ALT=".COMCOMPANY">
```

The width and height of the logo are embedded in the tag. The viewer's browser uses this important information to more quickly lay out the page according to the image's size requirements. If no width or height values are present in the tag, the browser takes longer to display the page because it must manually check the image size.

In this case, this logo is linked to a URL, and BORDER=0 has been added to notify the browser not to add a border around the graphic, identifying it as a link.

You should include ALT information in case the viewer's browser does not support graphics or animated GIFs. The word or group of words within the quote after ALT= appears in the viewer's browser if it can't display your image, as shown in figure 7.55).

Setting the HTML Table and Serving Fonts

Tables have helped designers cope with HTML and make the best of its limited technology to lay out some decent pages. To give you an idea of the kind of assistance tables can offer, figures 7.56 and 7.57 are examples of the .comCompany site with its table borders set to 1 (they are set to 0 by default, which makes them invisible).

Tables are extremely easy to implement and work with. You first start by defining them:

```
<TABLE WIDTH=520 BORDER=0 CELLPADDING=0 CELLSPACING=0>
```

The <TABLE></TABLE> tag defines the table in its entirety. The WIDTH setting is based on a fixed size, in this case, 520 pixels wide, and will not stretch to fit larger monitors nor shrink to accommodate smaller ones. BORDER determines whether you will have a border around your tables (as depicted in figures 7.57 and 7.58) or not (set BORDER=0). CELLPADDING determines the amount of space between the inside of the border and the contents of each cell. (Tables act much like spreadsheet cells, in that you determine the number of cell rows and columns.) CELLSPACING determines the amount of space between each cell, measured from cell border to cell border. After you complete the overall table settings, you can move on to assigning individual rows and columns to the table. Think of rows as the entire next line of text in this chapter. Think of columns as blocks of space within each row (all having to line up vertically with columns widths set above and/or below them). Given this information, the settings shown in figure 7.57 would yield a 2-column table with three visible rows of information.

The <TR></TR> tag defines each row within the table. The following example outlines the first visible row in figure 7.56:

```
<TR><TD WIDTH=200><IMG WIDTH=180 HEIGHT=35 SRC="blank.gif" ALT="[]"></TD><TD WIDTH=350><A
HREF="about.htm"><IMG SRC="slogan.gif" WIDTH="349" HEIGHT="36" BORDER=0 ALT="internet solutions
for everyday business problems"></A></TD></TR>
```

7.56

The .comCompany home page with table borders set to 1.

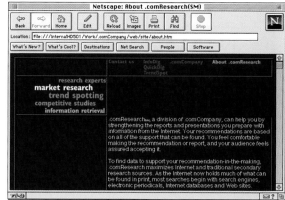

7.57

The .comCompany 2nd page with table borders set to 1.

It calls for a table row and creates the first cell within that row, <TD WIDTH=200>, which means, "Create a table data cell 200 pixels wide." If you wanted the cell to have a colored background, you could assign one to it at this point. <TD WIDTH=200 BGCOLOR="#FFFFFF"> would give you the same cell, except it would have a white background color. After the cell, a blank spacer is called for to designate that there will be no image in that cell. This is done to maintain the structural integrity of the table. The cell is closed off at this point by the </TD> tag, and the table's second cell is created <TD WIDTH=350>, signaling a 350-pixel wide cell, in which the "SLOGAN.GIF" image is called with a BORDER=0 descriptor because it's linked to the "ABOUT.HTM" page and does not require a box around it. The second cell is closed with the </TD> tag, and the row is ended with the </TR> tag.

The following is the rest of the HTML that makes up the .comCompany home page:

```
<TR><TD WIDTH=200 ALIGN=right><IMG WIDTH=155 HEIGHT=80 SRC="logoani2.gif" BORDER=0
ALT=".comCompany"></TD></TR>

<TR><TD WIDTH=180><IMG WIDTH=180 HEIGHT=1 SRC="blank.gif" ALT="[]"></TD>

<TD WIDTH=320><FONT FACE=helvetica, arial>Welcome to .comCompany! An Internet-based company that
provides Internet-related services to assist all types of businesspeople with everyday
needs.<BR><BR><A HREF=about.htm>Step inside</A> to get a peek at the services .comCompany provides
now.<BR><BR>Keep coming back to see what services .comCompany intends to provide in the very near
future. This Web site and the ways .comCompany can help your business will change frequently.
Bookmark this page so we can help you keep up with us!<BR><BR><FONT SIZE=-3
COLOR="#666666">Copyright <FONT SIZE=3>&copy;</FONT> 1997, .comCompany LLC, all rights
reserved.<BR>.comResearch, InfoDig, QuickDig and TrendSpot are Service Marks of .comCompany
LLC.</FONT></TR>

</TABLE>
```

Notice that the <FONT FACE> tag has been applied to the HTML body copy. Choosing typefaces for the web is tricky business because no standards have yet been set in terms of cross-platform font consistency. For now, Helvetica, Times, Courier, and Palatino are sure bets on the Mac, and Arial, Courier, and Times New Roman are common on the PC. By specifying <FONT FACE=HELVETICA, ARIAL>, chances are that Mac users will see the copy in Helvetica and PC users will see it in Arial (if Helvetica is not installed). There are no assurances, however, that every user will have these fonts installed in their computer. The moral here is DESIGNER BEWARE! when it comes to assigning fonts to HTML text. If you assign a font face other than the standard Helvetica, Arial, Times, Courier, or Palatino, you run the risk of your viewer's browser substituting a font that may not look attractive with your design. One good resource for obtaining cross-platform, web-friendly fonts is Microsoft's TryeType Font page at **http://www.microsoft.com/typography/fontpack**.

Obtaining Feedback with Forms

You can find an excellent introductory online tutorial that contains designer applications of HTML forms at *HotWired*'s Webmonkey site (**http://www.hotwired.com/webmonkey/html/97/06/index2a.html**).

For information on how to create actual functioning forms, you need to visit the Common Gateway Interface (CGI) page (**http://hoohoo.ncsa.uiuc.edu/cgi/**), where you can find many references to online documentation about PERL and CGI (both of which are beyond the scope of this book).

For our immediate purposes, however, let's take a look at .comCompany's "contact" page, where users are urged to send the company e-mail with their personal data and information requirement.

Effective forms must:

- **Communicate as something to be filled out.** It is nice to have contrast between the background and foreground entry fields, so that they stand out to the viewer's eye as areas into which to type info.

- **Be easy to navigate.** A good form is easy to fill out and obtains the most amount of information while staying as short as possible, to make filling it out less time-consuming for the user.

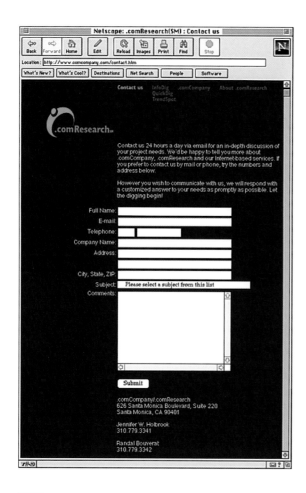

7.58

The .comCompany "contact" page.

Figure 7.58 demonstrates a beautifully simple form that utilizes contrast along with the structure of tables to obtain information from visitors and potential .comCompany clients. The following is the HTML code that produces the form in figure 7.58:

```
<HTML>

<BODY BGCOLOR="#003300" LINK="#ff9900"
➡VLINK="#ff9900" ALINK="#ff9900"
➡TEXT="#ffffff">

<HEAD>

<TITLE>

.comResearch(SM) : Contact us

</TITLE>

</HEAD>

<center><form method="POST" action=
➡"http://www.comcompany.com/scripts
➡/polyform.dll/Comcompany_ContactForm">

<table width=550 border=0 cellpadding=0
➡cellspacing=0>

<tr><td width=200><IMG WIDTH=180
➡HEIGHT=35 SRC="blank.gif"
➡alt="[]"></td><td width=350><IMG
➡SRC="contact.gif" WIDTH="324"
➡HEIGHT="35" border=0 alt="navigation"
➡USEMAP="#trendspt"></td></tr>

<tr><td width=200 align=right><a
➡href=home2.htm><img WIDTH=155
➡HEIGHT=80 src="research.gif" border=0
➡alt=".comCompany"></a></td></tr>
```

```
<tr><td width=200><IMG WIDTH=180 HEIGHT=1 SRC="blank.gif" alt="[]"></td>

<td width=350><font face=helvetica, arial>Contact us 24 hours a day via e-mail for an in-depth
➡discussion of your project needs. We'd be happy to tell you more about .comCompany, .comResearch
➡and our Internet-based services. If you prefer to contact us by mail or phone, try the numbers
➡and address below. <BR><BR>

However you wish to communicate with us, we will respond with a customized answer to your needs as
➡promptly as possible. Let the digging begin!

<br><br>

</font>

</tr>
```

```
<tr><td width=200 align=right><font face=helvetica, arial>Full Name:</td><td width=350><INPUT
➥TYPE="text" NAME="FULLNAME" SIZE=40></td></tr>

<tr><td width=200 align=right><font face=helvetica, arial>E-mail:</td><td width=350><INPUT
➥TYPE="text" NAME="E-MAIL" SIZE=40></td></tr>

<tr><td width=200 align=right><font face=helvetica, arial>Telephone:</td><td width=350><INPUT
➥TYPE="text" NAME="AREACODE" SIZE=5 MAXLENGTH=6><IMG WIDTH=3 HEIGHT=1 SRC="blank.gif"
➥alt="[]"><INPUT TYPE="text" NAME="PHONE" SIZE=15></td></tr>

<tr><td width=200 align=right><font face=helvetica, arial>Company Name:</td><td width=350><INPUT
➥TYPE="text" NAME="CONAME" SIZE=40></td></tr>

<tr><td width=200 align=right><font face=helvetica, arial>Address:</td><td width=350><INPUT
➥TYPE="text" NAME="ADDRESS" SIZE=40></td></tr>

<tr><td width=200 align=right></td><td width=350><INPUT TYPE="text" NAME="CONAME2"
➥SIZE=40></td></tr>

<tr><td width=200 align=right><font face=helvetica, arial>City, State, ZIP:</td><td
➥width=350><INPUT TYPE="text" NAME="CSZ" SIZE=40></td></tr>

<tr><td width=200 align=right><font face=helvetica, arial>Subject:</td><td width=350><SELECT
➥NAME="SUBJECT" VALUE="dont mind" SIZE= 1 ALIGN=left>

<OPTION SELECTED>Please select a subject from this list

<OPTION>InfoDig

<option>QuickDig

<option>TrendSpot

<option>Please Contact Me ASAP

<option>Other</SELECT></td></tr>

<tr><td width=200 align=right valign=top><font face=helvetica, arial>Comments:</td><td
➥width=350><TEXTAREA NAME="Comment" ROWS=10 COLS=72 wrap></TEXTAREA><BR><BR><input type=submit
➥value="  Submit  "></form></font></td></tr>

<tr><td width=200><IMG WIDTH=180 HEIGHT=1 SRC="blank.gif" alt="[]"></td>

<td width=350><font face=helvetica, arial>.comCompany/.comResearch<br>

626 Santa Monica Boulevard, Suite 220<br>

Santa Monica, CA  90401<br><br>

Jennifer W. Holbrook<br>

310.779.3341<br><br>

Randal Bouverat<br>

310.779.3342<br>

</font>

</tr>

</table>

</center>
```

```
<MAP NAME="trendspt">

    <AREA SHAPE="rect" COORDS="219,-1,321,9" HREF="about.htm">

    <AREA SHAPE="rect" COORDS="129,0,202,9" HREF="home.htm">

    <AREA SHAPE="rect" COORDS="73,24,128,34" HREF="trend.htm">

    <AREA SHAPE="rect" COORDS="73,12,119,21" HREF="quick.htm">

    <AREA SHAPE="rect" COORDS="73,0,111,9" HREF="infodig.htm">

</MAP>

</BODY>

</HTML>
```

As you can see in the HTML code for .comCompany's contact page, tables are used to help move the viewer's eye through the information, as well as to create an invisible dividing line that helps designate where the user will be inputting data.

I personally code my forms in HTML, although you can also use PageMill. Learning how to do forms in HTML is as easy as:

- Studying how others do it, as in the above HTML example.
- Designing a form in PageMill and viewing the HTML to see how it was done.

For more examples of effective visual forms usage, visit the *Click Here* web site at **http://www.rpirouz.com/click**.

As a designer, learning how to make CGI forms functional is not as important as learning how to structure well–thought-out forms that are nicely organized and easy to fill out. If you are an individual web designer, I recommend that you ask your Internet Service Provider to help you set up a CGI script to process your forms. If you work in a design studio or advertising agency, chances are you have access to in-house or out-sourced programming wizards to make your CGI dreams come true.

That's the Ticket

We've analyzed the strategic, conceptual, visual, and down-n-dirty, step-by-step processes of designing a web site. The next chapter deals with more advanced issues, such as using the Java, JavaScript, and Macromedia Director Shockwave technologies for solving communication problems.

8

Engage... Full Throttle Ahead

Advanced Web Design Techniques

After the overall communication strategy is laid out to reflect the site's key purpose and the initial look and feel of the site has been conceptualized and designed, it is time to consider the finer details—those finishing touches that make web sites technologically up-to-date, interactive, and a joy to navigate.

Without a fundamental understanding of the basic design principles and a strategic visual communication design philosophy (covered in Chapter 3, "Click This"), no "advanced technology" can make you a better designer. In fact, the technologies are merely tools in the skilled communicator's electronic toolbox. It is important to understand the tools and to know precisely when and for what purpose each is to be utilized. Simply using advanced technology for the sake of it indicates a lack of concept and/or strategic thinking (unless the technology is used in a completely experimental setting to judge user response, for example).

This chapter covers some advanced HTML specific to designers' needs, covers the ever-popular JavaScript and some of its designer strengths, introduces basic Java development, and concludes with a step-by-step Macromedia Shockwave demo.

Fancy Schmancy HTML

"Without a fundamental understanding of the basic design principles and a strategic visual communication design philosophy, no 'advanced technology' can make you a better designer."

Designer HTML comes in limited varieties, simply because HTML is a programming language written by non-visual designers who never expected it to be used to create the stunning phenomenon known as the World Wide Web. Certain little goodies, however, have been discovered and implemented over time by designers to bypass some of HTML's limitations.

The Meta Refresh Tag

Using the client-pull mechanism by which the client (the user's PC) pulls information (the HTML page) from the server (the Internet connection), you can tell your user's web browser to show a page for a given number of seconds, then automatically send your user to another page (hence, the term, *refresh*).

Designers have used this easy-to-implement HTML technology to present users with introductory web pages or quick "brand pitch" pages, where the product slogan or brand image is displayed for a brief period before the user is sent to the site's home page.

The Meta Refresh technology is also used for what is called *interstitial ads*. When users select a specific link, for example, they are immediately presented with a full-page web ad that appears momentarily, which then sends users to their intended destination (more on advertising in Chapter 9).

Figure 8.1 represents bookdeal.com's introductory page, which remains visible for 10 seconds. At **http://www.bookdeal.com**, the user is presented with an animation that begins with the words, "You can't do that…" being scratched out (as if with a pencil) and the words, "watch me." appearing right after, as if being typed by a typewriter keyboard. Meanwhile, if users want to bypass the animation, they are free to click-through the animation, which takes them to bookdeal's home page at **http://www.bookdeal. com/home/home.htm**. In this example, the Meta Refresh tag is used to sell a certain image—that of a positive individual, who despite all odds, believes in his or her idea to self-publish.

8.1

bookdeal.com intro page.

The following is the entire intro page HTML code:

```
<HTML>
<HEAD>
<META HTTP-EQUIV="refresh" CONTENT="10; URL=home/hello.htm">
<TITLE>bookdeal.com</TITLE>
</HEAD>
<BODY BGCOLOR="#000000" LINK="#000000" ALINK="#000000" VLINK="#000000" TEXT="#000000">
<BR><BR><BR>
<CENTER>
<A HREF="home/hello.htm"><IMG WIDTH=297 HEIGHT=56 SRC="cant.gif" BORDER="0" alt="Watch me..."></A>
</CENTER>
</BODY>
</HTML>
```

Please note the Meta Refresh tag and its usage in the above example. To use such a tag in your HTML, take the following into consideration:

- Use the META tag within your <HEAD></HEAD> tags.
- The number following CONTENT= represents the number of seconds before the page Refreshes; in the above case, 10 seconds.
- Be aware of users who have slow connections. If you are using Meta Refresh on a page with many graphics, be sure to allot enough time in the CONTENT= area that people who have slow connections can view your graphics. There's nothing worse than being taken to another page before the graphics finish loading—a pure waste of your users' time. Solution? Limit your Meta Refresh pages to one or two small graphics (the CANT.GIF graphic in the previous example is 2.9k).
- The data following URL= designates the destination URL … make sure that it's a correct and functioning address.
- Provide an alternative "out" for your users to bypass the intro—some people don't like having to wait for a Refresh tag. For example, you can create a link in your intro page that tells users to "click to bypass," or simply make any graphic on the intro page hot so that when users click on it, they are taken to the next page without having to wait for the Meta Refresh tag to kick in.

The Meta Refresh tag can add a nice choreographed touch to your web presentation. By being aware of your limitations and taking advantage of the technology's strengths, you can create positive first impressions that help bring users back.

Visual "Submit"

8.2

HTML's default Submit button.

If you've ever filled out an HTML form (or designed one yourself), you've probably cursed HTML's lack of control over how your SUBMIT button looks. HTML's Submit default is the oval button (fig. 8.2).

HTML's default Submit can be adequate for sites that are more analytical in nature, and whose audience is more mainstream. For example, .comCompany's contact page uses HTML's default Submit button.

HTML's default Submit button looks good in the setting (fig. 8.3) because of the simplicity of the overall page layout as well as the communication hierarchy established between the identity, navigation, fill-in form, and finally, the Submit button. Take a look at figure 8.4, however, and you'll notice an immediate eyesore.

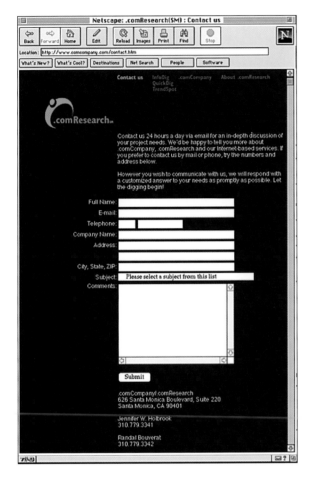

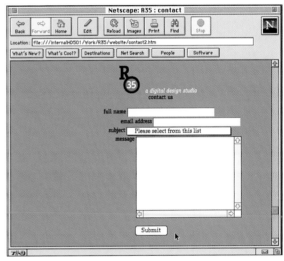

8.3

The .comCompany contact page.

8.4

R35's contact page using the standard HTML Submit oval.

The R35 site's contact page (**http://www.r35.com/contact.htm**) is an example of where the standard HTML Submit button can be quite ugly in terms of what it adds to the overall look and feel of the page. Notice that because of its white nature (on the Macintosh platform), it immediately begs for attention and pulls the viewer's eye down the page, when in fact the top of figure 8.4 contains the most important information: the company logo and the fill-in form. In this case, HTML's standard button interferes with the site's communication hierarchy. Because of the subtle use of scale and type in figure 8.4 (the unique typography consists of imported GIF images with which the standard Submit typeface conflicts), the Submit button has to go. Figure 8.5 illustrates the solution.

Traditionally, when ending a form in HTML, you need to input the following tag to place the Submit button:

```
<INPUT TYPE=SUBMIT VALUE="SUBMIT">
```

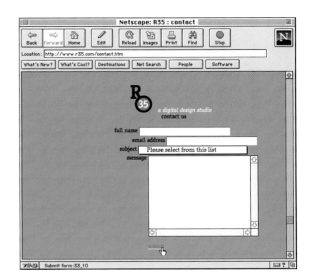

8.5

R35's contact page using a visual Submit graphic.

This tells HTML to dig into its shallow chest of buttons and drag out the big oval. You tell HTML what the button should say—in this case, VALUE="SUBMIT"—it could very well be VALUE="GO," or whatever else your heart desires.

Figure 8.5 demonstrates a welcome solution to the default dilemma. Notice how the Submit button in this example is no longer an oval—in fact, it's no longer an HTML form button! It appears in the same font as the rest of the typography because it is a graphic. Here are some things to consider when designing a graphic Submit button:

- It can be GIF, animated GIF, or JPEG.
- It is not restricted to any particular size.
- It works with Netscape 2.0 / IE 3.0 browsers or better.
- Make sure that it communicates that it's a Submit button—don't get carried away.

In figure 8.5, notice how beautifully the Submit button works within the communication hierarchy compared to figure 8.4. For added security, so that users know it's a link, a white line blinks on and off right under the word "submit" in figure 8.5 (thus the animated GIF). How is it done in HTML?

```
<INPUT TYPE="IMAGE" SRC="IMAGE.GIF" BORDER="0">
```

That's all there is to it. Instead of TYPE=SUBMIT, TYPE="IMAGE" tells HTML that you'd like to use an image for your Submit button (nice of those engineers to offer us this handy workaround). SRC="IMAGE.GIF" tells HTML the name of your image file (it could be SRC="IMAGE.JPG" as well). You'll have to add BORDER="0" so that no border appears around it (unless you want one).

The HTML Submit alternative can help to smooth out the flow in the communication hierarchy of your page as well as to maintain consistency in your site's overall look and feel.

Lists, HTML Bullets, Block Quotes, and Graphic Bullets

Indented lists with bullets are easy to create in HTML. The <UL>, or "Unordered List," tag can create HTML-based bullet-lists depending on your choice of a disc (default solid bullet), circle (hollow circle), or square (hollow). In HTML, creating an unordered list can look something like this:

```
<UL TYPE=CIRCLE>
<LI>ITEM NUMBER 1</LI>
<LI>ITEM NUMBER 2</LI>
<LI>ITEM NUMBER 3</LI>
</UL>
```

where <UL> begins the list, TYPE determines the bullet-style (circle, disc, or square), and each List Item <LI> is a bulleted item. Figure 8.6 shows the results of the above HTML.

8.6

HTML <UL> tag example.

The following HTML from a larger document introduces the next level of indentation, Block Quotes used along with an Unordered List:

```
<UL TYPE=SQUARE>
<STRONG><LI>AMERICAN HONDA</LI><BR></STRONG>
<BLOCKQUOTE>
BANNER AD CAMPAIGNS<BR>
HONDA COLLEGE MICROSITE<BR>
HONDA CLASSIC<BR>
LA MARATHON XII<BR>
</BLOCKQUOTE>
<STRONG><LI>VIRGIN RECORDS / AMNESTY
➡INTERNATIONAL</LI><BR></STRONG>
<BLOCKQUOTE>
INTERFACE DESIGN FOR "GET UP-STAND UP" WEB SITE<BR>
</BLOCKQUOTE>
<STRONG><LI>CALIFORNIA INSTITUTE OF TECHNOLOGY</LI><BR></STRONG>
<BLOCKQUOTE>
IDENTITY DESIGN<BR>
WEB ARCHITECTURE / DESIGN<BR>
</BLOCKQUOTE>
```

Figure 8.7 illustrates the above code as translated by a browser.

The <BLOCKQUOTE> tag is a wonderful tool to use when wanting to indent an entire paragraph or list of text without using bullets. What if you wanted to create a bullet list without having to be limited to HTML's circle, disc, or square? Figure 8.8 demonstrates just that.

By using graphics saved using a transparent background (GIF89a format), you can create your own colorful bullets based on whatever shape you chose. In figure 8.8, it was more aesthetically pleasing to design a bulleted list using .comCompany's predetermined color palette rather than relying on standard uneditable HTML tags.

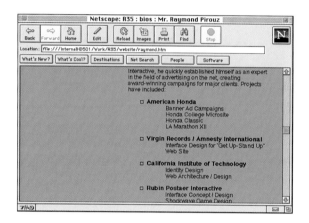

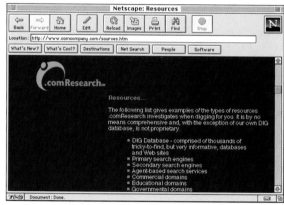

8.7

HTML <BLOCKQUOTE> example.

8.8

.comCompany's resources page.

The following is a sample of the HTML code that went into designing figure 8.8:

```
<TD WIDTH=350><FONT FACE=HELVETICA, ARIAL><STRONG><FONT
➡COLOR="#669933">RESOURCES...</FONT></STRONG><BR><BR>

The following list gives examples of the types of resources .comResearch investigates when digging
➡for you. It is by no means comprehensive and, with the exception of our own DIG database, is not
➡proprietary.<BR><BR>

<BLOCKQUOTE>

<IMG SRC="square.gif">DIG Database - comprised of thousands of<BR><IMG WIDTH=10 HEIGHT=10
➡SRC="blank.gif" ALT="[]">tricky-to-find, but very informative, databases<BR><IMG WIDTH=10
➡HEIGHT=10 SRC="blank.gif" ALT="[]">and Web sites<BR>

<IMG SRC="square.gif">Primary search engines<BR>

<IMG SRC="square.gif">Secondary search engines<BR>

<IMG SRC="square.gif">Agent-based search services<BR>
```

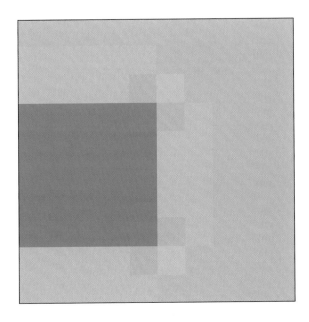

8.9

.comCompany's square.gif graphic.

Notice that a 350-pixel wide table data-row has been started, with fonts assigned to the text. The <BLOCKQUOTE> tag begins the list indent, followed by an IMAGE tag calling the square.gif graphic (fig. 8.9).

Notice that the square.gif graphic consists of a solid green box atop a transparent background, which serves as a built-in spacer (recalling the spacer.gif in Chapter 7, "Propeller Hats On"). In this example, there is no need to place a SPACER between the bullet graphic and the item text.

Lists and block quotes used in combination with standard HTML or graphic bullets are powerful information design tools in communicating structured and ordered data. As a web designer concerned with clear, persuasive communication, you should utilize every available resource to best transmit your message to the intended audience.

Designer JavaScript

Netscape's cross-platform scripting language, JavaScript has enabled programmers and designers to enhance the web experience. Unlike Java, Sun Microsystem's intensely powerful cross-platform development tool (covered in the "Java" section later in this chapter), JavaScript resides within your HTML document and can be immediately enjoyed without much processing time, the need for plug-ins, or third-party modifications.

Netscape's JavaScript Guide (fig. 8.10) is available at **http://home.netscape.com/eng/mozilla/3.0/ handbook/javascript/index.html**. Visit this site to learn more about JavaScript and other online JavaScript resources. Because of JavaScript's overwhelming acceptance by the web community, it has become the scripting language of choice by both programmers and designers who do code.

Project Cool at **http://www.projectcool.com/developer/** is an excellent online JavaScript resource that provides many scripts free of charge (all you have to do is retain their copyright message within your code).

JavaScript Tip of the Week at **http://www.webreference.com/javascript/** is another excellent online JavaScript resource if you'd like to learn more (this site provides step-by-step lessons for each tip).

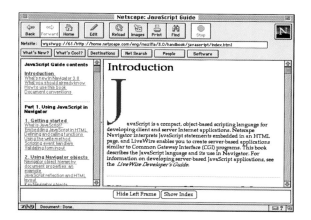

8.10

Netscape's JavaScript Guide.

8.11

Project Cool Developer Zone.

Note

As far as books are concerned, there are more than 50 JavaScript books on the market. Here are a couple I would recommend to begin with:

PLUG-N-PLAY JavaScript (New Riders Publishing—Packed with ready-to-use scripts on a CD-ROM) ISBN 1-56205-674-3

JavaScript Manual of Style (ZD Press) ISBN 1-56276-423-3

All the resources you need to learn and use JavaScript are literally all over the place, and I'd suggest you take advantage of them.

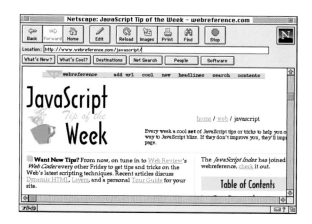

8.12

JavaScript Tip of the Week.

What's so great about this technology, and what can you do with it?

JavaScript is an extremely powerful scripting language whose core power can only be utilized by an experienced C++ object-oriented programming wizard. However, designers can tap into some of JavaScript's power to:

■ Add an extra level of feedback (beyond the pointing finger) when users roll over text or image links.

■ Force the browser to open new windows.

■ Replace one image with another as a user's mouse rolls over it, creating rollover effects for the web.

■ Create pull-down menu selections that take users to their desired destinations of choice.

The above are just a few of the many web enhancements that JavaScript allows designers to mingle with. Since there is no way to cover them all in this book, I concentrate on illustrating the above four examples in this section.

Extra Feedback Where It Counts

The easiest piece of JavaScript you'll ever code is the status message feedback. The *status message* is a component of your web browser that appears at the bottom of the interface, usually letting you know where a button links to. In figure 8.11, the status message is displaying the "Document: Done." message that lets you know that the page has finished loading.

By using this technique, you can add more information about the nature of your link. Instead of seeing **http://www.mypage.com/hobbies/cats/persian.htm**, your viewers can see, "I love cats … especially fluffy Persians." This can add an extra level of interaction between you and your users, as well as allow some opportunity for using creative writing to entice users to click.

In figure 8.13, notice that the cursor has been positioned over the "examine our creative director's digital portfolio." link and has changed to the pointing finger to indicate the link. Traditionally, you would see the URL location of the link down in the status message area. In this case, however, we see "concept: content: design." which is the title of the link destination. This extra piece of feedback provides the user with a foreshadowing of what is to come (remember high school lit. class?). Here's how it's done:

```
<A HREF="http://www.rpirouz.com" onMouseOver="window.status='concept : content : design.'; return
true">
```

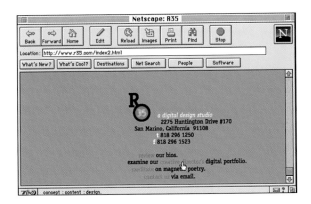

8.13

R35 status message feedback.

In your <A HREF> tag, after the destination URL, you will need to add the onMouseOver tag, which you will need to follow with your custom message, and end with the "return true" statement. That's all there is to it. The onMouseOver tag is a piece of JavaScript that tells your browser that when the user's mouse is over something, do something—in this case, display a message in a specific area.

By customizing the feedback that your links offer visitors, you can add more descriptive, creatively copywritten, enticing messages that make interacting with your site more enjoyable.

Opening New Windows

JavaScript allows you to force your viewer's browser to open a new window when clicking on certain links. Let's take a look at some reasons why you'd want to take advantage of this technology:

- Keep users at your page instead of letting them go—opening new windows allows users to examine the links from your page without leaving your site.
- Create a mini-window housing links to various destinations within your site (like a remote control).
- Open new windows to show larger, close-up versions of images on your site that would otherwise take up too much room.

Opening new windows is a two-step process, so let's look at the first step. You first must define the parameters of the new window early in your HTML code. Common HTML coding etiquette recommends that all script definitions take place within the <HEAD></HEAD> tags. JavaScript is a strict programming language that makes subtle uses of characters and coding conventions foreign to designers. For our purposes here, you just need to know the key areas that you must alter in order to get the results you want.

Note

To find out why JavaScript is coded the way it is, or to learn more about programming, I suggest taking courses in PASCAL (a programming language) and C++, after which you will know the HOWs and WHYs of JavaScript. Until then, you should be content with using existing code and modifying it to meet your needs.

The following example is a piece of JavaScript code that defines the open window function:

```
<HEAD>
<SCRIPT>
<!--//
FUNCTION OPENWIN() {
window.open("","X",'toolbar=0,location=0,directories=0,status=0,
menubar=0,scrollbars=1,width=600,height=400, resizable=1');
}
//-->
</SCRIPT>
</HEAD>
```

Between the <HEAD></HEAD> tags, <!--// and //--> hides the script from appearing on older browsers that don't support JavaScript. The function I named OPENWIN (you can name it whatever you like) calls for a 600×400 pixel window to open, with the following settings: Window name is "X," no toolbars, location window, directories, status message, and menu bar (0 means NO), while scroll bars are to be present, along with the window being resizable (1 means YES).

Calling the script into action takes place in the <A HREF> tag:

```
<A HREF="destination.html" onMouseOver="window.status=your custom message here'; return true;"
onClick=openwin() target="x">
```

Notice that this code combines the previously covered status window technique with this new technique. OnClick tells JavaScript to do something (translated by the = sign) when the user clicks. In this case, the something that the code instructs JavaScript to do is the function OPENWIN( ), which was defined earlier in the <HEAD></HEAD> tag, and targets the window whose name the code defines as "X."

If you do not want to incorporate the status message technique into the previous example, simply remove the tag so that your code looks like this:

```
<A HREF="destination.html" onClick=openwin() target="x">
```

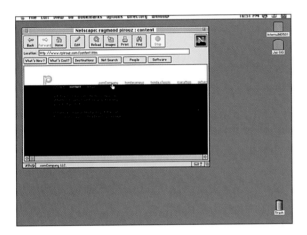

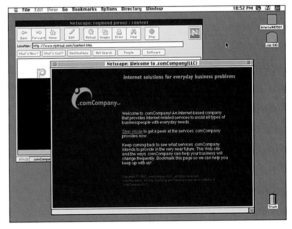

8.14

Getting ready to click on a link that opens a new window at the **http://www.rpirouz.com** site.

8.15

After clicking on the link shown in figure 8.14, a new window opens to reveal the link's destination and leaves the original page in the background.

That's all there is to it. Figures 8.14 and 8.15 show the open window function in action:

Notice the mouse cursor shown in figure 8.14. It's indicating a link (you know that because it has changed to the pointing finger) and giving the user feedback in the status message window. When the user clicks on the link, the screen shown in figure 8.15 appears, where a new window matching the specifications defined early in the page's HTML code have set up a window through which the target site is presented WITHOUT LOSING SIGHT of the link's origination page. This is a very important technique in keeping users at your site. If you provide links to many areas through JavaScript's window open function, you can give users access to other areas on the Net but at the same time prevent them from straying too far. Notice in figure 8.15 that the new window does not contain any of the navigation implements present in its parent window. Instead, it serves as a stage on which the link is presented to the user, so that when the user is done, he or she can close the window (by simply clicking on the window's close box) and the page returns to the front. Navigating through newly opened windows is actually easier than having to navigate through a site that makes you remember where certain pages were. With windows, you can keep them open and cascade them on your screen, keeping track of many web pages at once. When you open a new window, the previous page does not go away—rather, it remains in the background.

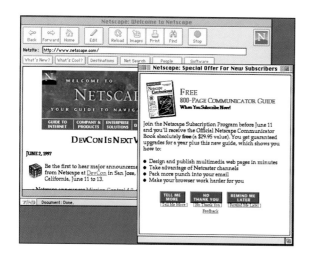

Figure 8.16 demonstrates the use of JavaScript's window open function to confront users with advertising as soon as they enter your home page.

8.16

Using the OnLoad JavaScript function to open another window as soon as users enter the site.

The Netscape site has taken a bold step by providing first-time visitors with an advertisement for a free book (for joining the Netscape Subscription Program before June 11). You can make new windows appear as soon as visitors enter your site by adding a piece of JavaScript code to the <BODY> tag within your home page HTML:

```
<BODY BGCOLOR="#666600" LINK="#333300" VLINK="#333300" ALINK="#333300" TEXT="#000000"
OnLoad=adwin()>
```

The above addition, the OnLoad function tells JavaScript to do something after your page finishes loading. When you define your JavaScript code within your <HEAD></HEAD> tags, key in the following:

```
<HEAD>
<SCRIPT>
<!--//
FUNCTION ADWIN() {
window.open("thepage.htm","X",'toolbar=0,location=0,directories=0,status=0,menubar=0,scrollbars=0,
➥width=300,height=400, resizable=0');
}
//-->
</SCRIPT>
</HEAD>
```

"A *rollover* is a descriptor for the act of physically moving your mouse to position your cursor over something on the screen (the word "roll" comes from the actual rolling action of the ball inside your mouse). So, if I told you to roll over an icon, I would mean for you to position your cursor over that icon... that's all."

In the previous example, FUNCTION ADWIN( ) gives a name to the JavaScript function, so that later on in the code, you can refer back to it by name (for example, if you add "ONCLICK= ADWIN( )" to an <HREF> tag so that it looks like this: <A HREF="HTTP://WWW.MYSITE.COM" ONCLICK=ADWIN( ) TARGET="X">, JavaScript will analyze the ADWIN( ) function and will open up a new window when the link is clicked). I made up the word ADWIN (for add window). It's completely arbitrary; you can name it anything you like. THEPAGE.HTM is the HTML file that will appear in the new window. You do not have to specify a target window if you're going to call only one new window. Of course, you can customize all of the page variables (toolbar, menu bar, height, width, and so on) according to your particular needs.

JavaScript Rollovers

Users appreciate feedback based on their actions, and rollovers allow designers to create compelling, engaging web experiences for their visitors. Rollovers lend importance to the revealed image and demand user attention. A number of different JavaScript coding techniques are available for creating rollovers, and they all can get hairy (especially when dealing with many rollover images). I suggest that you refer to the resources I pointed out earlier in this section (especially Project Cool at **http://www.projectcool.com/developer/**) and study them all to determine which technique works best for you. The personal rollover technique I use is derived from an online webmonkey tutorial at **http://www.webmonkey.com** that I tweaked and modified to fit my needs.

My personal web site at **http://www.rpirouz.com** takes advantage of JavaScript rollovers. In planning the JavaScript rollover strategy for my web site, I decided to reveal a piece of my design philosophy every time a user rolls over one of the site's three major links—concept : content : design. More specifically, I decided to reveal a design philosophy relevant to each keyword (as opposed to creating rollovers simply for the sake of creating rollovers). By revealing a piece of my personal design philosophy to my target audience (potential clients), I present a piece of me every time my audience rolls over a link, providing them with insight into my ideology.

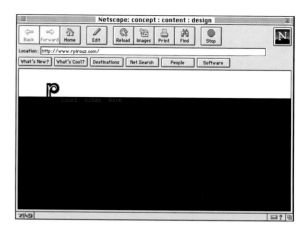

8.17

The Raymond Pirouz home (**http://www.rpirouz.com**).

Figure 8.17 illustrates my home page in its most simple form. If a user rolls the mouse pointer over one of the three links, a JavaScript code is triggered to reveal an image directly beneath the links. There are a couple of points to consider when creating rollovers with JavaScript:

- If you are going to reveal one image in place of another, both images must have the same height and width pixel dimensions.
- You can create a rollover that reveals an image somewhere other than the image you rolled over.
- Carefully plan out the aim of your rollover (don't create rollovers for the sake of it—anytime you enhance the communication or assist the user by adding feedback, you're doing good).

Having taken the above points into consideration, let's take a look at the components that make the JavaScript rollover in my site possible.

Figure 8.18 shows a placeholder for the image shown in figure 8.19, which is one of the design philosophies that appears when a user rolls over a link. I need to implement a placeholder in this scenario because when the user rolls over a link, I don't want the new image to appear at the exact same location as the link, but rather, I want the image to appear somewhere other than where the user rolls over.

8.18

Solid black rollover placeholder.

8.19

Rollover result image replaces the placeholder.

In simple English, I define the rollover function within my <HEAD></HEAD> tags (as usual) and then in the <A HREF> tag for my links, I tell HTML to send a JavaScript signal to the placeholder image and replace it with another image, based on the link my user has rolled over.

Having gone over the JavaScript choreography, or plan of action, let's now look at how the plan translates to code:

```
<HEAD>

<SCRIPT>

<!--//

function rollOver (imgNum,imgSrc)

{

   if (document.images)

   {

      document.images [imgNum] .src = imgSrc

   }

}

//-->

</SCRIPT>

</HEAD>
```

In the above example, I have defined the rollover function within the <HEAD></HEAD> tags. Notice that this is my interpretation of code that I've read about in my online experience. You may consider using another style of JavaScript coding to get the same results (refer to the previously mentioned references).

```
<A HREF="concept.htm" onMouseOver="rollOver (4,'philos1.gif');window.status='advertising for the
web audience.'; return true;"onMouseOut="rollOver (4,'philos0.gif');">concept</A>
```

The above code tells HTML to send the JavaScript code and reveal the image shown in figure 8.19 when the user rolls over the link, "concept." In this case, the onMouseOver="rollOver(x,'$name$.gif')" tag is used, where x is the number of the image to be replaced and '$name$.gif' is the file name of the image that is to replace x. Please note that the JavaScript code counts all of my images (in order of placement within my HTML document), from 0 on. Therefore, the first image in my page is number 0 to JavaScript, the second image number 1, and so on. In the above example, the placeholder image is the fourth image that appears in my HTML (hence, the use of the number 4 in the JavaScript tag). So, basically, the above <A HREF> tag begins to say, essentially, "When the user's mouse goes over this link, replace image number 4 with philos1.gif."

Figure 8.20 illustrates the result of this example. Notice that in the HTML, a semicolon (;) breaks the code and places a window status message within the HTML. You can see this message in figure 8.20, "advertising for the web audience." Notice how I have integrated several JavaScript goodies into one tag by using semicolons in the HTML. Semicolons are used by JavaScript to separate messages so that JavaScript understands where a message ends—and where another begins. The onMouseOut command tells JavaScript to replace the placeholder image (philos0.gif) with the current image when the user's mouse moves away from the link. Without the onMouseOut code, the new image would replace the placeholder image indefinitely.

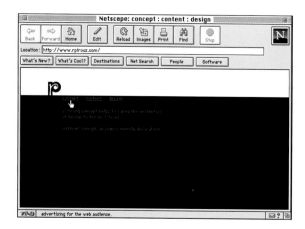

8.20

As the user rolls over a link, an image appears below it.

By implementing the above example (or other examples you run across on the Net or in books) into your own designs and modifying them to suit your particular needs, you can dramatically enhance the quality and memorability of your web site through the use of JavaScript and rollover technology. When raw HTML becomes an outdated form of web page design, and everything (even JavaScript) is designed in a WYSIWYG HTML editor that really works, keep in mind that if designed with a communication-enhancing purpose, rollovers are a powerful asset that can enhance your page, as well as provide visitors with immediate feedback.

JavaScript Pull-Down Menus

Combining traditional HTML forms capabilities with some JavaScript know-how, you can create cool little JavaScript pull-down menus from which users can select destinations within your web site. Pull-down menus are an excellent and easy way to add interactivity and organization to your site.

Traditionally, pull-down menus in forms allow you to select one of several choices presented to you in a vertical bar that opens to reveal all your choices when you click on it.

The following are some key advantages for incorporating pull-down menus within your site:

- They create an immediate sense of interactivity.
- They prompt user response.
- They are easy to implement.
- They are cross-platform/cross-browser friendly.
- They help to categorize and tuck-away numerous selections until called-upon by the user, thus allowing for more white space in the site's overall design.

Figure 8.21 illustrates such an HTML menu. Notice that the copy within the selection box urges user interaction. It is important to take every opportunity you have in communicating with your audience seriously. By providing "call-to-action" messages such as that in figure 8.21, you drive your users to interact with your page, rather than hope that they discover your hidden treasures (unless, of course, your site is experimental in nature and hiding things is one of your goals).

The HTML and JavaScript code for this example is rather painless. The following HTML code generates what you see in figure 8.21.

```
<HTML>
<HEAD>
<TITLE>
JavaScript Pull-Down Menu
</TITLE>
<SCRIPT>
function gotosite(site) {
    if (site != "") {
            self.location=site
    }
}
</SCRIPT>
</HEAD>
<BODY BGCOLOR="#000000">
<FORM NAME="menu"><SELECT NAME="CHOICES"
ONCHANGE="gotosite(this.options[this.selectedIndex].value)">
<OPTION SELECTED>Please select a choice
<OPTION>_____
<OPTION VALUE="1.htm">Choice #1
<OPTION>_____
<OPTION VALUE="2.htm">Choice #2
<OPTION>_____
<OPTION VALUE="3.htm">Choice #3
<OPTION>_____
<OPTION VALUE="4.htm">Choice #4
<OPTION>_____
<OPTION VALUE="5.htm">Choice #5
<OPTION>_____
<OPTION VALUE="6.htm">Choice #6
</SELECT>
</FORM>
</BODY>
</HTML>
```

Between the <HEAD></HEAD> tags, I define the JavaScript function GOTOSITE, which basically takes the menu information and sends the user to the corresponding page. Within the HTML <BODY>, I define the form by giving it a name and using the OnChange function that tells JavaScript to execute a command when the menu selection changes. The <OPTION SELECTED> tag displays a message to the audience (preferably enticing them to make a selection). The <OPTION> tags define each of the user's options, which contain values that correspond to the URL destination for each choice. Notice how every other <OPTION> tag contains an underscore line (___). This technique creates a division bar between each option. I prefer to use this technique because it helps to break up and distinguish each selection within the selection window.

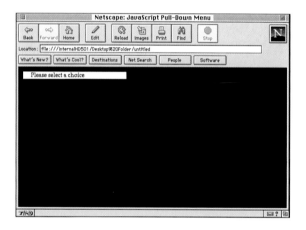

8.21

A sample pull-down menu prompting user interaction.

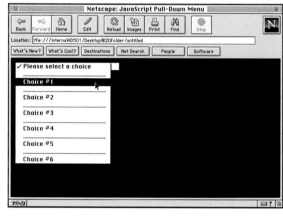

8.22

A sample pull-down menu with Choice #1 selected.

> **Note**
>
> You could hide all of the JavaScript code within this segment from users who don't have JavaScript by adding the <NOSCRIPT></NOSCRIPT> tags around the code.

Figure 8.22 reflects user interaction with the menu and a selection of Choice #1. In this example, when the user releases the mouse button atop a selection, the JavaScript code sends the user to the location of the selection. If the user were to release the mouse button while over Choice #1 (fig. 8.22), the preceding JavaScript code would take the user to 1.HTM.

There is a ton of information out there on JavaScript and its many wonderful uses. Please take it upon yourself to examine this area of web design and incorporate JavaScript into your next project.

Java

Sun Microsystems (**http://www.sun.com**) developed Java as a platform-independent programming language. Unlike JavaScript, Java is much more difficult to "fiddle" with. When you compile Java applets, the compiler relies on the presence of certain files (called *classes*) to smoothly convert your raw programming data into a functional applet. Once you jump through all the hoops, however, your Java applet may be viewed on ANY MACHINE that supports Java applets, which includes Macintosh, PC, and UNIX. Java is truly cross-platform and cross-browser safe (Both Netscape and Microsoft Explorer browsers support Java).

Although the hard-core programming technology behind Java is built on solid foundations, few tools exist that bring the raw programming power of Java to the masses. As technology evolves, however, we will see more Java integration (as announced by Macromedia: Director 6 will incorporate Java).

Symantec's Internet Tools

For now, Symantec (**http://www.symantec.com**) is one of the leading suppliers of Java development tools for both Macintosh and Windows 95/NT users. Figure 8.23 illustrates Symantec's Internet Tools page (**http://cafe.symantec.com/index.html**). Notice that three products are available for the Macintosh (Café, Visual Café, and Visual Page) and three for Windows95/NT (Café, Visual Café, and Visual Café Pro). At Symantec's site, you can receive free trial downloads of their software as well as order their Java development tools directly. For designers, I recommend Visual Café. Be warned, though: It is a good all-around WYSIWYG Java development tool, but it also has a learning curve, so make sure you have some time to devote.

Macromedia's AppletAce

Macromedia's AppletAce is another WYSIWYG Java development tool that is very limiting yet extremely easy to use. Figure 8.23 illustrates Macromedia's AppletAce web site at **http://www.macromedia.com/software/appletace/**. AppletAce is available as a free download for both Windows and Macintosh, and enables you to create Java applets such as banners, bullets, charts, and imagemaps.

8.23

Macromediaís AppletAce.

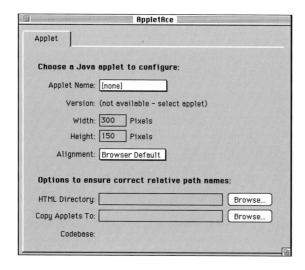

8.24

AppletAce's default interface.

For the purposes of this example, we look at a hypothetical Java banner design using Macromedia AppletAce. The program admittedly is basic, limiting, and buggy, but it does offer an excellent opportunity for designers to acquaint themselves with Java technology—and best of all, it's free.

When you run the program, it presents you with some choices (fig. 8.24). Basically, AppletAce works like this: It offers you choices upon choices and then provides you with a finished piece of HTML code that calls on Java class functions provided with the program. You can place the HTML on your home page, transfer the home page (along with the Java classes specific to the applet of your choice) and wham bam, you have Java on your home page. When you select "Banners," under "Applet Name," AppletAce gives you the screen shown in figure 8.25.

The Applet mode (fig. 8.25) allows you to key in the applet properties. You're going to create a banner that's 468 pixels wide by 60 pixels high.

The Text mode (fig. 8.26) begins to reveal the limitations posed by AppletAce. Although the limitations here derive from HTML's limitations, Java need not be limited by any browser, given its extremely powerful nature. Since AppletAce is a relatively simple program with limited customizable features, however, you just get an input box in which type a text message for the banner. You can change the font (limited by browser default fonts), size, color, style, and effect.

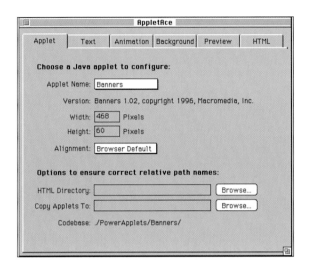

8.25

AppletAce - Applet.

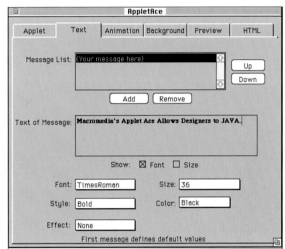

8.26

AppletAce - Text.

The Animation mode (fig. 8.27) refers to the way in which the previously keyed-in text appears and disappears through the banner. While on the screen shown in figure 8.28, choose ZoomIn for the text's appearance, and ZoomOut for its exit and leave the Frames information at its default settings.

The Background mode (fig. 8.28) allows you to select a GIF or JPG file (no animated GIFs) as the banner's background image. If you don't want a background image, as in this case, you can select a background color, which I have done, and a "URL when Clicked," which will send the user to that specific URL if he or she clicks on the banner.

The Preview mode (fig. 8.29) allows you to look at your banner as it would appear on a browser. This is a great feature built into this software and saves the headache of having to switch programs to test results.

The final AppletAce mode, HTML (fig. 8.30), provides the code that calls on specific Java classes (in this case, Banners.class) to make the banner a reality on your web page.

8.27

AppletAce - Animation.

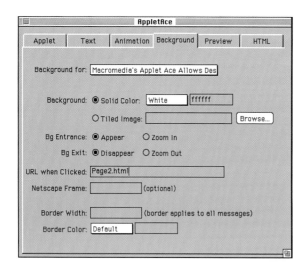

8.28

AppletAce - Background.

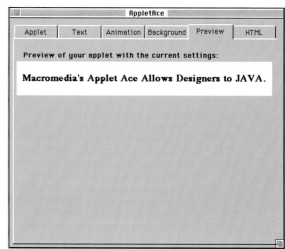

8.29

AppletAce - Preview.

"The key in
successful
web site design
and technology
integration is
education and
experimentation."

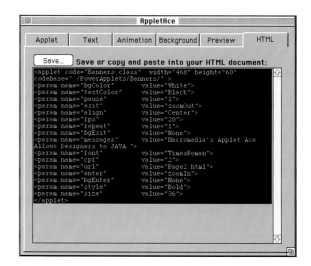

8.30

AppletAce - HTML.

Note

Please note that this section in no way attempts to serve as a tutorial on how to use Director, nor does it attempt to demonstrate Director's awesome power potential. The program is extremely complex and requires an entire book (if not several) to completely delve into its power. This section merely attempts to demonstrate how you can translate a design concept into a working Shockwave file in a general step-by-step manner.

Before continuing, please note also that the following Shockwave example is not Lingo-intensive, because I designed it. I am a designer and have a limited knowledge of programming. Therefore, the program limits me in what I can produce as a designer without a programming staff. Carefully consider this early in the conceptual development of your web site. If you need to have Shockwave files for your site, consider whether you can program the Lingo yourself. Designers often come up with wonderfully unexecutable ideas. By learning enough Lingo to understand how difficult the more complex coding becomes, you can become a shrewder designer. If it comes down to it, you can always hire a freelance programmer to help you, or get help from a friend who knows Lingo.

By experimenting with AppletAce and checking out Symantec's line of visual Java development software, you will be one step ahead of other designers who will wait until the technology is handed to them on a silver platter. The key in successful web site design and technology integration is education and experimentation. If you do both, you're bound to succeed.

Director Shockwave

In this section, I present a step-by-step approach to using Macromedia Director 5.0 to design a Shockwave file. Major improvements have been promised for Director 6, but the fundamental design issues associated with creating interactive media will stay the same.

As with any major program, Director has a long list of loyal fans who hang out on the web. An excellent online resource for finding out more (or asking questions if you get stuck) is Director Web, at **http://www.mcli.dist.maricopa.edu/director/**.

The Director Web's home page gives you many links to explore, as well as e-mail discussion groups you can join (expect to get at least 20 e-mail messages a day, if not more).

The Concept

As with any carefully thought-out design project, you need a concept before you begin any production. The R35 web site attempts to communicate a calm, serene, meditative atmosphere through its use of limited graphics, warm colors, and tranquil music. R35's Shockwave requirement consists of a magnetic poetry game, wherein users are presented with beautifully rich, contemplative music, as well as random (movable) words with which to form spontaneous poetry.

A magnetic poetry game enhances R35's image while providing visitors with an entertaining and thought-provokingly spontaneous—and pacifist—activity (you don't have to shoot things to have fun).

The Limitations

The immediate limitation that Director places on designers is that without a good understanding of Lingo (Director's programming language) it is difficult to create anything "shockworthy."

Intermediate Lingo knowledge (or a programming partner) is the minimum requirement for even beginning to think about using Director as a development tool.

After you cross the Lingo hurdle, you need to think about filesize considerations. You can end up with enormous Shockwave files if you're not careful. Consider the following:

- Create your artwork in Photoshop. I generally export my PICT files with an 8-bit/System/Diffusion palettes to cut-down on filesize. (You could create director files that are much lower in bit-depth—hence much smaller files—but you limit your color usage and have to manually create a custom palette in Director. A major drag).
- Save AIFF or WAV sound files as 8-bit/11 MHz or lower (the lower the better).

Director Step-By-Step

Upon launching Director, the first and most important thing to do is to set the Movie Properties.

In the Movie Properties dialog box (fig. 8.31), you can set the dimensions of your Shockwave presentation (You need these dimensions later in your HTML when you <EMBED> the code.) In this dialog box, you also can set the background color of your presentation. For the magnetic poetry example, I leave the background white and keep the Default palette set at System - Mac. (When the viewer's browser opens up the Shockwave file, it automatically converts the palette over to IBM if the viewer's on a Windows machine.)

When you click on OK in the Movie Properties dialog box, you get the screen shown in figure 8.32, which is the stage upon which you compose your presentation. Notice that I work with the Cast and Score windows, as well as the Control Panel and the Tool palette, visible. These windows are the essential tools with which I create and survey the presentation as it progresses.

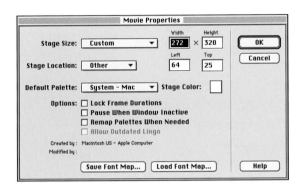

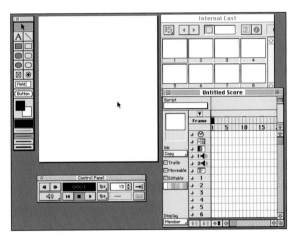

8.31

The Movie Properties dialog box.

8.32

Stage with the Cast and Score windows, the Control Panel, and the Tool palette present.

> ### Tip
>
> **Global variables** are pieces of reserved memory within the life of the presentation that store values.

Immediately after the stage opens, you key in the *Movie Script*, which is the piece of Lingo programming that sets the stage.

Every piece of Lingo code begins with an "on…" and ends with "end" (you can see several instructions given between these two words in the Lingo code shown in figure 8.33). The first instruction sets the soundLevel to 7 (the maximum volume setting). The next instruction defines a global variable (magnet). Before you can use global variables, you have to define them. The command fillMagnet in the Movie Script creates a function that recalls the global variable (magnet), and puts a random number from 4 to 48 into a variable (x). You will see where this is put to use later.

Next, you import your graphics and sound into your presentation, using Director's Import function (under FILE). Figure 8.34 demonstrates importing the music file. Notice that I do not link the music file to my presentation. By unchecking the "Linked" box, I import the music file directly into my presentation, where it becomes a piece of code that I can compress into Director's Shockwave format.

After you import the sound file, by clicking on its corresponding Cast Member graphic (in the Cast Window) and clicking on the circular blue "Information" button, the screen shown in figure 8.35 comes up, which allows you to hear the music as well as designate whether you want it to loop. For the purposes of this presentation, I would like the music to loop and have made the selection to that effect.

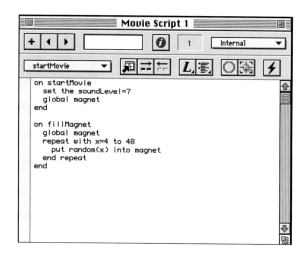

8.33

The Movie Script.

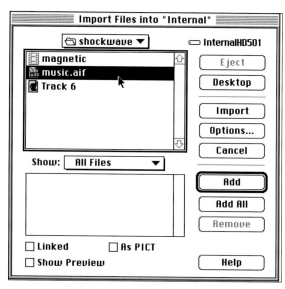

8.34

Importing sound into Director.

Director's Score window is a time-based display of all the presentation components, from graphics to audio, video, and so on. The Score window is composed of vertical frames and horizontal channels. One piece of presentation information takes up one frame in a channel. Figure 8.36 demonstrates a two-frame presentation wherein the music is introduced in both frames. It is important to place the music in every frame in which you want the music to appear. Because I'd like the music to play throughout the entire presentation, I place the music into both frames, in the Sound 1 Channel.

8.35

Sound Cast member properties.

All of the cast members for the magnetic poetry presentation are visible in figure 8.37, Director's Cast window. Notice that the magnetic pieces are nothing more than individual graphic cast members (45 total). Notice also that all of the scripts are also present in the Cast window (as they too are cast members).

The magnetic poetry presentation's initial interface is designed and layed out using Director's Paint feature (fig. 8.38). Notice that Director's Paint feature provides many of the same basic drawing and editing tools that you find in Photoshop. After you create the interface, Director places it on the stage (fig. 8.39).

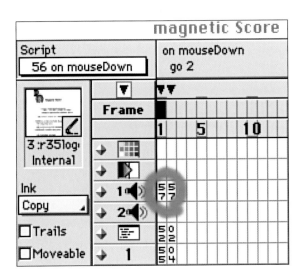

8.36

Placing the music within the Director's Score.

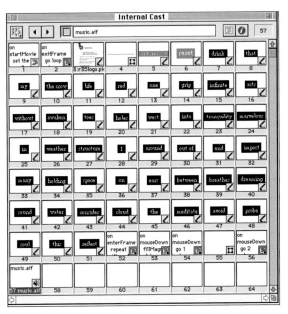

8.37

Director's Cast window.

8.38

Director's Paint window.

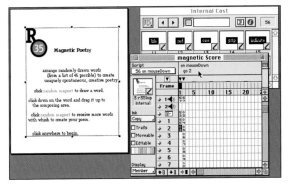

8.39

The magnetic poetry opening page placed onto Director's stage.

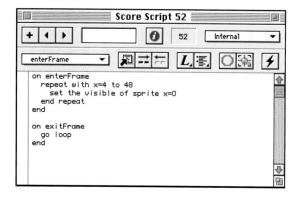

8.40

The Score Script of frame 1.

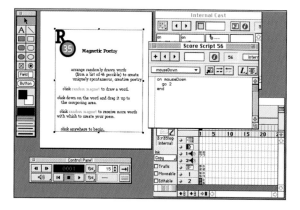

8.41

Turning the cover graphic into a button.

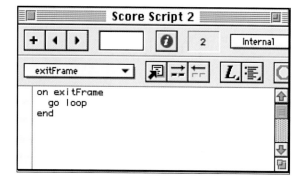

8.42

The Score Script of Frame 2.

Notice that in figure 8.39, the graphic is selected and shows up in the second sprite channel of the first frame. You need to tell director to pause at this frame so that the viewer has a chance to read the instructions and interact with the page. I do this by dragging out a down-pointing arrow atop the frame columns and positioning one over Frame 1 and another over Frame 2. These down-pointing arrows are identifying frame markers that Lingo uses. To tell Director to pause at this screen, you need to script some Lingo.

Each frame can have Score Script, which you can program via Lingo to perform many functions. Figure 8.40 demonstrates a piece of Lingo that I wrote to keep the visitor at the first frame. You do that by using the on exitFrame, go loop command. It tells Director to loop back to the last marker position it saw upon leaving the frame. Since the last market position it saw is on the same frame from which it exits, the presentation remains on the first frame until instructed (using Lingo) to do otherwise. The "enterFrame" portion of Frame 1's Score Script tells Director to turn the sprite channels of frames 4 through 48 invisible (0 equals off, or invisible, while 1 equals on, or visible). I show you why this is important shortly.

To instruct Director to take the user away from the first page and into the heart of the demonstration, you need to add interactivity to the cover graphic, turning it into a button that, when clicked, executes a Lingo command. I do this by selecting the graphic (fig. 8.41), clicking on the pull-down Script menu (on the upper-left corner of the Score), and choosing "New Script." Figure 8.41 illustrates the Lingo command that executes upon user interaction. The on mouseDown script tells Director to execute a command when the user clicks. "go 2" tells Director to go to frame number 2, thereby leaving the first frame through user interaction.

Because the rest of the presentation occurs in the second frame, you need to place another "on exitFrame, go loop" statement into the Score Script of Frame 2.

In the second frame, the user is presented with the option to draw a random word from the possible 45. You do this by first setting up the interface, creating a random magnet button (which when pressed draws a random word) and a reset button (which when pressed clears the page and restarts everything), and by placing all the magnets on the stage and making them MOVEABLE (by selecting them on the Score window and clicking in their respective Moveable check boxes, as shown in figure 8.43).

Figure 8.44 reflects the Score window of the magnetic poetry presentation. Notice that the cells in Frame 2 are filled to capacity. This is because each graphic takes up one cell, and there are 45 words (or graphics) plus the interface elements that fill up Director 5's Score window limited to 48 items (Director 6 dramatically removes this limitation). Notice also that because all of the word graphics are present in Frame 2 of the presentation, users will see them all when they first enter the frame. You don't want this, because the goal of the presentation is to have users draw random words. Hence, the Lingo in the Score Script of Frame 1 instructs Director to turn sprite channels 4 through 48 invisible.

After you make the magnets invisible to the user, you can use Lingo to make them visible randomly. Figure 8.45 demonstrates the Score Script of the random magnet button, which when clicked on, selects a random number from 4 to 48 and makes that graphic visible so that the user can move it around and compose his or her poetry.

Figure 8.46 demonstrates the Score Script of the reset button, which when clicked on, sends the user to Frame 1, resetting the presentation.

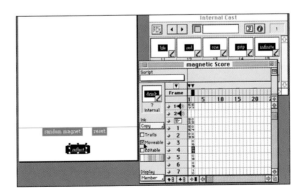

8.43

Setting up the second frame.

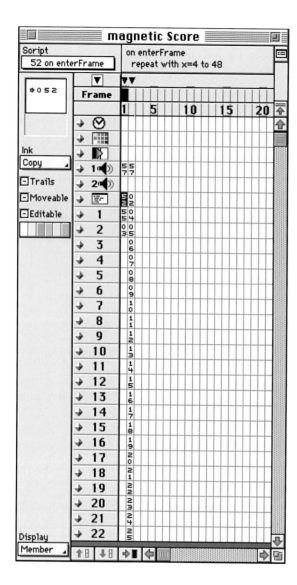

8.44

Director's Score window.

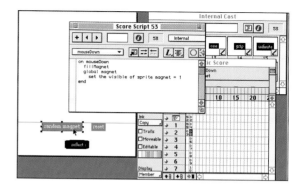

8.45

Making the magnets visible.

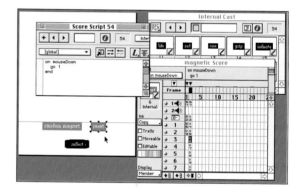

8.46

Resetting the presentation.

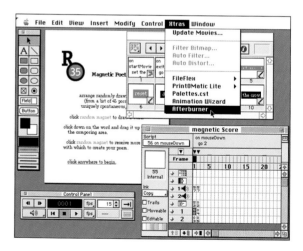

8.47

"Shocking" the presentation in Director 5.

After you key in all the Lingo and are ready to save the presentation as a Shockwave file, you have to select the Afterburner Xtra (Xtras, Afterburner) to create Shockwave files from within Director 5 (Director 6 does not require that you use the Afterburner Xtra). The resulting file size of the Shockwave presentation is 277k, which is large, but acceptable for a Shockwave presentation (the bulk of which is the looping 1.5-minute music file).

Once you create the Shockwave DCR file, you're ready to add a link to it. Figure 8.48 demonstrates such a link. Please take the following points into consideration when you link to a Shockwave file:

- Mention its size; some viewers may not want to sit through the download.
- Provide ample warning that the file requires the Shockwave Plug-in; your HTML <TITLE></TITLE> is a good place to start.
- Offer a link to the Shockwave plug-in for users who may not otherwise have the plug-in before they go to the link that contains the file.

Upon clicking the Experience the tranquillity (277k) link, the user is presented with a new window (using the JavaScript new window command, which I discussed earlier in this chapter) that contains the Shockwave presentation.

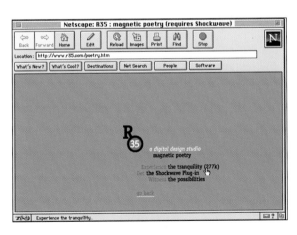

8.48

The R35 site with a link to the magnetic poetry page.

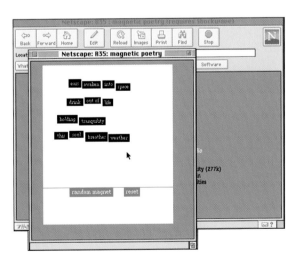

8.49

R35's magnetic poetry presented in a new window.

That's the Ticket

Conceptual and strategic thinking, coupled with the use of technologically appropriate communication vehicles, are the foundation on which successful web sites are built. Unfortunately, no matter how good the preceding principle sounds, it is not always enough. In the fiercely competitive world of the Internet, it takes that extra step—marketing savvy and know-how, coupled with creative promotion techniques—to get users coming through the floodgates. The rest of this book deals with creative marketing strategy translated into "webvertising" (advertising on the web) to help you get the most out of your targeting potential. Keep reading—it's not over yet.

9

Capitalism in Utopia

Although the Internet began quietly enough as a U.S. national security operation in light of the cold war, it accidentally grew into a humble global village of linked networks used mainly by scientists and researchers. To them, the Internet must have been an almost utopian technology: an unregulated mode of communication through which the Earth's brightest minds could freely share information for the advancement of the scientific and research communities.

> **Note**
>
> To learn more about the origins of the Internet, read *Where Wizards Stay Up Late* (ISBN 0-684-81201-0).

The graphic representation of this near-utopian model of human communication (made possible by first-generation browsers) gave birth to the World Wide Web. Identified by early web pioneers as the electronic "manifest destiny," the web's popularity quickly transformed it into a booming metropolis of interconnected supercomputers hosting local access providers who host corporate and home-based webmasters and netizens. Imagine going from the quiet of "starry nights" to the bustle of "honking horns and flashing lights."

Culture Speak

Throughout its swift evolution, the web has established its own online culture, code of ethics, and visual language. The more popular visible iconic representations of this cultural phenomenon are the "smiley face" : -) and the "wink" ; -). However, many invisible (almost moral) codes also have evolved within the online culture, some of which can be summarized as follows:

- Information on the web **should be free**.
- **Commercialization** is frowned upon.
- Web citizens (often referred to as netizens) would rather **barter** than pay for intangible goods or services.
- Traditional "rules-of-the-game," such as national boundaries and local, state, federal, and governmental regulations, **should not apply** to the Internet and the World Wide Web.
- A polite **"may I"** is all it should take to use intellectual property belonging to someone else—no lawyers necessary.
- The web should be **free from taxation** and support the right to **free speech online**.

Although the above are general representations of online culture, they reflect a state of mind based on the Internet's origins as a medium of communication through which the FREE flow of intellectual information went unchecked and (for the most part) unregulated.

> **"You have to somehow draw users to your site by letting them know that it exists and by convincing them that it's worth visiting."**

What does an evaluation of Internet culture have to do with online marketing and promotions? From a marketing (and realistic) standpoint, web sites can succeed only if netizens *visit* them. As a developer of successful web sites, it is your responsibility to compel the Internet audience to visit your site. Simply conceiving of and building the ultimate web site is not enough. You have to somehow draw users to your site by letting them know that it exists and by convincing them that it's worth visiting. One way to do this is to incorporate traditional advertising strategies into an online model (specific to the culture and expectations of netizens) and develop a campaign strategy.

As an advertiser, you must KNOW your audience and be able to speak their visual language to effectively compel them. One of the key steps in knowing your audience is understanding the nuances of their culture. If you understand the online culture, which differs significantly from the mainstream "live" culture, you are one step closer to creating compelling Internet advertising that draws visitors. Of course, the underlying cultural beliefs referenced above should not drive your online advertising strategy or message. They should form no more than the foundational thinking on which to base your advertising campaigns.

Webvertising?

Webvertising, the act of marketing and advertising on the Net, encompasses the following components (items in **bold and italic** denote grass-roots marketing/advertising strategies that YOU can accomplish without a major cash layout):

- ■ *Site Announcement.* You must inform the search engines and online Yellow Pages of your existence (this is the first place visitors begin their search for information).
- ■ *Link Swaps.* Contact the webmasters of sites with which you share a common theme and offer to place a text link to their site within your site if they agree to return the favor.
- ■ **Banner Advertising.** Conceive of and develop still images or animated GIF images (called banners because of their 468×60 average dimensions—although no "defined" standard sizes exist) that are placed within search engines or other web sites (from whom you have purchased "air time") to draw users away from the site content and compel them to click on the banner, causing them to leave their original location.
- ■ *Barter Ads.* Contact the webmaster of a site that you feel attracts potential interested parties and offer to place a banner for that site on your page if the webmaster agrees to do the same OR join an online banner exchange group (discussed later in this chapter).

- **Interstitial Ads.** Offer advertising space to potential corporations that are willing to spend money on your site by forcing users to view ads in between content pages (made possible by the META REFRESH tag, which I discuss in Chapter 8, "Engage… Full Throttle Ahead").

- *Internal Banner Advertising.* Create banner ads for your own site, leading users to YOUR content instead of someone else's.

Although the above serves as a good general overview of webvertising components (there are many more components, enough to warrant an entire book on this subject alone), you should definitely be aware of some online marketing and webvertising resources essential to your further understanding of the subject:

- **Promote-It! (http://www.iTools.com/promote-it)** provides an extensive online resource listing of marketing and promotion resources.

- ClickZ (**http://www.clickz.com**) is an online webvertising and marketing resource that provides insightful articles about the subject and links to many online resources worth checking out.

9.1

ClickZ:Internet Advertisers and Marketers Resources and Information.

Begin exploring the world of online webvertising by visiting the above links. Refer to the "Advertising Resources" listing that I provide in Chapter 10 for further links. As you will find in your online travels, buying advertising space on the Net can be extremely expensive for the average individual or small business (generally, rates start at $100 per week and go up to $10,000 or higher per week based on the web site, its popularity, and so on.). Although you may not be a blue-chip player, on the Internet you're as BIG as you say you are. I will shortly cover how to incorporate some of the aforementioned webvertising components to promote your site.

Going Against the Grain

One of the most important considerations to take into account when developing an online ad campaign is the fact that netizens HATE webvertising.

This is an interesting phenomenon because advertising revenue is the KEY FACTOR that has helped keep the "commercial, graphic" web alive. Without advertising revenue, designers could not afford to spend countless hours developing for the web. After all, the only people who are really PAYING to keep the major sites on the web (and all the hype surrounding the web) alive are advertisers. Every time you see a banner ad, or a sponsor logo, or MSNBC's *THE SITE* for that matter, know that they are being funded in part by advertising dollars.

> "You literally have two seconds to get the attention of your potential audience."

While some sites don't require advertising dollars because they make a killing selling products online (**http://www.amazon.com**), other sites are purely information-based (**http://www.wired.com**) and rely mainly on advertising dollars to help pay the "electricity bill."

Given the fact that the online community hates banner ads and webvertising in general, know that you literally have two seconds to get the attention of your potential audience and five seconds total (including the initial two seconds) to compel them to click.

Later in this chapter, I go into creative strategies to get users to click.

Visibility Is Key

What if you built the ultimate web site and no one came? You can reduce the chances of a vacant web site by registering your site with the major search engines. This is the simplest form of webvertising (and an important first step) that takes very little planning and can quickly get you "out in the mix." Although registering with search engines is an important first step, please note that effective webvertising requires that you execute as many of its components as possible for maximum visibility. Registering with search engines alone is not enough, and I discuss other components shortly.

Major Search Engines

Note

For a good overview of the major search engines and how to use them, point your browser to *The Spider's Apprentice*, as shown in figure 9.2 (http://www.monash.com/spidap3.html).

Before I go into further detail, I need to clarify a distinction between search engines, spiders, and online directories/indexes. Search engines can be thought of as Internet libraries, housing the location of each web site that is within its card catalog. Some search engines use automated spiders to go out and gather links by crawling from link to link and bringing back data (like AltaVista), while others depend on user input for data collection into their online directories/indexes (like Yahoo!). Although data-collection schemes differ from engine to engine, search engines all offer the same service: to provide users with links to information sources based on keywords submitted by the user in search of information.

According to *Search Engines Up the Wazoo II* (**http://pw2.netcom.com/~edangel/search2.html**), more than 70 search engines are on the web. However, there are only a handful of major engines visited by the majority of users online.

9.2

The Spider's Apprentice—Search Engine Details.

In my opinion, listing your site with the following seven engines can potentially give you exposure to about 85–95% of the Internet audience (that is, if they go to the search engine and look up certain keywords that will bring up your site as one of possibly hundreds to thousands of competitors):

- Yahoo!
- Infoseek
- Lycos
- Hotbot
- WebCrawler
- Excite
- AltaVista

Yahoo! (**http://www.yahoo.com**) is one of the most popular directory/index-based search engines. Its online catalog is updated based on user submissions and contains literally millions of indexed pages. If you require information that is unavailable in Yahoo!'s directory, it automatically uses the AltaVista spider to locate the information you require. To add your site to Yahoo!, simply scroll down to the bottom of the home page and click on the How to Include Your Site link. A visual example of this follows later in the section "Going Solo with Yahoo!."

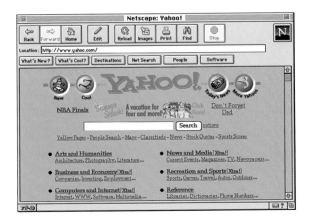

9.3

Yahoo! (Text and Artwork copyright © 1996 by YAHOO! Inc. All rights reserved. YAHOO! and the YAHOO! logo are trademarks of YAHOO! INC.)

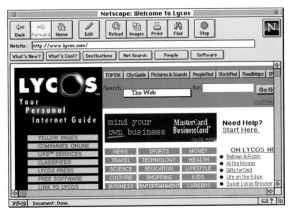

9.4

Lycos.

Infoseek (**http://www.infoseek.com**) is an excellent search engine. With millions of indexed pages, Infoseek is a simply designed yet powerful research tool. It is one of my personal favorites, and often returns the most relevant results based on my keyword inquiries. To add your site to Infoseek, click on the Add URL link located at the bottom left of the home page.

Lycos (**http://www.lycos.com**) contains more than 60 million indexed pages and attempts to offer more than just "search" services. I personally don't appreciate being bogged down by so many options on a page, but that's just my opinion—I just use the Lycos search engine and ignore the rest. To add your site to the Lycos directory, select the Add Your Site to Lycos link located at the bottom of the home page.

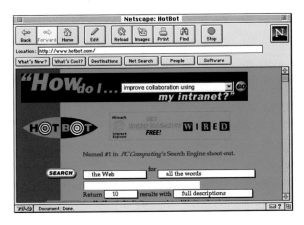

HotBot (**http://www.hotbot.com**) is *Wired* magazine's search engine with a high-tech design. Containing more than 50 million indexed pages, HotBot allows you to select the number of results you'd like it to return to you. To add your site to HotBot, simply click on the ADD URL button located near the bottom of the home page.

9.5

HotBot.

WebCrawler (**http://www.webcrawler.com**), owned by America Online, is one of the older and smaller search engines on the Net (with close to a million indexed pages). The reason that you should appear in WebCrawler's database is its HUGE user base. Because America Online subscribers use WebCrawler (and Excite), you can potentially expose yourself to millions of users simply by registering here. To add your site, click on either the Add URL button at the top right of the home page or on the Add URL text link near the bottom of the home page.

Recently acquired by America Online, Excite (**http://www.excite.com**) is AOL's proprietary search engine. With millions of indexed pages and America Online's user base, Excite is definitely worth registering with. To add your site, click on the Add URL text link at the bottom left of the home page.

9.6

WebCrawler. (WebCrawler and the WebCrawler Logo are trademarks of Excite, Inc. and may be registered in various jurisdictions. Excite screen display copyright ©1995-97 Excite, Inc.

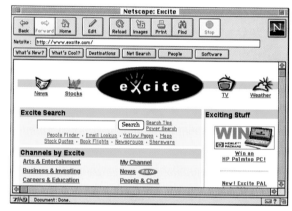

9.7

Excite. (Excite, Excite Search, and the Excite Logo are trademarks of Excite, Inc. and may be registered in various jurisdictions. Excite Screen display copyright © 1995-1997 Excite, Inc.)

Digital's AltaVista (**http://www.altavista.digital.com**) is one of the most powerful and speedy search engines on the web. With over 30 million indexed pages, AltaVista is the seventh and final search engine that I recommend you register with. Just click on the Add URL text link near the bottom of the home page.

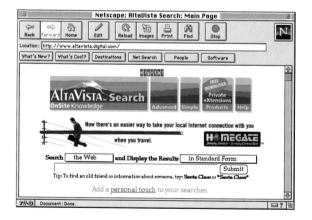

9.8

AltaVista.

Registering with Search Engines

Registering with seven search engines might take a good hour or so, considering that you quickly go from site to site, filling out all the information required for each search engine submission. If, however, you decide to let the 70-plus existing search engines know of your existence, it might take you a good couple of days (before you go crazy, that is). If you want to keep your sanity, I recommend using an announcement service such as Submit It! (**http://www.submit-it.com**) or *WebPromote* (**http://www.webpromote.com**).

Submit It! offers a free service, which adds your site to approximately 18 search engines (only three of which are really worthwhile in my opinion). If you want to take full advantage of both Submit It! and WebPromote's services, though, you'll have to pay a price.

For example, a $60 payment to Submit It! allows you to register two of your sites with hundreds of search engines (this is a VERY MANUAL operation, as each search engine asks for information in a unique fashion … there is no standard *one-form-submits-to-all* method—yet). Submit It! simply provides you with access to hundreds of search engines without you having to manually find each, locate the "Add URL" links, and so on. It's pretty much a do-it-yourself operation. Submit It! does, however, offer a consulting service that handles the submissions for you, but the fee is a hefty one (over $200). As far as fees are concerned, Submit It! charges lower fees than WebPromote. If you're on a budget, I'd recommend going solo and simply registering with the seven search engines I discussed earlier.

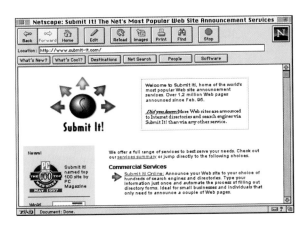

9.9

Submit It!

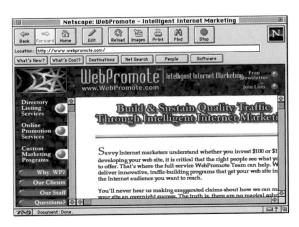

9.10

WebPromote.

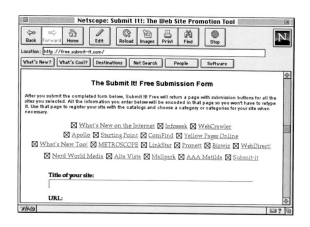

9.11

Submit It! Free Submission Form.

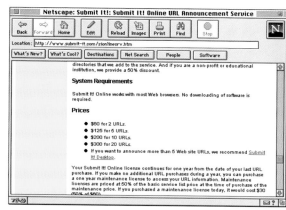

9.12

Submit It! Online URL Announcement Service.

Going Solo with Yahoo!

If you've decided to limit your site announcement to a handful of the most commonly visited search engines, you're not alone. I'm not so sure that announcing your site to EVERY search engine on the web will get you more visits. If the majority of netizens use the seven major search engines described earlier, it certainly seems like a waste of time to expend energy on the rest.

If you're going solo, all you have to do is take a look at one of the submission forms to get an idea of the kind of information you have to provide. I'm going to use Yahoo! as an example. After you go through one submission process, the rest are very similar.

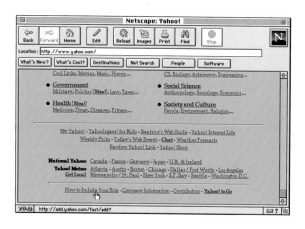

9.13

Yahoo! home page, with the cursor atop the "How to Include Your Site" link. (Text and Artwork copyright 1996 © by YAHOO! INC. All rights reserved. YAHOO! and the YAHOO! logo are trademarks of YAHOO! INC.)

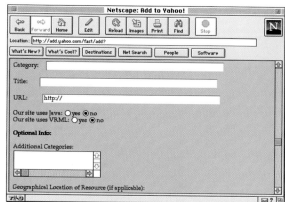

9.14

Yahoo!'s online URL submission form. (Text and Artwork copyright 1996 © by YAHOO! INC. All rights reserved. YAHOO! and the YAHOO! logo are trademarks of YAHOO! INC.)

Figure 9.13 represents the first step you would take to include your site in the Yahoo! index. After you click on the How to Include Your Site link, Yahoo!'s online submission form appears on-screen, as shown in figure 9.14.

This form asks for the following information:

- **Category.** Yahoo! indexes every URL within categories. This gets a bit tricky. You need to be sure to type the EXACT category name, along with its path from the Yahoo! home page directly to the location wherein you want your URL to appear. The best way to do that is to actually go to the location wherein you want your link to appear and then press the Add URL button at the top of the interface (fig. 9.15).

  For the purposes of this example, pretend that you'd like to add an URL listing to the Graphic Design Professional Organizations index listing in Yahoo!. You first go to this listing by choosing the appropriate section headings within Yahoo!'s categorical structure. Once there, you press the Add URL button, which results in the screen shown in figure 9.16.

  Notice that Yahoo! has automatically filled in the Category field based on the location from which you clicked on the Add URL button. No other search engine has ever forced me through this kind of maneuvering just to add an URL. However, because of Yahoo!'s popularity, it's worth the trouble.

- **Title.** This is the underlined listing name as it appears within the search engine (for an example, see American Institute of Graphic Arts in figure 9.15).

- **URL.** The site's Internet address goes here (http://www.etc…).

- Yahoo! next asks if the site uses **Java** or **VRML**. I believe they mention this fact within the listing if the YES radio buttons are selected.

The rest of the information fields are optional and you need not fill them out. It is important to fill out the Comments field, however, because it will appear after the Title (see BDA International in figure 9.15). Other search engines ask for keywords. Yahoo! does not, but you should formulate a series of keywords that best describe your site and its content for search engines that do ask for it. Keywords and a description are also important to consider for placing within <META> tags in the site's HTML document, which I discuss shortly.

By familiarizing yourself with the requirements of a sample site registry, such as the one described above, you have taken the first step into the online realm of webvertising.

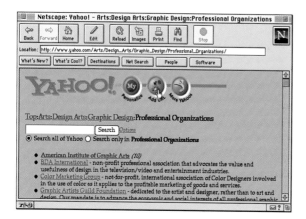

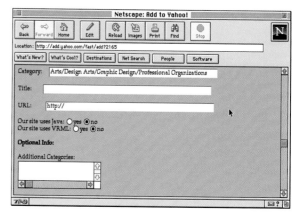

9.15

Adding a new URL listing to the Graphic Design Professional Organizations index listing within Yahoo!. (Text and Artwork copyright 1996 © by YAHOO! INC. All rights reserved. YAHOO! and the YAHOO! logo are trademarks of YAHOO! INC.)

9.16

Yahoo!'s online URL submission form with the Category field automatically filled in by the system. (Text and Artwork copyright 1996© by YAHOO! INC. All rights reserved. YAHOO! and the YAHOO! logo are trademarks of YAHOO! INC.)

Tip

Before you begin your announcement campaign, I suggest that you create a quick fact sheet. (You can create this fact sheet in any word processing program.)

Within the fact sheet, include any and all information that you'd like to reveal to the search engines—name, address, telephone numbers, site title, URL, description, keywords, and so forth. Then, when you have your browser open and you're ready to begin submitting your information to the various search engines, you can open the fact sheet and easily copy and paste the information into the forms provided by the search engines. This eases repetitive and unnecessary typing and maintains continuity and consistency across applications.

Getting Descriptive with the <META> Tag

You can enhance your listing within many of the search engines (including Infoseek, Lycos, HotBot, and AltaVista) by incorporating the <META NAME> tag. Basically, when certain search engines send their spiders out to find certain information, one of the things they look for is a <META NAME> tag within the <HEAD></HEAD> tags and after the <TITLE></TITLE> tags of an HTML document. Because so many of the search engine spiders look for the <META> tag within the <HEAD></HEAD> tags and after the <TITLE></TITLE> tags, it is very important to implement them correctly within HTML.

It is *extremely* important to:

- Place the <META NAME> tags within the <HEAD></HEAD> tags
- Place the <META NAME> tags AFTER the <TITLE></TITLE> tags

To find out more about the nuances of the <META> tag, look up **http://vancouver-webpages.com/META/**. There are two <META NAME> tags you should be concerned with when trying to enhance search engine results (both should be incorporated for best results):

- <META NAME="KEYWORDS"> This tag houses the keywords you choose to identify with your site's content. For example, if your site is an online cookbook, some of your keywords might be cooking, baking, cakes, BBQ, etc., etc.
- <META NAME="DESCRIPTION"> This tag houses a description of your site. In the cookbook example above, the description might be, "Cookbook.com is a virtual grill that fires up good, old-fashioned cooking 24 hours a day."

For example, the <META NAME> tags within my personal home page at **http://www.rpirouz.com** look something like this:

```
<HEAD>

<TITLE>concept : content : design</TITLE>

<META NAME="keywords" CONTENT="design, graphic design, advertis
➡ing, banner, banner ads, click-through, interface, interac-
tive">

<META NAME="description" CONTENT="Raymond Pirouz is an advertis
➡ing Art Director with an intimate understanding of interface
➡design for interactive CD-ROM and Web application, as well as
➡Internet advertising strategy and implementation.">

</HEAD>
```

When certain search engines send their spiders to my page, they get the following description:

"Raymond Pirouz is an advertising Art Director with an intimate understanding of interface design for interactive CD-ROM and Web application, as well as Internet advertising strategy and implementation."

They also are told that if the user of the search engine keys in the following keywords,

"design, graphic design, advertising, banner, banner ads, click-through, interface, interactive"

my page should be presented as one of the resulting matches to the query.

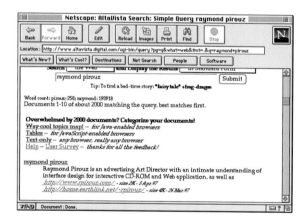

9.17

AltaVista search results for "raymond pirouz."

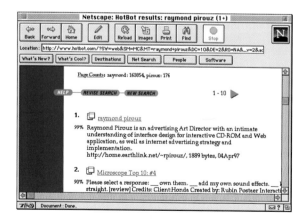

9.18

HotBot search results for "raymond pirouz."

Figures 9.17 and 9.18 demonstrate search results for the search query, "raymond pirouz" from the AltaVista and HotBot engines, respectively. Both results provide the copy that I included within my <META NAME="DESCRIPTION"> tag. Notice that while the AltaVista search result shows both my Earthlink as well as rpirouz.com URLs, the HotBot result only shows the Earthlink URL. All this means is that I have to resubmit an updated URL submission to HotBot so that its database can be updated to display the most current information.

Search engines do not really have the time (or computing power) to constantly cruise the Net and maintain/update changes that take place within the web. It is generally up to you to update search engines, directories, and indexes with your most current information.

By registering with the seven most popular search engines (Yahoo!, Infoseek, Lycos, HotBot, WebCrawler, Excite, and AltaVista), and by adding <META NAME> tags to your HTML documents, you can bring your site one step closer within reach of netizens on the prowl for information.

The Evolution of Advertising

What is advertising, and how has it managed to find its way onto the Internet? I attempt to answer this question by using some abstract examples, so please be patient. Advertising is the practice of introducing a product for which a need is created. The history of advertising is a long and complex story dating back to the creation of the first *need* brought about when the caveman saw fire for the first time and wanted it for himself. Nature's introduction of fire created a need in the heart of the caveman for its ownership. Therefore, it is safe to say that nature advertised fire to cavemen long ago in the history of man, creating a best-selling product ever since. Because everything has an opportunity cost, it is also safe to say that every time mankind lights a fire, he is giving up a possible alternative (putting on a jacket or eating vegetables instead of cooked meat, for example). Therefore, advertising creates a need for products and services whose purchase and use involve an opportunity cost.

The livelihood of our capitalistic system depends primarily on the production of goods and services and their sale to a class of consumers who must constantly be introduced to the next product, service, and cure-all. The advertising industry is responsible for creatively introducing consumers to new products and compelling them to make a purchase for the advancement of our current system.

The Players

"The advertising industry is responsible for creatively introducing consumers to new products and compelling them to make a purchase for the advancement of our current system."

In the game of advertising, there are three key players:

- **The Client (or Sponsor).** They have a product that needs to be advertised.
- **The Agency.** They are hired by the client to create the advertising and media-buying strategy and conceptualize the creative translation of strategy to visual imagery that creates a need for the product.
- **The Media.** They own the means of communication and need advertising revenue to keep them afloat financially. They reserve a portion of their communication vehicle (radio, TV, magazine, newspaper, web site, or whatever the medium) for advertising space, which they sell to the agency (or a separate media-brokerage service who mediates between the agency and the media), representing the client. The fees imposed by the media for the sale of advertising space are mainly based on their readership, listenership, or viewership (hence, the ratings systems).

Within the advertising agency, there are two major "sides" who generally work together to serve the Client's needs:

- **The Account Side.** They are responsible for maintaining the account, conducting most of the initial market research associated with representing a product or service to a specific target audience, and defining the scope, overall strategy, and creative brief.
- **The Creatives.** They are presented with the creative brief, which comprises of facts, figures, marketing statistics, and the communication strategy that must be converted to visual communication to creatively compel consumers to "buy" into the product or service.

Within the "creative" camp of an advertising agency, there are two major "sides" who generally work together to visually translate the marketing strategy:

- **Art Directors.** They are generally more "visual" and can draw, paint, and conceptually solve visual problems.
- **Copywriters.** They are generally more "verbal" and can write "copy" that creatively sells the "core-being" of the product or service.

Of course, there are some art directors who can "write copy," as there are copywriters who can "art direct." The creative side is often lead by a creative director who approves all the creative execution and ensures that the creative is "in-line" with the marketing strategy.

Where Advertising Meets the Web

On the web, advertising has emerged as the savior of the online experiment and the easiest revenue-generating resource for web sites (Media) with compounding ISP fees. With the exception of a few sites such as Amazon Books (**http://www.amazon.com**), which actually makes a profit by selling products online, most sites rely on advertising to maintain their costs. The online webvertising model takes a census of a site's potential user-base and sells "banner" space on sites with the most visitors. Therefore, sites like Netscape that receive thousands of hits per day can charge advertisers tens of thousands of dollars per week for ad space.

To create effective webvertising, it is important to understand that there are two major kinds of advertising:

- Advertising that creates a need based on a sense of insecurity and inadequacy
- Advertising that creates a need based on the inherent values (that is, the "core-being") of a product or service

The best kind of advertising creatively communicates that which is at the core-being of a product or service. "Honesty in Advertising" is a good example of the best kind of advertising. Products or services that sell themselves help to create the best ads (the Volkswagen ads of the '60s are a prime example).

The Banner Ad

The most prevalent form of direct webvertising, banner ads have been in business since the web became commercialized. Despite all the rumors about the "death of banner ads," banners have continued (and still continue) to be a prominent form of online advertising and brand positioning/promotion.

A *banner ad* can basically be described as a piece of visual communication (either animated or still image, with no "set" size standards) that is placed within a web site. Its goal is to attract the netizen (or distract browsing netizens) long enough to compel a "click-through." The term *click-through* comes from the act of clicking on a link, thereby taking the user "through" to another location (in the case of banner ads, to the advertiser's site).

Banner advertising serves two major purposes:

- Compelling users to click in order to take them away to the sponsor's site
- Promoting a positive brand image, reinforced through repetition

The banner ad is nothing but AN INVITATION TO VISIT THE SITE, which is the REAL WEBVERTISEMENT. Each site is an ad in its own right. There is simply not enough time to tell an entire story in a banner. Netizens don't like banners and will not spend more than two seconds (if that) to look at one. Banner ads are created to draw users to the meat of the ad—the web site.

Never in the history of advertising has creative communication been able to receive an "immediate" sense of success or failure. For the first time, advertising can be judged by the *click-through-rating*, which is a measure of the number of times a banner is clicked versus the number of times it appears to visitors. The industry-average click-through rating is somewhere between 1 and 2 percent. For every 100 banners, one to two get clicked, on average. Never in the history of advertising have advertisers had the chance to "test" the immediate user response to advertising, with the ability to change them on the fly if they don't receive positive click-through ratings.

Paying the Price for Banner Ads

Banner ads can be an extremely expensive webvertising endeavor and are usually practiced by blue-chip players, such as major technology companies and automotive distributors. Since most users expose themselves to the major search engines and browser software sites, advertising space on these services is VERY expensive. If you need to target a general audience, search engines and browser sites are your best bet. However, if you are trying to attract a very targeted audience, you may be able to find more affordable webvertising space by doing a little research.

Figure 9.19 represents Netscape's Sponsorship Rate Card (**http:// www.netscape.com/ads/ ad_rate_card.html**). According to this rate card obtained during the month of June 1997, it would cost $28,000.00 to display a 468×60 pixel banner that would appear 1,000 times in a technical section of the Netscape site over a one-week period (basically $28 every time the banner shows up). This is an extremely expensive investment that only the most well-off corporations can afford. The average consumer wanting to promote his/her product or service does not stand a chance in an environment such as this.

For those who can afford the online luxuries of purchasing banner ad space with search engines and browser sites, Internet-based media-brokerage agencies such as Web Wide Media (**http://www. webwidemedia.com**) and the DoubleClick Network (**http://www.doubleclick.net**) offer superb webvertising management and placement services. They mainly work within a network of participating sites and act as mediators between the advertiser and the web site wanting to sell ad space. This portion of webvertising is beyond my knowledge, but you can find all you want to know in Eugene Marlow's book, titled *Internet Advertising* (ISBN 0-442-02550-5).

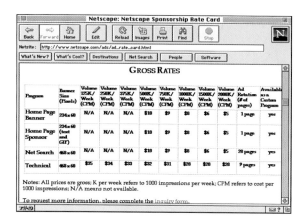

9.19

Netscape Sponsorship Rate Card. (Copyright 1996 Netscape Communications Corp. Use with permission. All Rights Reserved. This electronic file or page may not be reprinted or copied without the express written permission of Netscape.)

9.20

DoubleClick Network.

Creating Effective Banner Ads

Effective banner ads can be defined as those receiving high click-through ratings, while portraying a conceptually strong, aesthetically pleasing image that helps to reinforce a positive brand message for the product or service being advertised.

The Microscope web site (**http://www.pscentral.com**) is the Internet's only weekly web ad review that profiles some very interesting banner ad campaigns on the web. By visiting Microscope, you can browse through its archive and examine the excellent site editor critiques of a wide variety of banners ads. My only complaint about Microscope is its lack of click-through rating coverage. Although many of the banners profiled on the site are conceptually strong, there are no indicators as to how well they were received by the Internet audience. Simply creating a strong banner is not enough. It must perform well within the context for which it was designed before it can be deemed truly successful.

Here, we have arrived at what I call the "click-through dilemma." What is more important: A banner's concept and image or its success with netizens (measured in click-through ratings)? While it's important to create beautifully conceptual communication, it's also just as important to have audiences "click" on banners.

When it comes to creating successful banner ads, the common consensus is:

- The banner *must* say, "Click Here" on it (often referred to as a call to action).
- It should use the word FREE if such an offer exists.
- The bright color RED should be used to accentuate BIG type.

9.21

Microscope: Best Ads on the Web.

Unfortunately, things are never this easy. There are no set formulas for any kind of visual communication. Each problem is unique, as should each solution be unique. Assumptions, that create false senses of reality, such as there needing to be the words "Click Here" on a banner for users to know that they should click on it are extremely absurd. This implies that Internet users are dense and don't know that ads are meant to be clicked on. Researchers may have failed to realize that people don't click on banners because they don't like them … not because they didn't say "Click Here." Anyone who cruises the Net learns very quickly that as soon as their cursor changes to a pointing finger , they're over a link. this is merely ONE of many reasons NIT to have to leterally say "Click Here" on a banner.

Let's not forget that banners serve two functions: Enticing users to click and promoting a positive brand message about a product or service. Click-through ratings can't measure the latter and are therefore flawed for not taking into consideration the branding role that banner ads play.

Banner Click-Through Secrets

You don't have to say, "Click Here," to get users to interact with a banner. All you have to do is employ the following strategy into your design and you will have successful banners every time:

- **A strong concept.** Without a concept, you might as well just say "Click Here" in big, bold, red, flashing type.
- **Excellent art direction.** Image is everything. Creating a memorable first impression helps to reinforce a positive branding message.
- **Utilize the basic design principles.** Scale, contrast, typography, visual language, and white space are details that you must address if you want to design successful banners.
- **Creative copywriting.** Sell the core-being of the product or service and compel users to click with creative call-to-action messages.
- **Animation for the sake of reinforcing the concept.** If the banner needs to be animated, animate it! Make sure that it is necessary, and not gratuitous.

- **Small filesizes for quick load times.** Remember that you have only two seconds to get your audience's attention. Your banner should load extremely quickly (hence, a 1k to 10k filesize is preferable).
- **Be brief and to the point.** Banner ads are not there to tell a story; that's the job of the web sites that they lead users to. Just get them to click and the target web site will do the rest.

I will apply my strategy to the following sample banner design problem to illustrate how this works in practice:

Design a banner ad that measures 136 pixels wide by 186 pixels tall for ISDN service. It cannot animate. As a sidebar, the service is free for the first month.

9.22

The typical banner ad.

9.23

The successful banner ad.

Figures 9.22 and 9.23 showcase two possible solutions to the above communication problem. Figure 9.22 basically says all that needs to be said in order to get a response from users. The word "FREE" is extremely large, along with "CLICK HERE," which is bright red and almost disturbing. "ISDN" is unmistakably black, and "Click NOW!!!" is added at the bottom (in white) just in case the viewers don't know they should be clicking on the banner. Notice that this banner lacks any real concept. It involves no creative copywriting, no attention to detail, no art direction, and certainly no shame!

Figure 9.23 is a different story altogether. I created this banner in less than 30 minutes to prove that it is possible to spend a little more time in order to develop a beautifully compelling piece of visual communication. I hope you agree that the banner in figure 9.23 is a dramatic improvement over the one in figure 9.22. Imagine if I (or you, for that matter) spend a day on it instead of 30 minutes. Imagine how much better the banner ad can be!

Figure 9.23 has a concept behind it. Using the visual language of the fire alarm, I quickly put together what appears to be a red box with a piece of glass covering the word ISDN (which is grayed out to symbolize it being turned off) with a button below it (symbolizing the switch to turn it on) and a fluorescent cable (symbolizing the blazing ISDN cable ready to be ignited). The copy reads, "In case of a slow connection, BREAK GLASS." This piece of copy creatively applies what we know from our real world to the virtual online model, directing our frustrations at bottleneck modem speeds toward the glass, which can be shattered to let the anger out, thereby activating the ISDN (the solution to our connection-speed problems). Notice that I didn't have to say, "In case of a slow connection, CLICK HERE." In this case, "BREAK GLASS" is the same as "CLICK HERE." To break the virtual glass, the user would have to CLICK on it! This is an example of creatively solving a communication problem without resorting to the boring conventions of straight marketing verbage. All of what I explained to you is immediately absorbed by the human brain because of its inherent understanding of the visual language. In fact, if you study both figures 9.23 and 9.24, you will find that figure 9.24 is much more accessible and comforting to look at than figure 9.23.

If this were an animated banner, I would create it as I created the animating .comCompany graphics profiled in Chapter 7 (Animating the Brand). For a step-by-step tutorial on how to create an animating banner, please visit the *Click Here* web site at **http://www.rpirouz.com/click**.

Taking Banners "Internal"

What can average users learn from the banner ad? How can every-day users and content providers use the concept of the banner ad to promote their products or services on a grass-roots level?

The idea of banners, when incorporated into your own site, can help you market some of the content buried deep within your links. The concept of the banner is simply the following:

> *To create a compelling graphic that demands attention and takes users somewhere else when clicked.*

What if the banner promoted a page within your own site? What if the banner did not take your users away from your site, but rather, took them deeper within your site? After all, why would anyone want users to leave their site, even if you are getting paid for it?

Figure 9.24 represents what I refer to as an *internal banner ad*. Internal banner ads can be described as ads that take users within a site, rather than away from a site. The link profiled in figure 9.24 uses the visual language of a banner, yet looks very much like it belongs to, and was designed specifically for, the **http://www.lynda.com** web site.

In fact, upon clicking on the link, we are presented the page shown in figure 9.25, which is a page within the lynda.com web site that allows us to purchase Lynda's books online. It's a very good example of going beyond the banner, because Lynda uses the "banner" metaphor to get users to click on what's really a huge button graphic.

9.24

An internal banner ad within the Lynda Weinman home page.

9.25

www.lynda.com bookstore in association with Amazon.com.

LinkExchange–Grass-Roots at Its Best

With more than 100,000 members and growing, LinkExchange (**http://www.linkexchange.com**) is the web's largest advertising network. Best of all, it's free to join and begin using its services.

After you sign up and submit a non-animated 400×40 pixel GIF banner promoting your site, and include the HTML code that LinkExchange provides for you to place within your web site, you can begin to take advantage of LinkExchange's 100,000-strong user base. For every two times a LinkExchange banner is displayed on your site, you receive a credit that translates to one exposure of your banner somewhere within the 100,000 LinkExchange member sites.

LinkExchange offers ways to purchase credits, called the LinkExchange "Friends" program, where for $50 or more, you receive x number of credits that are applied to your account, increasing your site's exposure rating dramatically.

LinkExchange is definitely the best and most affordable way to promote your web site to millions of potential viewers.

Having to add a link from an exchange service such as LinkExchange can sometimes be a pain, especially if you have to compromise your site design for the sake of having a banner ad on your page.

Figure 9.27 displays my Earthlink personal page (**http://home.earthlink.net/~rpirouz**) with a LinkExchange banner. Notice that the banner is near the bottom of the page so that it is clearly not part of the initial design scheme, yet falls within the overall design structure of the page. I personally tend to shy away from exchange services simply because they force you to place their banners on your page. This is a completely personal choice on my part. You may be more tolerant of banner ads on your home page if you sell a product that you're willing to compromise in order to get more visitors to your site without having to lay out the big bucks to advertise with top search engines.

9.26

LinkExchange.

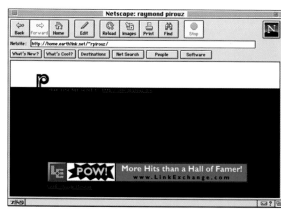

9.27

My personal site with a LinkExchange banner.

Exchanging Visitors for Clicks

One interesting phenomenon that is associated with advertising on your site is the fact that you literally ask your users to leave. By clicking on an ad within your site that is not an internal banner ad, your users are off to your site sponsor (the advertiser whose banner appears on your site). This can be considered a raw deal because you may receive anywhere between 1 and 2 cents per click, yet you lose one user with every penny or two. Is this really worth it? For sites that have millions of hits per week, such as the Netscape or Microsoft sites, it may very well be, because those users are bound to return for product updates, and other information. For your site, however, this may not be your best bet.

One recommendation that I have minimizing the loss of your visitors is to alter the HTML that many banner programs may give you so that when the banner is clicked on, users do not leave your site. You can accomplish this small feat by using the JavaScript Window Open command, discussed in chapter 8 (Opening New Windows), or by simply adding a "TARGET=_blank" tag to the end of the <A HREF> tag that the banner exchange service provides. A sample would look like this:

```
<A HREF="HTTP://WWW.BANNEREXCHANGE.COM" TARGET=_BLANK>
```

The "target=_blank" tag forces your browser to open a new window when the user clicks on the banner so that your site remains in the background and does not fade away.

Some banner exchange programs do not want you to alter the HTML that they provide you, but I think that's to deter people from damaging the code. If you know what you're doing, I see nothing wrong with making a minor adjustment such as allowing a new window to open, as in the case of figure 9.28.

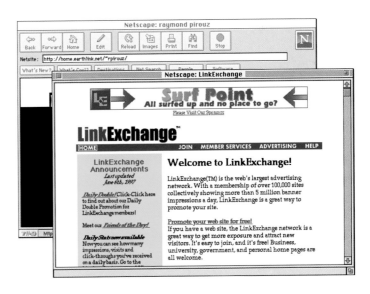

9.28

My personal site with a new window opened as a result of clicking on an exchange banner.

That's the Ticket

I've covered online marketing, promotion, and banner advertising tricks, while taking a look at how banners can be incorporated for grass-roots marketing projects to lead users deep into a site instead of away from it.

The following chapter concludes this book with a resource listing of places to obtain further information on the web.

10

Helpful Online Resources

The following online web design resources are categorized by subject and are designed to be used for research and learning purposes. Because of the ever-changing nature of the web, there is no way to guarantee that all the links provided herein will be functional. If you happen to run across a link that is no longer "live," please feel free to let me know by sending e-mail to (**rpirouz@rpirouz.com**). I will be more than happy to update link location changes on the *Click Here* web site (**http://www.rpirouz.com/click**).

Click Here Contacts

Click Here web site
- (http://www.rpirouz.com/click)

Raymond Pirouz, author
- (http://www.rpirouz.com)

Lynda Weinman, editor
- (http://www.lynda.com)

Award Sites

Masscommunication Awards
- (http://www.masscommunication.com)

The Clio Awards
- (http://www.clioawards.com)

The One Show
- (http://www.oneshow.com)

Cool Site of the Day
- (http://cool.infi.net)

The High Five
- (http://www.highfive.com)

Internet Professional Publishers Association - Design Excellence
- (http://www.ippa.org)

Microscope Home Page: Best Ads On The Web
- (http://www.pscentral.com)

CGI Resources

Matt's Script Archive
- (http://www.worldwidemart.com/scripts/)

The Common Gateway Interface
- (http://hoohoo.ncsa.uiuc.edu/cgi/)

Books Online

New Riders Publishing
- (http://www.mcp.com/newriders/)

Hayden Books
- (http://www.mcp.com/hayden/)

The DezineCafé Bookshop
- (http://www.sativa.com/bookshop/)

Amazon Books
- (http://www.amazon.com)

Browser Software

Netscape
- (http://www.netscape.com)

Microsoft
- (http://www.microsoft.com)

Design Education

Art Center College of Design
- (http://www.artcenter.edu)

California College of Arts and Crafts
- (http://www.ccacsf.edu)

California Institute of the Arts
- (http://www.calarts.edu)

Cranbrook Academy of Art
- (http://oeonline.com/~crdesign/)

Minneapolis College of Art and Design
- (http://www.mcad.edu)

Parsons School of Design
- (http://www.parsons.edu)

Pratt Institute
- (http://www.pratt.edu/)

Rhode Island School of Design
- (http://www.risd.edu)

San Francisco State Multimedia Studies Program
- (http://msp.sfsu.edu/online)

School of Visual Arts
- (http://www.sva.edu)

School of Visual Concepts
- (http://www.SVCSeattle.com)

Design Software Companies

Adobe Systems Inc.
- (http://www.adobe.com)

Macromedia
- (http://www.macromedia.com)

MetaTools Inc.
- (http://www.metatools.com)

mFactory
- (http://www.mfactory.com)

Design Organizations

Cooper-Hewitt National Design Museum
- (http://www.si.edu/ndm/)

National Endowment for the Arts
- (http://arts.endow.gov)

Communication Arts
- (http://www.commarts.com)

American Institute of Graphic Arts
- (http://www.aiga.org)

The Graphic Artists Guild
- (http://www.gag.org)

American Center for Design
- (http://www.ac4d.org)

Director Resources

Director FAQ
- (http://www.mcli.dist.maricopa.edu/director/faq/)

Clevermedia's List of Lingo Resources
- (http://clevermedia.com/lingolinks.html)

Director Web
- (http://www.mcli.dist.maricopa.edu/director/)

JavaScript Resources

JavaScript Tip of the Week
- (http://www.webreference.com/javascript/)

Netscape's JavaScript Guide
- http://home.netscape.com/eng/mozilla/3.0/handbook/ javascript/)

Project Cool
- (http://www.projectcool.com)

Typography

Microsoft Typography
- (http://www.microsoft.com/truetype/css/content.htm)

Adobe Type
- (http://www.adobe.com/type/)

Agfa
- (http://www.agfahome.com/products/prodfam/type.html)

Bitstream
- (http://www.bitstream.com)

The Font Bureau, Inc.
- (http://www.fontbureau.com)

The Font Shop
- (http://www.fontfont.com)

Monotype
- (http://www.monotype.com)

Emigre
- (http://www.emigre.com)

The Goudy International Center
for Font Technology & Aesthetics
- (http://www.rit.edu/~goudyctr/goudycenter.html)

typoGRAPHIC
- (http://www.subnetwork.com/typo/)

Web Design Resources

Web Page Design for Designers
- (http://dialspace.dial.pipex.com/town/parade/np17/wpdesign/)

CNET features - how to - HTML tips and tricks
- (http://www.cnet.com/Content/Features/Howto/Htmltips/)

Yale C/AIM Web Style Guide
- (http://info.med.yale.edu/caim/manual/)

Web Review
- (http://www.webreview.com/)

A Beginner's Guide to HTML
- (http://www.ncsa.uiuc.edu/General/Internet/WWW/HTMLPrimer.html)

Webmonkey
- (http://www.webmonkey.com)

Webvertising Resources

DoubleClick
- (http://www.doubleclick.net)

ClickZ
- (http://www.clickz.com)

Four Corner's Effective Banner Design
- (http://www.whitepalm.com/fourcorners/effectivebanners.shtml)

LinkExchange
- (http://www.linkexchange.com)

Submit It!
- (http://www.submit-it.com)

The Online Advertising Discussion List
- (http://www.o-a.com)

Web Wide Media
- (http://www.webwidemedia.com)

CyberAtlas
- (http://www.cyberatlas.com)

Adweek Online
- (http://www.adweek.com)

Advertising Age
- (http://www.adage.com)

R

R35 (digital design studio), 16-17, 32-33

R35 web site, 16

Raymond Pirouz (author) web site example, 72-75, 238

refreshing (META tag), 176-178

regions, creating, 161-165

registering web sites (search engines), 216

  AltaVista, 218

  HotBot, 217

  Infoseek, 217

  Lycos, 217

  registration forms, 220-222

  Submit It!, 219

  WebCrawler, 218

  WebPromote!, 219

  Yahoo!, 216

Rhode Island School of Design web site, 239

rollovers, 70, 100, 189-192

rotating images (Photoshop), 154

rows (HTML tables), 167-168

Rubin Postaer Interactive web site, 92-93

Rubin Postaer Interactive web site example

  animation, 96

  target audience

    captivating, 100-102

    enticing, 96-100

S

sales time (webvertising), 215

San Francisco State Multimedia Studies Program web site, 239

Save As command (File menu, Photoshop), 121

Save command (File menu, Photoshop), 121

scale, 46

  Microsoft site, 51

  Netscape site, 47

  Photoshop, 154

  pixels, 111

  Web design, 40-41

School of Visual Arts web site, 239

School of Visual Concepts web site, 239

scientific hues, 38

Score window (Director), 202-203, 206

search engines, 55

  banners, 55-56

  disinformation, 62-63

  Excite, 61-62

  Net Search (Netscape), 56

    Excite, 58-59

    Infoseek, 60

    Lycos, 57

    template, 57

    WebCrawler, 58

    Yahoo!, 59

  site announcements, 213

  webvertising, 216

    AltaVista, 218

    HotBot, 217

    Infoseek, 217

    Lycos, 217

    META NAME tag, 223-224

    registration forms, 220-222

    Submit It!, 219

    WebCrawler, 218

    WebPromote, 219

    Yahoo!, 216

  Yahoo!, 60-61

Search Engines Up the Wazoo II web site, 216

secondary hues, 38

security (applications), 105

server-side imagemaps, 161

SGI (gamma), 23-24

Shockwave (Director), 130, 199-200

  Afterburner Xtra, 207

  bandwidth, 101

  Cast Window, 201-203

  content, creating, 131

  enterFrame, 204

  interactivity, adding, 204

  limitations, 200

  magnets, hiding, 205-206

  movie properties, configuring, 200

  Movie Script, 201

  on exitFrame, go loop, 204

  Paint feature, 202-203

Score Window, 202-203, 206

  View Source-Copy-Paste protected, 105

  see also Director

Shockwave Support Center web site, 106

Shockzone web site, 106

simplicity (web design), 67-68

site announcements (webvertising), 213, 219

site depth, 75-77

sites, 239

  Adobe, 12, 239

  Adobe Systems, 115

  Adobe Type, 239

  Advertising Age, 240

  Adweek Online, 240

  Afterburner Xtra, 132

  Agfa, 239

  amazon, 81

  Amazon Books, 88, 226, 238

  American Center for Design, 239

  American Institute of Graphic Arts, 239

  Art Center College of Design, 238

  Beginner's Guide to HTML, 240

  beZerk, 103

  Bitstream, 12, 239

  bookdeal, 111, 177

  Cabernet's CGI Cellar, 106

  California College of Arts and Crafts, 238

  CGI Made Really Easy, 106

  CGI Scripts, 106

  Clevermedia's List of Lingo Resources, 239

  Click Here, 154, 238

  ClickZ, 214, 240

  Clio Awards, 238

  CNET features - how to - HTML tips and tricks, 240

  CNN Interactive, 105

  .comCompany, 144

  Common Gateway Interface, 106

  Communication Arts, 239

  Cool Site of the Day, 238

  Cooper-Hewitt National Design Museum, 239

  Cranbrook Academy of Art, 238

T

Paint Shop Pro
WEB
Techniques

C ompetition on the web runs high, and in order to compete, you have to know how to create. Web graphics are essential elements of great web pages, and more users are discovering Paint Shop Pro as a powerful tool for creating eye-catching web images. With *Paint Shop Pro Web Techniques,* you'll learn to use Paint Shop Pro to create images and achieve effects you never thought possible. Awarding-winning web designer T. Michael Clark takes you through step-by-step tutorials that show you how to maximize the use of Paint Shop Pro as a truly competitive web graphics creation program. In nine full-color chapters, you learn about color choices and graphics quality, backgrounds and borders, how to create stunning titles, and how to work with third-party filters. You learn to achieve such effects as embossing, drop shadows, chromes, 3D, bevels... and much more.

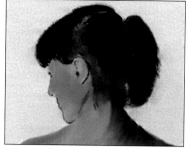

Introduction

Chapter 1 A Brief Overview of Paint Shop Pro

Chapter 2 Color Quality

Chapter 3 Graphics Quality

Chapter 4 Essential Elements of Your Web Page

Chapter 5 Getting Your Message Across

Chapter 6 Backgrounds and Borders

Chapter 7 Filters

Chapter 8 Special Techniques

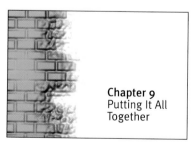

Chapter 9 Putting It All Together

REGISTRATION CARD

Click Here.

Name _____ Title _____

Company _____ Type of business _____

Address _____

City/State/ZIP _____

Have you used these types of books before? ☐ yes ☐ no

If yes, which ones? _____

_____

How many computer books do you purchase each year? ☐ 1–5 ☐ 6 or more

How did you learn about this book? _____

Where did you purchase this book? _____

Which applications do you currently use? _____

_____

Which computer magazines do you subscribe to? _____

_____

What trade shows do you attend? _____

_____

Comments: _____

_____

_____

Would you like to be placed on our preferred mailing list? ☐ yes ☐ no

☐ **I would like to see my name in print!** You may use my name and quote me in future New Riders products and promotions. My daytime phone number is: _____

New Riders Publishing   201 West 103rd Street ◆ Indianapolis, Indiana 46290 USA

Fax to **317-817-7448**

Fold Here

BUSINESS REPLY MAIL
FIRST-CLASS MAIL PERMIT NO. 9918 INDIANAPOLIS IN

POSTAGE WILL BE PAID BY THE ADDRESSEE

NEW RIDERS PUBLISHING
201 W 103RD ST
INDIANAPOLIS IN 46290-9058

Chapter 1: The Big
Picture: Sending
Graphics Over the

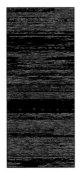

Chapter 2: The Big
Squeeze: Compression

Chapter 3: Bit Depth
and Palettes Once
and For All

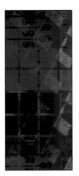

Chapter 4: Molding
Images for the Web

Chapter 5:
Backgrounds and
Texture

About
Photoshop
Web Techniques

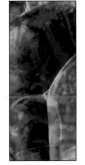

Chapter 6:
Transparency

Photoshop Web Techniques shows you how to harness the power of Photoshop as a web graphics tool. Author Scott Hamlin comprehensively covers several Photoshop techniques through hands-on tutorials and real world examples, as well as provides several "Beyond Photoshop" sections to show you how to incorporate your graphics into such popular web-based technologies as JavaScript and Shockwave. In 11 full-color chapters, you'll learn everything you need to know about creating web graphics with Photoshop and using those graphics to create web pages that will leave your visitors always wanting more.

$50.00 USA/$70.95 CAN/£46.99 Net UK (inc of VAT)
ISBN: 1-56205-733-2

Chapter 7: Working
with Text

Chapter 8: Bullets
and Buttons

Chapter 9: Imagemaps:
The Old and the New

Chapter 10:
Creating Images for
Shockwave Files

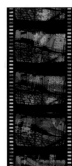

Chapter 11: Web
Animations with
Photoshop

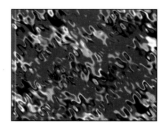

CH 1—PLANNING

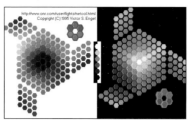

CH 2—PALETTES & WEB

CH 3—TEXTURES

Interface Design
with Photoshop

REAL WORLD

CH 4—BEVELING

offers direct, step-by-step creation of Web and multi-media interface elements in Photoshop. Each chapter focuses on an important aspect of interface design, including textures, beveling, embossing, and more. With each chapter providing full coverage of one element, you receive all the textual and visual information you need to plan and design interfaces unrivaled by your competition. From the planning stages to creating unique variations, this book will show you how to use Photoshop's power and utilities to your best advantage.

CH 13—SLIDERS

CH 5—EMBOSSING

CH 12—STOCK IMAGERY

CH 6—GLOWS & SHADOWS

CH 11—3D IMAGERY

CH 7—CHROME, GLASS, PLASTIC

CH 10—DISTORTIONS

CH 9—VARIATIONS

CH 8—BORDERS